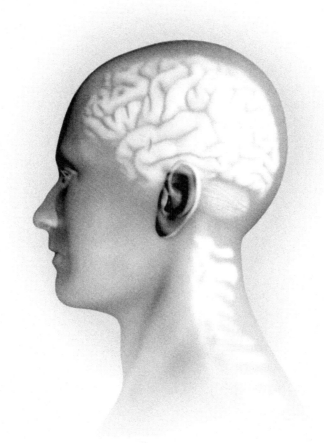

FEELINGS

GYŐZŐ MARGÓCZI

FEELINGS

THE NEED FOR A NEW SCIENCE

Budapest, Hungary
2016

Translation made ont the basis of
Margóczi Győző: Érzések

English translation: Gábor Szkórits-Tala & Dóra Keresztiné Kövér
Copy editor: Patricia Hughes

ISBN 978-963-12-4878-4
Available from Amazon.com and other book stores

CONTENTS

FOREWORD

to the third edition

Dear reader,

Let me start my foreword with a tale. Have you ever heard the tale of the "hundredth monkey effect"? You haven't? Then I will tell it to you.

Once upon a time, somewhere over the rainbow, or rather somewhere on this side of the Pacific Ocean, somewhere in the Japanese Sea there was an island where a population of monkeys were trying to keep body and soul together when benevolent scientists started observing them. In order to win the monkeys over, the scientists gave them sweet potatoes to eat. The monkeys however, did not really like the food scattered around in the sand of the beach because the sand stuck to the potatoes and was cracking under their teeth. One of the young monkeys, though, realised that if she washed the food she could get rid of the sand and enjoy the treat undisturbed. As time passed, more and more monkeys learnt this masterstroke. The interesting thing was that, after a certain time, even monkeys living in the neighbouring islands had mastered the trick.

From the events above, many people have drawn the conclusion that there might be a certain "morphogenetic field" that is capable of forwarding information between living creatures even without physical contact, especially if more than a certain critical number of individuals, i.e. the critical mass, already have that particular bit of information. Using the analogy of today's computerised world, it is something like when we upload some information from our computer to the cloud. Anybody can download that information if they look for it in the right place but if a sufficient number of people have already uploaded the same information, finding it and downloading it becomes increasingly easier. Something that seems to support this theory is the fact that it has been observed several times throughout human history that in many cases scientists discover things around the same time even though they have never heard of each other or about each other's field of research.

Whether the tale above is simply a fairy tale or it has some truth in it, I do not know, but something happened now in 2015, two weeks before my 60th birthday, that made me think. I started reading the book *Descartes's error* by Antonio R. Damasio, published in 1994, and when I got as far as the chapter *Somatic marker hypothesis*, I suddenly started wincing. "Oh my God! I discovered the same thing in 2007!" How is it possible that I, a nobody from Hungary with only a degree in electromechanical engineering in my pocket, discovered the same thing in my spare time in the evenings or in the mornings before going to work – even if only 13 years later – as the well-known professor with decades of clinical and scientific experience in his well-equipped institutions and laboratories supported by dozens of full-time assistants? This is peculiar to say the least. Okay, you may say "Every dog has his day". Fair enough: I just stumbled upon it. But how do you explain the fact that I gave the same name to the phenomena as Prof Damasio? He used the term 'somatic marker' whereas I used 'marker feelings'. What is the probability of this happening just by chance? Well certainly not too big. Naturally, the two books started from totally different bases, discussed totally different problems and gave totally different explanations to certain phenomena.

These facts alone, however, would not have given sufficient stimulus to rewrite my book and publish a new edition of it. The reason I had to rework my book is partly because, although Prof Damasio and I were writing about the same phenomenon, we were writing about two different sides of the same thing. And the two sides cannot exist without one another as each sheds light only on one side of the problem. The two halves together give us the full picture. They can only describe the entire phenomenon together and this is the only way to understand the full picture. Another natural reason is that in the past eight years the picture I drew has developed in detail and clarity. And the third, and probably the most important, thing is that – as it is shown in the subtitle of my book – I would like to call the attention of the world to the immediate necessity of creating a new branch of science. This new branch should fill in the gap somewhere between the fields of neurology and psychology. The new branch is the science of feelings which we may call sensology. This science will not deal with the neurobiological details of the generation of feelings. Just as chemistry does not deal with the generation of individual elements, leaving it for physics, and concentrates on the combinations that can be created from the elements found in the periodic table, similarly, sensology will have to concentrate on the various combinations and interplays of the feelings found in us.

What can the new science give to humankind? Much more than you would think at first sight. The fact that it can give an explanation for phenomena neither neurobiology nor psychology could explain before is obvious. However, it is much more important that the entire way of thinking of humankind will be transformed with the development and spread of sensology. New perspectives will open up and a much more refined, transparent and, most of all, peaceful world will come into being. You can read more on this in my book Words (© 2015 Győző Margóczi, Budapest, ISBN 978 963 12 1585 4).

I originally meant my book Feelings to be a popular science book and I wrote it in the appropriate style and language which some of you, who are accustomed to the scientific style, may find irritating but I can assure you that my style does not alter the factual content of my book in any way.

INTRODUCTION

Dearest reader,

When a child is born, she definitely does not know much about the world. She will put together her view of the world from bits and pieces and she will try to form all those bits and pieces into a uniform image. She has to do this because she has to adapt to the world and how could she adapt to it if she did not know what to adapt to?

It is a jigsaw puzzle, you know, the picture toy that you can buy in the toy shop around the corner. The maker of the toy took a nice colourful image and cut it into small pieces and jumbled them. Life is a jigsaw puzzle where our own life is at stake. Some of the pieces we find and put together during our life but others are given to us already put together in bigger chunks by our parents and teachers. Those of you who have played with a jigsaw puzzle will know that you always select the bits that match the ones you have already put together. If a new bit does not fit the existing image, you simply put it aside and disregard or even discard it. We tend to adhere stubbornly to the fragments we have already put together regardless of whether it is in line with reality or not. The bigger the fragment we have to give up, the more it hurts. That is why billions of people never give up their own images.

I have put together an image myself. It may not be perfect and it might not answer each and every question of life but I hope it may give others help in creating their own images.

I am not asking you, my dear reader, to demolish the image you have put together so far. All I would like to ask is that you have a look at my picture and do not throw it away immediately just because you have found a bit that does not fit your picture. Do not put my book down! Read it through, please, and examine the entire picture thoroughly. I am convinced that the visitor who only checks the first picture of an exhibition, the one that is closest to the entrance, makes a mistake. If you look at the entire exhibition and still go back to the first picture, you can do it in good faith because now you know that this is the best and the most beautiful picture. And if you like another picture more, you will also be satisfied because you have found something better and more beautiful. I believe that one develops by understanding different views of the world.

When astronauts take pictures of the Earth from outer space, they take pictures in different frequency ranges of light. Each frequency range will reveal different details for the researchers. They put different filters in front of the lens. When making my picture, I also used a special type of filter: human feelings. It is human feelings whose thorough analysis can yield a new and unusual picture of us, humans. I am asking my reader not to read this book as a dry, scientific work. Try to feel the feelings and phenomena I describe for yourself instead. Apart from the things to understand, this book also offers things to feel and you can get the fullest picture through understanding and feeling the book. If you do not do it like that, you will do exactly what the musicologist in the story did who read each and every study and analysis about a given piece of music, only he never listened to the piece itself. This is how he lost the point. This book was written to help people and if it can help only one of them, it was already worth writing it.

The Author

APPLE PIE

(What does a dessert have to do with a book like this?)

The whole thing started on a summer afternoon. It was hot and stuffy, the air did not move at all. The parasols in the garden of the cake shop were desperately trying to fend off the attack of the sun, but with little success. I had a sip of my drink and looked at it again. We had been looking at one another for about 10 minutes. Me and the apple pie. "I love apple pie" I thought and I reached for my fork. But then I heard an inner voice.

"You don't love apple pie, do you?! If you loved it, you wouldn't eat it."
"Stop joking! I know if I love apple pie or not."
"If you truly loved it, you would put it under a glass bell, you would fill the glass bell with rare gas and put the whole thing into the fridge."
"And why on earth would I do that?"
"To save the apple pie, of course."
"Why should I save it?"
"That's the point! You don't care at all about the fate of

21

that poor apple pie, you only want to feel its taste in your selfish way; you only want it to generate a pleasant feeling in you, yourself, and don't care at all if this would result in the devastation of that poor apple pie!"

I thought that was true. But did it also apply to others? For example, the couple at the other table: did they really love one another? Or did they only like the feeling they generated in one another? What did the word 'love' mean? What was the actual feeling behind it? And what was a feeling, for that matter? Well, that is how it all started.

1.

CONDITIONS OF EXISTENCE

(Is everybody familiar with the conditions of their existence?)

If someone starts building a house, they never start by build-ing the roof. Why would anyone do such as silly thing? They would only make their life more difficult and, at the end, the whole thing might collapse on top of their heads or they would create a deformed monster of a building. Therefore a master builder always starts with the foundation. The more solid the foundation is, the better the chances are of creat-ing a reliable building. Naturally, you must not throw stones randomly on top of each other later on either. The building stones have to connect with one another nicely and accu-rately and then you may be able to create something valu-able. So, I think we should also start with the foundations.

If you want to get an answer to the questions of human existence, it makes the most sense to start with the general conditions of existence. Yes, I know! The works of genera-tions of philosophers would fill libraries on this issue. What is more, even if you read all of them, you still would not nec-essarily get an answer that satisfies everyone. Nevertheless I still take courage (quite a lot of courage, by the way) and try to define the general conditions of life on my own account, trying to make my definition more or less acceptable for ev-eryone regardless of their worldview.

The conditions of existence:

1) The first condition of existence is energy. Everything that exists consists of energy, or a special form of energy: matter. From the religious point of view, God is nothing else but the first and, at the same time, the ultimate and most sophisticated energy.

2) The second condition of existence is birth or creation, because nothing in our world lasts forever and everything has its beginning and end. In the religious approach, God is an exception because he has existed from time immemorial and he created the world that is, in turn, already mortal.

3) The third condition of existence is order. Every existing being is defined by a certain order. Each has its own internal order and structure.

4) The fourth condition of existence is the preservation of this internal order. Something can only exist if it preserves its internal structure and order. If it does not, it is not what it used to be any more. The existing structures are not equally rigid or flexible. They can tolerate lesser or greater changes as long as these changes are within a framework typical of the given system.

5) There are some external factors and also internal factors, generated within the same system, which may act against the preservation of order.

6) In order to maintain the system, we continuously need to collect information about the outer world and the system itself.

7) We need to evaluate the collected information.

8) We need to act upon the evaluated information in order

to maintain the integrity of the system. We need to correct and compensate for the effect of external and internal forces aimed at changing the system.

So far so good. But how shall we proceed? I would suggest we skip the detailed explanation of the first 3 points: the first 2 because they belong to the fields of physicists, philosophers and theologians; the third because it belongs to the fields of biologists and research physicians. Let us try to concentrate on point (4) which, in our case, is about preserving the integrity, unity and health of the human body and soul. First, let us limit our discussion to the preservation of the integrity of the human body and then let us deal with psychological factors later on in order to ensure better intelligibility.

2.

HIERARCHY OF NEEDS

(What kind of needs do we have?)

1. The need for energy supply

As I mentioned before, both external and internal factors may threaten the integrity of the system. Since we are talking about the human body, let us take this as the origin, the zero point of our coordinate system. What are the internal forces, generated within this system, that threaten the health of our body? One of these factors is ageing which, in the long run, leads to our organism becoming incapable of living. It makes sense not to discuss this factor because, according to our present state of knowledge, we cannot do much about it. There is, however, another factor we continuously encounter day by day. This is energy consumption. Our body can only function and operate by using energy. Our body uses energy both when we are having a rest and when we are engaged in physical activity. Of course, the consumption is much higher in the latter case. But the energy is not used only for moving. Since we need a certain optimum temperature in order to maintain our metabolism, we also need to thoroughly regulate our system of body temperatures. If we do not replace the energy we have used or, in more simple terms, if we do not eat, do not drink and do not breathe, we will die. Therefore, we can declare that the first, and probably the most important, need of our life is the need for a supply of energy.

2. **The need to get information**

You will see that our needs are organically connected with one another: one is a consequence of the other and they create an indissoluble functional unit. The same applies to the need for getting information. However, I need to point out one thing: although I use the word 'information' to describe this need, this term is not entirely correct, but let us use this one for better intelligibility for the moment.

a) Internal information system

> In point 1 we saw that the human organism needs an energy supply. But when? And how much? We cannot eat all the time and we cannot eat endless amounts of food, either. We need an internal information system on the basis of which we can tell when and how much energy and nutrients we should take. At the same time, this system is responsible for controlling the internal operation of our organism. The internal information system collects and evaluates information from within our body.

b) External information system

> But the existence of an internal information system is not enough. Apart from knowing if we need energy in a given moment, we also need to be able to find food in our environment and tell whether that particular food is edible or not. So we need an external information system as well. Although the external information system is also within our body, it is directed towards the external world, it collects data from the external world and it interacts with the external world.

3. **The need for safety**

After eating and drinking well, we now only need to be careful to avoid something punching a hole in our skin. Or, in more scientific terms, now we can concentrate on the outer world because we have an excellent external information system which we can use not only for searching for food but also to avoid external factors threatening our physical and psychological integrity in order to save our life. What could these external factors be? A gorge, a venomous snake, a burglar or your mother-in-law. Anything that can present a threat for you.

5. **The need for a group**

Yes, I know! I also learned mathematics and I know number 4 comes after number 3 and not number 5. Still, let us leave out point 4 for the moment for the sake of better intelligibility. The need for a group comes from the need to avoid external threats and from the fact of easier adaptation to the environment. The chances of survival of individuals grow significantly if they form a group. Whether it is a learned or inherited need is difficult to tell. I myself think it is more likely to be an inherited need, but education and family play an important role in it in the case of people. There are many examples of this in the animal world. If you observe the life of small fish, you will see that individual fish hatch at different times and at a distance from one another and they live without parental supervision so there is no one they could learn this kind of behaviour from but they still organise themselves in shoals. How the same thing takes place in the case of humans I have no idea but the result is obvious. On the one hand we do not feel good alone, on the other hand – and history proves it – the chances of survival of people organised in tribes, nations or countries are much better than those of their solitary counterparts. Not to mention the social division of labour and the incredible economic success and improved standards of life achieved by it.

6. **The need of meeting others' expectations**

Naturally, the need of meeting others' expectations comes from the needs of previous levels: it is the organic consequence of the fact that we want to belong to a group. If we want to belong to a group we need to meet certain parameters: the expectations and requirements of the group. If we do not do that, the group will not accept us, they will outlaw us and we will stay alone.

7. **The need of meeting our own expectations**

One of the cornerstones of one's peace of mind is meeting your own expectations, satisfying your own norms.

8. **The need for self-realisation**

Self-realisation is nothing else but a multifactor optimum game the factors of which are: the external world which we need to take into consideration; the capabilities that we have; the first five needs that we have to satisfy; our fellows whose expectations we need to meet; and our own self-image, the integrity of which we need to protect in order to ensure that we can face our own image in the mirror while we are shaving or doing our make up.

4. **The need of reproduction**

And here comes the missing need number 4: the need of reproduction. This is an odd one out for several reasons. One of them is we need to see that, for a developed individual, reproduction is not an essential of life. He can preserve his integrity even if he does not reproduce himself. Why do we still say this is a need? Because it is a "factory preset" of our genes. We simply cannot disregard the irresistible urge for reproduction. Another reason is that this need is only activated during a certain period of our life: only the seeds of it are present in our early childhood and only the remains of it are there to be found in our old age. A third reason is that so far we have only been discussing point 4, i.e. the preservation of structure, out of the conditions of existence and this need belongs to point 2, i.e. the point of birth and creation. However, we need to pay attention to the fact that the needs are built one on top of another. If we did not have the need of reproduction, we ourselves would not exist and we would not have to think about condition 4. of existence, the preservation of structure, because we would not have anything to preserve.

The organisational unity and order of importance of our needs is a consequence of these needs being built on top of one another. The most important one of them, naturally, is energy supply or, in more simple terms: eating. If we starve to death, there is not much need for the rest. An individual will satisfy her primary needs first and will only seek satisfaction of needs of higher levels then. The need of reproduction is not an "essential of life" for individuals so this one can be left out from the hierarchy of needs but the individual may suffer from her unsatisfied need.

We can give up satisfying our primary needs for the short term in order to realise our higher level needs but we cannot do so in the long run. For example, I can cancel a lunch in order not to miss an important meeting but I will not care about any meeting – unless it is about getting food – if I know I will not have anything to eat in the foreseeable future.

Certain events can satisfy, or threaten, multiple needs at the same time. In such a case, individuals seek to satisfy as many needs as possible. A good example of this is finding or losing a job. There are, however, special cases when individuals, seemingly disregarding the hierarchy of needs, are ready to sacrifice their lives for ideals. We will see later on that this is also in line with the hierarchy of needs.

3.

THE INFORMATION SYSTEMS OF OUR ORGANISM

3.1 Bases of neurological regulation

(Does everybody remember what they learnt in biology?)

As we saw the need for information took the distinguished second place in the hierarchy of needs. We also found out that there is a need for an internal and an external information system. We will now turn our attention to the human nervous system. The nervous system is nothing else but one of the data systems of the human body. The other important "telecommunication" system of the human body works on a chemical basis but in this book we will concentrate primarily on the nervous system. The nervous system ensures the flow of data for the harmonic operation of organs and the coordination of our movements; the nervous system makes it possible for us to sense the world around us and enables the operation of our big control centre, the brain.

Let us now go back for a short time to the school bench and try to recall what we learnt about the nervous system in biology classes. The basic building block of the nervous system is the nerve cell. In Figure 1 I have tried to show the basic structure of a nerve cell called the neuron.

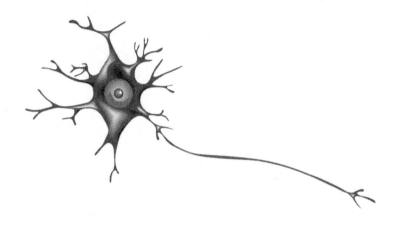

Figure 1

According to various estimates, the number of neurons in the human brain totals between 10,000,000,000 and 1,000,000,000,000.

As you can see, a number of short arms protrude from the nerve cell: they are called dendrites. The dendrites are the data collection arms of the nerve cell that collect inputs for it. Through its dendrites, the nerve cell takes impulses from neighbouring nerve cells. There is a long, thin, pipe-like arm coming from the nucleus: this is the axon with the axon terminals on its end. Through the axon, the nerve cell sends signals towards the neighbouring nerve cells. So the axon is nothing else but the output of the nerve cell. The length of an axon may range from a couple of hundredths of a millimetre up to 1 or 2 metres. The speed of an impulse from the dendrites to the end of the axon is somewhere between 1 and 100 kph. The axon of the nerve cell may be in connection with several dendrites at the same time, creating a jungled network. The axon terminals, i.e. the output of a nerve cell, and the dendrites, i.e. the inputs, of neighbouring nerve cells do not connect directly: there is a small gap between them. This small gap is called the synaptic gap and the entire connection point is called a synapse. When in rest, these synaptic gaps isolate and separate nerve cells from one another. When, however, an impulse arrives to the axon terminal, a special substance, generally known as a neurotransmitter, splits off the axon terminals and, crossing the gap, starts to stimulate the next nerve cell and then, after having passed the impulse on, quickly decomposes or gets withdrawn separating the two nerve cells again.

But what does the entire process look like? A nerve cell starts working, i.e. gives an impulse, if an impulse, or an appropriate combination of impulses, arrives to its inputs, the dendrites. Then, an impulse runs through the axon, reaches the synapses and there the neurotransmitters, through the synaptic gaps, pass it on to the next nerve cell.

Why did I consider it important to describe all these processes? Well the most important thing to understand here is that you need time for the completion of these processes. You need time for the neurotransmitters to disappear from the synaptic gaps and also for the generation of a sufficient amount of them for the transfer of the next impulse. These regeneration times limit the speed of the discharge of the nerve cells. According to our present knowledge, individual nerve fibres are capable of producing a maximum of about 1000 impulses a second and even that they can only do for a short time because then they get exhausted. This is going to be an important factor later on, so let us call it the maximum law.

Let us now examine how these nerve cells are organised into data channels. Let us have a look, for example, at the nerve fibres connecting the tongue and the brain. These are the fibres that forward the data related to the flavours sensed by our tongue to the brain. This is what Figure 2 tries to show.

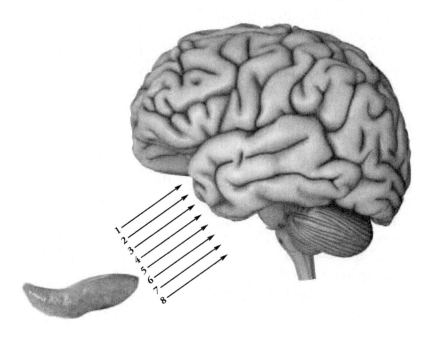

Figure 2

Let us do an imaginary experiment now. Let us give numbers to some of the nerve fibres and let us observe how they operate. Let us take 2 or 3 grains of sugar in our mouth. We will feel a mild sweet flavour, and we will experience that, for example, nerve fibres 1, 4 and 7 get activated and start sending frequent impulses to the brain. Now let us take a spoonful of sugar into our mouth. We will feel a strong, pronounced sweet flavour and will also experience that it is still nerve fibres 1, 4 and 7 that are active, only the number of impulses going through them has increased. Now let us rinse our mouth with clear water and let us wait a little. Then let us squeeze a little lemon juice into a spoon, let us shake it off and suck the remaining lemon juice off the spoon. We will feel a mild sour taste and will experience that now nerve fibres 2, 5 and 6 get activated while the others remain at rest. Now let us take an entire spoonful of lemon juice into our mouth. We will see that it is still nerve fibres 2, 5 and 6 that are the active ones, only the number of impulses going through them has increased.

What consequences can we draw from our imaginary experiment? Well, the most straightforward finding is that we can describe every feeling with two main indicators: one of them is the quality of the feeling and the other one is its intensity or strength of the feeling. Another important finding is that different feelings use different nerve paths to get to the brain: the feeling of sweetness travelled on nerve fibres 1, 4 and 7, whereas the feeling of sourness travelled on nerve fibres 2, 5 and 6. The next conclusion we can draw is that the strength of a stimulus is proportionate to the number of impulses passing through the nerve paths: the stronger the stimulus, the more impulses pass through the nerve fibres. Now, would this mean that if, let us say, 10 impulses a second pass through nerve fibres 1, 4 and 7 as a result of taking one teaspoon of sugar, then 100,000 impulses a second will pass through the same fibres as a result of eating a kilogram of sugar? No. This is where the maximum law mentioned previously comes into play. The nerve cells are incapable of producing more impulses than the maximum number of impulses typical of that particular type of nerve cell. So it does not matter if we pour 1 kilogram of sugar into our mouth, we will still not feel it as sweeter than the single teaspoon of sugar. (It does not make any sense to do the experiment anyway. I have not met anyone who could store 1 kilogram of sugar in his mouth and it is quite a pain in the neck to clean the room afterwards. And, anyway, you would look really silly with 1 kilogram of sugar in your mouth.)

Composite feelings

While sweeping up the sugar and mopping the floor (I told you not to try it, didn't I?), we can think about what happens if we add a few drops of lemon juice to our teaspoon of sugar and eat it. The results are obvious. The nerve fibres sensitive to both types of feelings – i.e. both nerve fibres 1, 4 and 7 and nerve fibres 2, 5 and 6 – will activate while we will feel a new sweet-and-sour taste. Composite or, in a more simple term, complex feelings are generated if the nerve activation patterns generating the individual components of these feelings overlap one another.

The taste of a certain type of food is the total of the tastes of its components. If the basic tastes adding up to create the new taste are of equal strength, it is impossible to decompose the new taste to its components. This is also true for other channels of feelings. Smells and sounds can be combined in the same way. It is also important to point out, however, that certain feelings do not influence one another. For example tasting some food does not have any impact on my hearing. So we need to draw the conclusion that you can only create composite feelings within certain groups of feelings.

The law of the difference threshold

The next important law that needs examination is the law of the difference threshold. In 1834 Ernst Weber, a German philosopher, carried out some interesting investigations. In one of his experiments, a subject in a dark room was constantly shown a light spot of a certain intensity. Besides the constant light spot, another light spot was shown from time to time for short periods. The subject was told to signal if the light spot shown from time to time was stronger than the constant one next to it. The experiments showed that the weaker the constant light spot serving as the basis of comparison was, the smaller the increase of intensity needed for the subject to perceive the light spot shown from time to time as stronger. The stronger the constant light spot serving as the basis of comparison, the greater the increase in intensity that was necessary for the subject to see the occasionally emerging light spot as brighter. Webber completed the same experiments with regard to various feeling-channels. He had similar findings all the time. So if you listen to the radio fairly loud already, you will have to turn the volume up much more in order to hear the music as louder.

3.2 External information system
(Can we do it differently from how we learnt it?
What is a feeling?)

In order to ensure better understanding, let us first have a look at the external information system of our organism. No one can question the fact that, in order to preserve our integrity and save our lives, we need to collect information from the external world. How do we do it? The different data channels are often referred to with the words 'seeing', 'hearing', 'tasting', 'smelling', 'touch' and 'sense of temperature'. The problem with these words is that their definition is inaccurate and therefore misleading or difficult to interpret. Since this book is not meant to deal with word creation and language development, it will be easier, instead of creating new words, to define what these words mean in my interpretation.

Seeing: the nervous activity triggered by electromagnetic radiation between the wavelengths of 400 and 700 nm.

Hearing: the input feelings triggered by the vibrations of air in the frequency range of 20 to 20,000 Hz.

Tasting: the input feelings triggered by the chemical parameters of the substances getting into the mouth.

Smelling: the input feelings triggered by the chemical parameters of vapours and gases getting into the nose.

Touch: the incoming feelings triggered by the pressure on the surface of the skin.

Sense of temperature: the input feelings originating from the changes of the kinetic energy of the cells making up the surface of the skin.

In the definitions above, the term 'input' is used in its system technology meaning. The careful reader must have noticed that I did not use this term in connection with seeing. Why? Because seeing is not a feeling.

I think it is time to try and define the notion of 'feeling'. What is a feeling? Well, studying the related scientific literature, you will find a number of different, and often contradictory, definitions for the notion of 'feeling'. Now we will try to cut the Gordian knot and give the simplest possible answer. The answer is really very simple: feeling is what we feel. Period: that is all. If I wanted to be blunt, I would say feeling is anything that "tickles". Naturally the word 'tickle' is not meant in the literal sense here.

Seeing requires very complex nervous activities. The sense of temperature only requires two types of nerve cells, the receptors of cold and the receptors of hot, to be activated, which are open-ended neurons located right below the skin surface. I have not found any reference to the number of these receptors in the scientific literature but there must be far fewer of them than of the neurons of seeing. According to some estimates, the optic nerve contains as many as 1,000,000 neurons. These neurons however do not only differ from temperature sensing neurons in their numbers, but also in the complexity of their functions and in the complicatedness of the processing of incoming data. Our sense of temperature can only tell us whether the surface of our skin is warming up or cooling down at any given moment. Whereas seeing can give us information about the colour, shape and size of objects, the relation between the sizes of different objects, the spatial orientation of objects, the spatial orientation of these objects in comparison with one another; the spatial position and orientation of objects in comparison to us, the observer; the movements of objects; the direction of the movements of objects; the speed of objects and the changes in the speed of objects. We cannot express or experience this enormous amount of data through nervous activities at the level of feelings. If I wanted to explain the situation in the language of technology, I would say the bandwidth of the nervous activities at the level of feelings is not broad enough to forward the amount of data produced by seeing. Based on the above we can declare that seeing is a data collection process that is not a feeling.

And after excluding seeing from the circle of feelings so nicely, let me quickly contradict my statement made above. How can I do that? Why not? Physicists cannot decide either if light is a substance or a wave. If they are allowed to do so, should I not be allowed to do so? Joking aside, if we disregard the "trifle" that seeing does not "tickle", then, from the system technology point of view, seeing serves the same purpose as "regular" feelings, i.e. it provides information about the world around us so, functionally speaking, it is indeed a feeling.

3.3 Internal information system
(Why did little John fall into a pit?)

Is it necessary to be aware of each and every nervous action? Is it important for us to know exactly what is happening in our organism? The answer is no. The human nervous system has a special part, called the sympathetic nervous system. This system controls the operation of glands, breathing, the beating of the heart, the veins, the liver, the kidneys, the stomach and the intestines. This entire internal system works like a properly programmed automation. It can do so because our internal organs are connected to one another on the basis of a strictly defined constant internal order. It is very important to emphasise the word constant. Our veins connect to our heart today exactly the same way as they will tomorrow. The connection between the stomach and the intestines does not change from month to month either. Why is it important to emphasise the word constant? Let us do an experiment. A good housewife knows exactly where salt, pepper, pots and rolling pins are in the kitchen. Now let us blindfold our housewife and let us ask her to produce the salt. She will raise her hand and automatically, without hesitation, take the salt off the shelf. What is happening here? The lady gave the following orders to her hand:

1) Open fingers!
2) Raise arm in a 45° angle!
3) Take one step ahead!

4) Close fingers!
5) Take one step back!

This series of movements could be successful because she knew the exact place of the salt and she had carried out the same series of movements several hundreds of times. She did not have to get and evaluate new data; everything was running smoothly. If, however, we put the salt only an inch away from its place, she would not be able to find it. That is why being constant is so important.

The situation is pretty similar in the human body. The organs are arranged in a well-defined constant connection with one another. There is a meticulously prepared and thoroughly tried and tested script of cooperation in operation between them. There are no new or unexpected situations. If you want to make the example of the housewife even more accurate, we do not even need to give an order, i.e. we do not even have to ask the housewife to take the salt off the shelf, the housewife will know automatically what she has to do, when and why. Everything in the human body is fully automated and runs smoothly without us even having to know about it.

What is the case with the external world? Well, everything in the external world, dammit, keeps changing all the time! This is the nature of the external world. Using the example of the housewife again, it is as if we kept putting the salt into a new place all the time. Automations do not work in the external world.

How can you reconcile the well-coordinated, automatic internal system with the constantly changing external world where established automations do not help at all? Let us take the example of the processing of nutrients. Nutrients are processed in the human body in a perfectly automated way. Nutrients enter the stomach where gastric juices start working, then the nutrients are sent to the intestines where the process of absorption starts, and so on and so forth. Everything does what it is supposed to do. The closed system works properly and it does what it needs to do, and when it needs to do it, automatically. Yes, but at one point you run out of food to be processed and the energy level of the body starts decreasing. Naturally, your organism – just like any properly operating machinery – automatically activates its reserves and starts decomposing adipose tissues. Anything our body can do within the system, it will do automatically without us knowing about it. However, it cannot cope automatically with things outside the system, i.e. the external world. What can it do? It sends an alarm signal. But what sort of a signal can it be?

Let me tell you a joke. Once upon a time, there was a very, very deep pit. Just because it was so deep, signs were put all around it for safety reasons. They said 'Careful! Deep pit!' and also 'It is strictly forbidden to go close to the edge!' On a nice sunny day, little John was walking there with his parents, and since he was a naughty and restless boy, he "naturally" started to frisk about around the edge of the pit. His parents told him off immediately:
"Little John, you see that sign, don't you? It says 'deep pit'. Don't play on the edge of the pit because you will fall off!"
"Ah!"
"Johnny, I told you not to play on the edge of the pit because you will fall off!"
"Ah!"
"My son, Johnny! How many times do I need to repeat that you should not play on the edge of the pit because you will fall off?"
"Aaaaaaaaaaaaaah!!!"

What happened here? Did Johnny receive a signal saying he must not play on the edge of the pit? Yes, he did. He was warned in writing and he was also warned in words multiple times. What did he do? He simply disregarded the warning signals. How could we solve this problem? Let us install an electric fence on the edge of the pit. You know, this is a wire that gives a high-voltage electric shock if someone or something touches it. It is perfectly safe, it only causes an unpleasant feeling. This is used for guarding cows and horses without human supervision (in order to prevent them from falling down into the pit).

What would we achieve with this solution? Not only would little John get information about not going close to the edge, but the information itself would also keep him away from the pit. Apart from its informative value, the information in this case would also have a directing, guiding and controlling power. And what does the human organism do? Exactly the same. Sends an alarm signal in the form of a feeling. Feelings do not only have informative roles, but also have controlling and guiding ones. They have a driving force which tries to guide us in a certain direction.

Attention! This is a very important point! When you are hungry, you do not only get a signal that the energy level of your organism is too low, but you are also forced to eat. We simply cannot disregard the signal, i.e. the feeling. Based on the above, you can draw the conclusion that the internal information system of our organism does not give an intelligible signal as long as it can automatically cope with a given task. We only receive such a signal when we need to involve the external world in some way or another (Only relatively few feelings are exceptions to this rule). This does not only apply to the processes of metabolism, it is also true for different illnesses or injuries. The organism signals that there is a problem with the given body part and that we should not load it or we should treat it carefully until its recovery is complete.

4.

CLASSIFICATION OF FEELINGS

4.1 Need-indicating feelings
(How do we know if we need something?)

Having mentioned the electric fence, let us now change to a cowboy simile. One of the groups of feelings works like a clumsy cowboy who does not know where a good pasture for his cows lies. He does nothing apart from cracking his whip and chasing his cows. Where they should go, he himself does not know; he is only cracking his whip. It is up to the cows whether they find the pasture or not, or whether they starve to death or not. This is how hunger chases us people, and then it depends on our cleverness if we find food or not.

There are five similar cowboy groups, which are related to the needs for energy supply, information, safety, reproduction and group. Combinations of cowboys, or feelings, serve the satisfaction of each of these needs. The need for a supply of energy is served by hunger, thirst, air hunger, the feelings of cold, hot and fatigue, as well as the feelings related to the necessity to empty roughage. We will call these feelings need-indicating feelings since these feelings indicate to us when a given need is not satisfied. A common feature of need-indicating feelings is the unpleasantness that urges us to get rid of them one way or another. However, need-indicating feelings must exist in two forms. That is to say, it is not enough to know that a given need is not satisfied, you also need to be aware if it has already been satisfied. If we take eating as an example, we also need to feel when to stop eating. In the case of eating, it is the feeling of being full that stops further food intake. So the feeling of being full is a need-indicating feeling.

Based on the above, we can declare that need-indicating feelings at both top and bottom limits must belong to the needs for energy supply, information, safety, reproduction and group. An exception to the rule is the need-indicating feelings related to emptying roughage where, due to the nature of things, there is only one need-indicating feeling as we cannot over-empty ourselves.

The careful reader will have noticed that we listed eight needs in the discussion of the hierarchy of needs, whereas in this chapter we have only mentioned the first five of them in connection with need-indicating feelings. There is a simple reason for this: we only have indicating feelings for the first five of those needs or, using a technological term, only these five needs have limit switches. The remaining needs are totally different in nature from the first five.

4.2 Orienting feelings
(Could someone orient me as to what orienting feelings might be?)

So far we have seen that people are, on the one hand, forced by their feelings to satisfy their needs and, on the other hand, helped by their feelings in their orientation in the external world. Okay, but what helps us in choosing among things? What makes us decide to do this and not that? If we are hungry, we start walking around to find food. With the help of our information system, we can nicely navigate in the world around us and we may find some food that offers a sweet feeling, some that offers a salty feeling, some that offers a bitter feeling, and indeed some that offers a sour feeling. Which one will we eat? "What a silly question!" my dear reader may be thinking now. "Of course, the one that tastes the best!" Yes, but sometimes it is the feeling generated by the sweet food, sometimes the salty, sometimes the bitter and sometimes the sour that we find the most pleasant at a given moment depending on what we have eaten before, how long since we last experienced the given taste and what type of food our organism wants at that moment. One day we prefer salty, the next day we prefer sweet. Well, which is the most pleasant feeling then? Be careful! The chemical properties of the given food generating a particular feeling of taste are always exactly the same. They do not change, not even slightly. On the basis of this, we must state that there is nothing like the most pleasant feeling of taste and there is nothing like a more pleasant feeling of taste either: there are only different feelings of taste. There are the feelings of sweet, salty, bitter and sour. Then why do we find one taste better than another? Let me tell you the secret: we do not find one feeling of taste more pleasant than another, all that happens is a new feeling appears which is very difficult – and takes much experience – to separate from the incoming feeling. Since the incoming feeling and the new feeling are both feelings, they will overlap one another and start interfering with one another. Functionally speaking, this new feeling guides us and tells us which incoming feeling – taste in our example – to prefer at a given moment. Let us call this feeling an orienting feeling.

In the case of sight, which is not an actual feeling, it is easier to separate orienting feelings from the incoming data. If we see a picture and see it is beautiful, the word 'beautiful' means that the picture generated a nice aesthetic feeling in us. In this case the emerging aesthetic feeling is nothing else but an orienting feeling. This is the feeling that helps us decide which picture to look at: a picture that is beautiful to us or a picture that is disgusting to us. Do not forget that the aesthetic feeling is created in us, and exists in us and not in the picture. This feeling belongs to us and not to the picture. The picture is as it is. It is nothing more than a combination of surfaces selectively reflecting incoming electromagnetic radiation of different wavelengths. When we return next time, we may not find the picture as attractive although the picture itself will not have changed. We have changed and the orienting feeling generated in us has changed. So, while looking at a picture, we can easily differentiate the image we see from the orienting feeling emerging in us, but it is more difficult to separate the taste of the food from the related, pleasant or unpleasant, orienting feeling while we are eating.

Why do we need orienting feelings? Well, orienting feelings define how we behave in connection with the different phenomena of the external world. Whether we should avoid or disregard a certain thing or whether we should try to get it or make contact with it. Going back to the example of finding food: it is the orienting feeling that will define whether we reject a given food, react in a neutral way to it, or want to eat it. To ensure better understanding, let us try to show it in Figure 3.

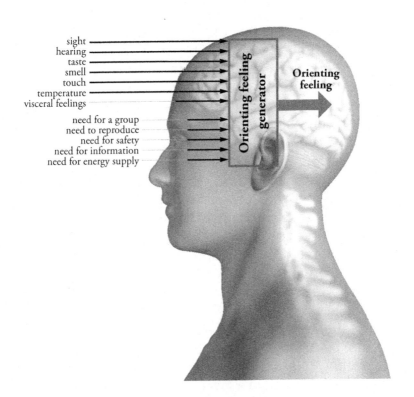

sight
hearing
taste
smell
touch
temperature
visceral feelings

need for a group
need to reproduce
need for safety
need for information
need for energy supply

Orienting feeling generator

Orienting feeling

Figure 3

In the top left of Figure 3, you'll find the input channels of data coming from the external world. The data are present in these channels in the form of feelings. Another channel is also shown in the picture: the channel of the feelings within the body that transports feelings coming from our joints, muscles and guts. We call these feelings visceral and somatic feelings. For the purposes of this figure, the word 'input' is used in its system technology sense. On the right-hand side, the output of orienting feelings is shown. The term 'output' is also used in its system technology sense. In the middle, you see an orienting feeling generator. How does this generator work? The starting point of the process is the need. The feeling of a need being unsatisfied at a given moment starts the process. The individual starts to satisfy her needs and, in the meantime, she collects data about her environment that are represented in her as sight and other incoming feelings. The data are processed and an orienting feeling representing the current physical and psychological status is generated in her. By reacting to the given incoming feelings, this orienting feeling is responsible for avoiding environmental impacts unfavourable for the individual and for finding favourable ones in order to satisfy the given need in the best possible way. The way it takes place is when the individual perceives an unfavourable, perhaps even dangerous environmental impact, an unpleasant orienting feeling is generated in her which she tries to terminate by avoiding the given environmental impact. When she meets something that is necessary or useful for her, a pleasant orienting feeling is generated in her and she tries to increase it by exposing herself to the given environmental impact to let it have its own way.

A consequence of the above is that orienting feelings never generate by themselves, they are always connected to incoming feelings. Naturally, it may happen that she evaluates the data arriving through a given channel as neutral for her and then no orienting feeling is generated. So the quality of orienting feelings may range between pleasant, neutral and unpleasant. Since data are arriving in multiple channels at the same time, orienting feelings are present most of the time. Times without any orienting feelings are rare. The individual will rank the orienting feelings and will choose the most pleasant for her. Have a look at Figure 4 below.

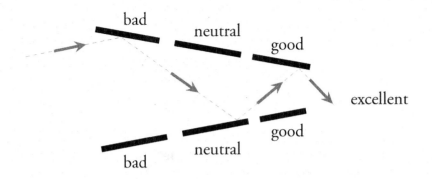

Figure 4

Orienting feelings, as we saw, are defined by incoming feelings, sight and the current internal status of our organism. Since very many basic feelings exist even within one single data channel, and these basic feelings form composite incoming feelings and interfere with composite incoming feelings from other data channels, all these feelings together create an endless ocean of incoming feelings. This ocean is then flooded with the practically infinite variations of data provided by sight, so the total of the variations of the input data flow is completely beyond comprehension. And to make the situation even less "simple", our organism generates the appropriate orienting feeling from this mass of data of the incomprehensible amount of variations in harmony with its current physical and psychological status – another factor of infinite variations. Therefore, two orienting feelings can never be the same, they can only be similar to one another.

So we can declare that the quality and intensity of an orienting feeling depend on three factors:

1) Our current physical and psychological status,
2) The quality of incoming feelings,
3) The intensity of incoming feelings.

As the first factor is completely dependent on the given

circumstances, it does not make much sense to look at it because the number of potential combinations is endless. We can carry out the examination of the remaining two factors best if we always consider one of them as a constant and consider the other one only as a variable.

Let us start with the easier case. Let us suppose that the intensity of a given incoming feeling is constant. For better intelligibility, let us examine the incoming feelings generated by sound waves. Let us set the volume control of our imaginary sound generator to the fixed volume of 20 dB and let us set the pitch to 1500 Hz which is easily detectable for the human ear. Now let us start changing the pitch constantly without touching the volume control. And let us monitor the orienting feelings generated in us. We will see that different pitches will generate pleasant and unpleasant orienting feelings in us (according to personal preference). Now let us find a pitch that generates a pleasant incoming feeling in us and let us fix our generator in this position. Now let us grab the volume control and start changing the volume, and monitor the orienting feelings generated in us. We will see that our orienting feeling perceived so far will change with the changes of volume. This is something we often experience in everyday life: it does make a difference if we listen to a romantic piece of music as a thundering march or listen to a military march as a distant whimper. How our pleasant orienting feelings connected to a certain pitch change in relation to volume depends on our individual personal taste.

So far so good. Now, however, let us take a special case that still happens quite often in everyday life. Let us suppose a pleasant orienting feeling is intensified with the increase of the volume. It often happens in everyday life that after experiencing pleasant orienting feeling we would like to experience the same feeling more intensely by increasing the intensity of the incoming feeling. And that is where the shoe pinches! Because at the moment we start increasing the intensity of the incoming feeling, Weber's law of the difference threshold starts working. What does it mean in our experiment? If we were listening to the sound generating a pleasant orienting feeling at a low volume so far, a small increase of volume will produce a pleasant increase in the orienting feeling in us. But if we were listening to the sound generating a pleasant orienting feeling at a higher volume so far, we can only trigger a pleasant increase of the orienting feeling with a large increase of the volume. What is the explanation? We simply do not perceive smaller changes of intensity in the case of higher intensity incoming feelings. As a result, orienting feelings will not change either, or will not change in direct ratio to the increase of the intensity of the incoming feeling. This fact, as we will see later on, plays an important role in people's lives.

As a matter of fact, there are three types of orienting feelings. One of them is comparable to a two-variable equation where one of the variables is the object, food, drink or phenomenon that triggers the effect and the other variable is the human being itself in whom the feeling is generated. But if we already know one of the variables and fix it, the equation becomes a single variable one. Translating all this into the language of feelings, if we select a given object, food, drink or phenomenon that we are examining, the parameters of these things will be constant and it will only depend on the internal status of the subject what feelings are generated in him. That is to say, the taste of the apple pie is always the same, while the orienting feeling generated in relation to it depends on the status of the person tasting it, so the system becomes a single variable one.

The second type of orienting feelings has three variables. These orienting feelings are usually responsible for ensuring the proper and appropriately timed implementation of a certain series of activities or behaviour in the appropriate order and way. Evolution attached pleasant orienting feelings to a part of many possible activities under certain circumstances thus ensuring that we are "interested" in implementing them. So we can only experience those pleasant feelings if we carry out certain activities under certain circumstances. That is to say the creation of the orienting feeling depends on three factors: the status of the person carrying out the activity, the external circumstances and the appropriate implementation of the activity. Using the example of a handshake, it does make a difference what psychological status we are in, whose hands we are holding and how we implement the handshake (it does matter whether you are shaking the hand of a friend or you are holding the hand of your lover). It is important point out that three-variable orienting feelings are not only generated in us genetically but can also be learned. During our lifetime, pleasant or unpleasant orienting feelings may be associated with certain series of movements depending on whether they lead to pleasant or unpleasant outcomes.

The third type of orienting feelings is the "floating" type. As a matter of fact, floating orienting feelings are nothing other than orienting feelings of six, nine, twelve etc. variables. The problem is that we only have three of these variables, the rest of them lie with the people our feelings are related to. That means no matter if we define the variables on our side, we cannot do anything with the variables of the other party because they depend on another person. And the opposite of this is also true! No matter if the other person defines her variables if I do not care about her variables. So, being dependent on two or even more people, these feelings hang, or float, in the air.

I think I should now explain what I am talking about. The floating type of incoming feelings is responsible for regulating human relations and is generated in human relations. Examples of this type of incoming feelings can be for example intimacy, trust, cordiality, devotion etc. These pleasant orienting feelings are meant to ensure that a certain type of relation is created and maintained between people. It makes no difference, however, if we select the feeling of intimacy, for example, and act accordingly, or whether we are in a state in which we could experience this feeling if our partner is not, or if he is not behaving in line with intimacy or if he is being awkward or if his psychological state is inappropriate, for example he is angry; or if the external circumstances are not suitable. In order to experience the feeling of intimacy it is also necessary that our partner takes the appropriate steps and is in the state of mind where he can also experience the feeling, and the external circumstances must also be suitable (external circumstances also include our behaviour).

I can best show the difference between three-variable and floating orienting feelings with the example of basketball. Three-variable orienting feelings are like simple basketball when our goal is just to put the ball into the basket with the appropriate series of movements. Floating orienting feelings are also similar to basketball with the difference that, in this case, somebody else is holding the basket and is running up and down with it as he will. You can only conjure the ball into the basket if you pay really close attention to the movements of the person running with the basket (and even then you may or may not succeed); if you ask the person to hold the basket still for you; if, for some reason, he wants to hold it still; or if you are simply lucky.

Typical floating orienting feelings are, for example, sexual orienting feelings but they can become three-variable feelings if our partner only plays a passive role in the act, or they can become two-variable in the extreme case of masturbation. Orienting feelings help in satisfying all kinds of needs but we will see that, due to the nature of our needs, floating orienting feelings will dominate in the case of higher level needs. It is logical since the contribution of others is also necessary for satisfying these needs.

Data coming from different channels might serve for the

satisfaction of one single need. Orienting feelings generated in connection with different data channels will form a final resultant in such cases. For example, if we suddenly feel the smell of a food that generates a pleasant orienting feeling in us, then we see the food which again generates a pleasant orienting feeling in us but then, when we taste it, its taste generates an unpleasant orienting feeling in us, in the end we will not eat it. In this example we saw the interaction of two-variate orienting feelings but three-variate and floating orienting feelings can also interact with one another. But whatever type the orienting feeling is, the general rules apply to it anyway. And the general rules are that even if all the external circumstances are the same, a different orienting feeling is generated every time and it disappears as soon as it has fulfilled its mission. But when does an orienting feeling fulfil its mission? This is what the next chapter sheds light on.

The cooperation of need-indicating and orienting feelings

As I mentioned earlier, multiple indicating feelings can represent one single need. Let us now use the example of the need for energy supply and, more specifically, the feeling of hunger. In order to better understand the cooperation of needs and orienting feelings, let us make a simple drawing. Look at Figure 5.

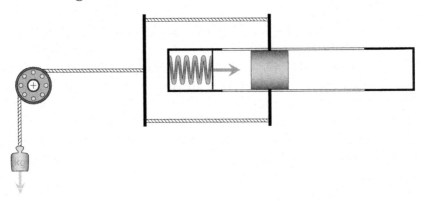

Figure 5

Imagine a cylinder with a push spring at one end and a piston in the middle with one handle at each side. The piston can move freely in the cylinder. Let us now tie a rope to the handles of the piston at each end. Then let us tie the two ropes together and let us attach a weight to their joint end. Now, let us sling the rope over a pulley equipped with a brake assembly, and apply the brake so that the weight will only slide down slowly. As the weight sinks down, it pulls the piston until it reaches the spring. As the weight keeps sinking and pulling the piston, the spring becomes compressed which gives an increasing counter-pressure to the piston as it tries to return it to its original position and restore the original status of the system.

Now let us try to interpret the figure above with regard to our needs. In the starting position our organism is in balance: it has the necessary amount of energy to function and stay alive. However, our organism, slowly but surely, will use up its energy reserves. This process is represented by the weight slowly moving downwards and pulling the piston. The lack of energy in our organism will reach a certain critical level and, upon reaching that level, it will send an alarm: "Careful! Low energy level!" This alarm is a feeling: the feeling of hunger. In our model this is the moment when the piston reaches the spring and starts compressing it. The alarm is symbolised by the force with which the spring tries to return the piston to its original position. The later we eat, the hungrier we become, i.e. the more the spring is compressed, the more intensively it tries to return the piston to its original position. Now let us eat a few bites. Food intake is represented by the force symbolised with the large arrow that is operative on the handles of the piston and that tries to return the piston to its original state of rest. Now let's look at Figure 6.

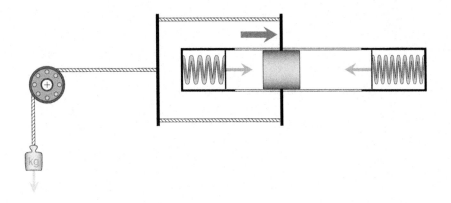

Figure 6

As the new force starts to operate and starts moving the piston, the force of the spring decreases. As we start eating, our feeling of hunger also starts decreasing. The energy supply of our organism starts getting back to its normal position and now we do not need the warning alarm any more. The feeling of hunger will reduce and terminate after a certain amount of time. Yes, but let us suppose we are voracious. I know, my dear reader, that you are not but now, for the sake of the experiment, let us act as if you were. So let us continue eating. As our stomach gets fuller, it just expands and expands. After some time, in order to prevent it from bursting, we need to stop eating. But when? We will receive a message. Needless to say, it arrives in the form of a feeling: the indicating feeling of repletion and fullness. The more we eat, the more uncomfortable we will find this feeling. The feeling of repletion is symbolised by the force of the spring placed at the right end of the cylinder in Figure 6. The more we compress the spring, the more strongly it will try to return the piston to its original neutral position, i.e. the more strongly we will feel the feeling of repletion. Now we can stop eating and we will see that our organism starts processing the incoming energy and the feeling of repletion slowly disappears and a neutral state sets in which, after a certain time, will again be replaced by the feeling of hunger and everything starts again from the top.

Now we will try to find out how orienting feelings work. Let us have a look at Figure 7

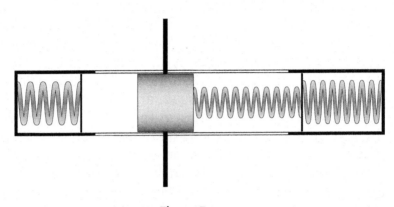

Figure 7

Figure 7 shows a cylinder with a piston in it. At the left end of the cylinder we put a push spring symbolising unpleasant orienting feelings. These are the ones that repulse us and keep us away from undesirable things. These are the feelings that we try to avoid. If we still cannot avoid undesirable things, the bigger impact those things have, the more strongly the unpleasant orienting feelings repulse us. We attached a pull spring to the piston from the right-hand side symbolising orienting feelings that we found pleasant. These pleasant feelings attract us and we strive to "get" and experience those feelings. The further away we get from these feedings, the more they attract us. The closer we get to them, the more their attraction reduces and, after a certain time, we do not find them attractive any more. And if we still keep receiving those feelings, they may even turn into negative and bad feelings which repulse us. These repulsive feelings are symbolised by the push spring at the right-hand side of the pull spring.

Using a specific example, let us imagine that we need to drink a glass of castor oil or, if you do not know castor oil, imagine a glass of lukewarm lard. The more we push it, the more terrible feelings will overcome us. This is the unpleasant feeling symbolised by the push spring on the left. If, however, it happens to be our favourite food and we have not eaten it for a long time, then we will want to taste it again. This feeling is symbolised by the force of the pull spring. If we ate our favourite food yesterday, we will find it less attractive and if we ate it an hour ago, we won't want to taste it at all. So the force of the pull spring also decreases. And if we had to eat it again and again, we might start to hate it, i.e. the push spring at the right-hand side would be activated. Although the taste of our favourite food does not change, since our organism is filled with the nutrients retrievable from it, the orienting feeling associated with the food that was pleasant in the beginning starts to decrease, then turns to neutral and then transforms into an unpleasant orienting feeling.

But this is the normal course of things. This is exactly the task of orienting feelings: to avoid things that are disadvantageous for us and to get things that are advantageous for us. Why should an orienting feeling last any longer? If we have already avoided the disadvantageous things and have obtained the advantageous things, why would we need them anymore? What would be the reason for their survival? Nothing. That is why orienting feelings disappear when they have completed their mission.

Let us now connect the piston representing our needs with the cylinder symbolising orienting feelings. Have a look at Figure 8.

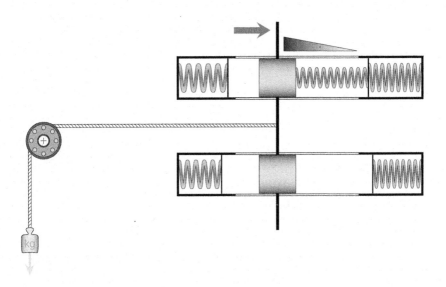

Figure 8

Let us fix the two pistons together rigidly because these things are connected within us as well. The initial state is a neutral position. No feelings tell us that we should satisfy any of our needs. If our channels of incoming feelings collect data about anything that can be useful for us, a pleasant orienting feeling may emerge to attract us. This is symbolised by the pull spring at the right-hand side of the top cylinder. As time passes, the internal balance of our organism gets upset. This is shown by the system of pistons moved by the weight. As our organism reaches a critical margin, it sends a need-indicating feeling about the necessity of satisfying a need. The more off-balance we are, the stronger the warning feeling is. This feeling is represented by the force emerging in the push spring at the left-hand end of the bottom cylinder. At the same time, feelings that we found pleasant and attractive anyway will become even more attractive. This is represented by the increase in the force of the pull spring operating on the top piston, due to the fact that it is pulled further apart.

Now let us satisfy our need. We indicated need satisfaction with the arrow symbolising an external force operating on the assembly of pistons. By satisfying our need, the intensity of the indicating feeling will decrease and then disappear just like the pushing force of the left-hand spring in the bottom cylinder. If we go on satisfying our need – even when it has ceased being a need because we do not need any more – the pleasant orienting feeling accompanying the satisfaction of the need will lose some of its power, i.e. the force of the pull spring operating on the top piston will reduce. If we continue the process further, an unpleasant warning feeling will appear whose function is to stop the process. This is represented by the right-hand spring in the bottom cylinder exercising a counterforce. The force of attraction on the top piston also disappears, and what is more, it may even turn into a repulsive force. Translating all this into the language of the need for energy supply: even if we are not hungry, we still like experiencing pleasant orienting feelings (that is why it is so difficult to stick to a slimming diet) which we will demand all the more if the feeling of hunger appears. With the increase of hunger, this demand gets even stronger. When we start eating, our feeling of hunger gradually decreases as does the pleasant orienting feeling. If we keep eating even when we are not hungry any more, the intensity of the pleasant orienting feeling will reduce, i.e. eating will not feel as good and we will receive a negative indicating feeling from our stomach that tells us to stop eating or we may burst. If we still continue eating, a point may come when the orienting feeling that was pleasant so far turns into a neutral, or even an unpleasant, orienting feeling and we may even grow to hate the given food for a lifetime.

But what is the case with food that generates an unpleasant orienting feeling in us? Figure 8 also answers this question. In a simple case when we are not talking about satisfying any need, only about enjoying pleasant orienting feelings, we try to avoid not too good or even unpleasant orienting feelings. These feelings repulse us with all their power: they push the pistons away from themselves. But if the demand to satisfy a need emerges, we are not that picky any more: the repulsive power of unpleasant orienting feelings decreases. The force of the weight is also against the force of the spring symbolising the unpleasant orienting feelings so the spring will be easier to compress. The "half a loaf is better than none" effect comes into play.

External circumstances can also influence the operation of the system. For example, if we are exposed to intensive physical stress, our energy reserves drain faster. If we are spending our well-deserved summer holiday on the beach lying in the sun all the day, we use less energy. We can best show the effect of external circumstances in a picture if we connect it to cylinders with a rigid linkage on the right and start moving them to left and right relative to the position of the fixed pulley with an external force. See Figure 9.

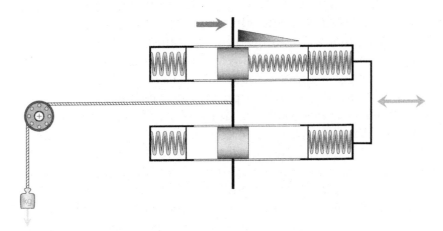

Figure 9

If you pull the cylinders to the right, the pistons get closer to the push spring on the left, which – based on the example of eating – corresponds with an increased energy use due to external factors, i.e. it results in the quicker appearance of the demand for need satisfaction. If you push the cylinders to the left, the pistons move further apart from the push springs on the left, which represents the state of lower energy use and the slower appearance of the demand for need satisfaction. The scheme above is generally applicable and holds true for every need or, to be more accurate, for every hardware type need. When I say hardware type needs, I mean the needs that are part of our "factory settings", i.e. the genetically encoded needs of human beings. These are the needs for energy supply, information, safety, reproduction and group.

In the case of software type needs like the need to meet others' expectations, the need to meet our own expectations or the need for self-realisation, we do not find indicating feelings. These needs are only activated under special circumstances. One of the big problems of human beings living in developed economies is that they do not use the cylinder of orienting feelings for its original function. In the olden days, the cylinder of orienting feelings was only an aid for satisfying needs, whereas today it is also the means of getting pleasure: something we cannot use unpunished. You can see that the cylinder of needs and the cylinder of the orienting feelings constitute an indissoluble unit. If we immerse ourselves in the pursuit of pleasure, it will have its physical consequences. Think of gaining weight, for example. What do you think you buy when you walk into a cake shop? Cakes? No! You buy pleasant orienting feelings disguised as cakes. Cakes are not primarily meant to satisfy the need for energy supply but simply serve the purpose of finding pleasure instead. Well, this seems to solve the riddle of the apple pie. We do not feel love while eating the apple pie. But what is love then? Soon you will be given an answer, my dear reader.

Multiple cylinders of orienting feelings might be attached to the same cylinder of needs where different orienting feeling cylinders represent the orienting feelings associated with different channels of incoming feelings. This is shown in Figure 10.

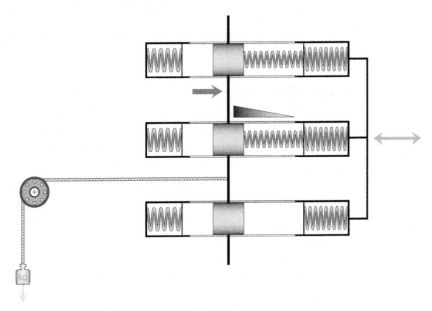

Figure 10

The cylinders do not always work in sync. They can modify the effect of one another and, sometimes, they can even work against one another. For example, the pleasant smell of food generates a pleasant orienting feeling, whereas its appearance may generate an unpleasant one. The mechanical model above, however – although functionally speaking it serves its purpose: it helps us to understand the relationship between need-indicating and orienting feelings – does not entirely reflect reality. Need-indicating feelings and orienting feelings in themselves are not sufficient to make humans actually act.

4.3 Strategic feelings
(Is it not only soldiers that have strategies?)

So far we have given an overview of the needs that are essential for our existence, and which feelings make us meet these needs, which feelings or incoming feeling channels help us orientate ourselves in the outside world, which feelings help us avoid the goals that are unfavourable for us, and which ones help us identify the favourable ones, which will help us satisfy our needs.

So, we have identified our objective with the help of orienting feelings. What should we do then? As we know, life is not a bed of roses. We normally need to act to make good things happen; we can't just sit back and do nothing. We have to struggle for everything. Strategy is important in this struggle. Generals give strategic orders in the battlefield. What are strategic orders? For example, an order to soldiers to occupy a certain town, or to avoid it because of the superior force of the enemy. Once the town is occupied, another order is given not to surrender if the enemy tries to reoccupy the town. The general, however, doesn't care about how the given task is fulfilled. That's none of his business.

It is not only generals who give strategic orders though, our minds also generate such strategic instructions in order to satisfy our needs. Orders are given to soldiers, those who execute them, in a written and oral form. But how do our minds give strategic instructions? They are manifested in the form of strategic feelings. In order to understand how it works in practice, let's have a look at Figure 11:

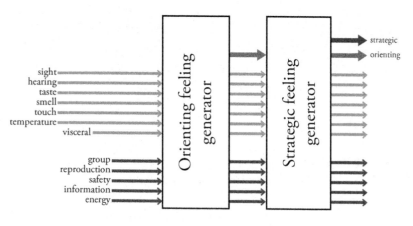

Figure 11

The figure demonstrates clearly that generally all the incoming feelings play a role in generating a strategic feeling,

including sight, the indicating feelings representing needs, and the orienting feelings. Sometimes, however, strategic feelings may be generated without need-indicating feelings as well, only through orienting feelings, as in case of an apple pie. At the same time no strategic feeling can be generated without orienting feelings, as the latter specify the goal of the whole process.

However, we need a bit of clarification here. One night my wife asked the following question: "Do we happen to have anything yummy in the house?" Oopsy-daisy! What does this question mean? That was when I realised that you can even desire things when there is nothing specific there to desire! More accurately, it was not a pleasant orienting feeling triggered by a specific food that started the process of desire. That is to say, the question was not: "Do we happen to have a slice of rum cake at home?" My wife desired the pleasant orienting feeling itself instead! So at that particular moment she was totally indifferent to whether it was an apple pie, chocolate cake or a Napoleon that triggered the pleasant orienting feeling in her, she only wanted to have something to do it (in the end we solved the problem with a bit of chocolate). But let us move on. Let me demonstrate with a short story how strategic feelings work.

On a sunny day, when the blue sky is full of fleecy clouds, a man is walking not too happily, as his need for energy supply is generating an indicating feeling in him in the form of hunger. As he is very hungry, he is collecting incoming feelings, as well as images about his environment. Then the gentle spring wind brings the smell of a roast chicken, which had been placed on a window sill by a housewife to allow the chicken to cool down to the proper temperature for lunch. The smell of roast chicken generates a pleasant orienting feeling in the man; that is when the first strategic order is given: Go and get it. This order is manifested in the form of a feeling: desire. As we know, desire is a sweetish, yet painful, all in all unpleasant feeling. Let's admit it, it's not good to long for something; sooner or later we would like to get rid of this feeling.

It is again worth paying attention to the orienting and diverting characteristics of the feeling. Desire will not tell us what to do, it will only encourage us to achieve our goals. Just like the general who does not care about how his soldiers get into the town to be occupied. All he does is yell at the soldiers, and it is the officers', the non-commissioned officers' and the soldiers' task to find out how to get into the town. Like all other strategic feelings, the strategic feeling of desire only makes sense under certain conditions. The general's strategic order to occupy a town only makes sense until the town is occupied; once the order is fulfilled, it is no longer relevant. The same is true for the strategic feeling of desire. We can only long for something until we get it. As soon as we have it, desire is over, as it has fulfilled its function.

Of course, desire as a strategic order has an opposite as well: rejection, loathing, disgust and shuddering, which are the various degrees of the same feeling. All these feelings suggest staying away from something, trying to avoid it. Disgust and its weaker variations are evoked by negative orienting feelings. Of course, disgust also discontinues once it fulfils its role, i.e. if we avoid what evokes unpleasant orienting feelings in us.

But now let us return to the roast chicken. Let us not bother how, but let us imagine the man is able to sneak up to the window sill and steal the dish with the roast chicken. That is when the next strategic order is generated: accept and keep it. The feeling equivalent of this order is joy. Joy is a pleasant feeling which encourages us to maintain a situation. But how? Again no mention is made of this. The strategic feeling of joy ends the processes guided by the strategic feeling of desire. As it is usually easy to fulfil an order given by the strategic feeling of joy, as well as to accept good and pleasant orienting feelings, once it has fulfilled its function, the strategic feeling of joy quickly dissolves.

The man, however, is clumsy, and drops the hot and greasy dish and the delicious chicken falls on the ground. What bad luck! That is when the next strategic order is given: hold on to it, don't let it go. The feeling equivalent of this order is non-physical pain, a feeling which wrings our hearts. This is the feeling we feel when we give up our favourite possession, when our girlfriends or boyfriends leave us or when a close relative dies. Of course, what the feeling is like and how strong it is depend on the situation, but all the above examples have the same origin and intend to fulfil the same function. The message and the order are as follows: hold on to it, don't let it go.

One of the biggest dramas of humankind may be that when we are able to get hold of something good, and the strategic feeling of joy tells us to accept and keep it, it is very easy to obey: all we need to do is accept the good thing. But once we have accepted it, the feeling of joy disappears, as it has fulfilled its role. However, if we lose a person who is dear to our hearts, if somebody we wholeheartedly love dies, we feel the strategic feeling of pain - hold on to them, don't let them go. What can we do then? Nothing. Nothing at all. Yet the pain will keep repeating to us to hold on to the person and not to let them go. And it will never stop, as it will never be able to fulfil its function.

And now let's return to the man and the roast chicken - the housewife's small, but rather aggressive dog pounces on the man, and starts to tear his trousers with its sharp teeth. Then comes the next strategic feeling: anger. Anger is nothing other than an order for aggression. What type and extent of aggression is quite another thing though. The strategic feeling of anger originates from the need for safety. However, we cannot always be careful enough to avoid what is dangerous for us. Sometimes we are cornered, and all we can do is try to neutralise and destroy the source of danger. Then we will feel anger, hate, hostility, indignation, fury, irritation and annoyance. The various degrees all encourage us to do the same thing: to attack, injure and destroy the enemy. However, there is a difference between the meanings of these words other than simply their degree. Anger is a primary feeling which, unless it can turn into aggression for whatever reason, will boil in us, i.e. we will start processing what happened, and as a result of this process we will feel hate, hostility, indignation, fury and irritation. However, these feelings are not "pure" anymore; they consist of a chain of tactical and technological feelings.

What characterises anger or feelings which encourage other types of aggression that originate from anger? What they have in common is that all aim at doing damage to the enemy, as well as causing physical or non-physical pain to them. It means that we will feel joy if the enemy is in pain, and feel non-physical pain when the enemy feels joy; so in order that we feel joy the person we have aggressive feelings towards should suffer. To achieve this goal we need to monitor the person's feelings, and we should be in synchronicity with them to be able to cause proper pain to this person. However, it usually requires little intelligence. The vast majority of people make do with a variety of simple, well-proven forms of aggression.

There are four types of aggression:

- Physical aggression is when we want to destroy the other person, or cause them physical injuries or physical pain. Physical aggression has several degrees too, and the degree is proportionate to the anger felt.

- Verbal aggression is when the other person's symbol of 'Self', the ego, and what they think about themselves are under attack, e.g.: when we reprimand and disparage them, or describe them with negative adjectives and thus cause them non-physical pain.

- Mental aggression is when we imagine hurting the other person either physically or verbally. In such cases the other person doesn't even know about the aggression.

- Unintentional aggression is evoked by a third party; it's a special type of aggression when a third person, an outsider, or a natural force will carry out the attack, doing the 'dirty job', without anybody ever commissioning that third person or the natural force. It is important to mention this fourth type of aggression, because it is the reason for gloating.

Aggression as an action can be a self-contained process or a subprocess as well. If it is a self-contained or main process, it is manifested by a combination of strategic feelings of its own, the strategic feeling set of which complies with usual strategic feelings: desire, disgust, joy and non-physical pain. Successful aggression is followed by joy. That's it. Accept it. Keep it up. However, while we commit aggression, we may have pleasant orienting feelings, i.e. we may have an agreeable orienting feeling with three variables when we hit, stab or shoot someone. Well, I know several kind-hearted readers are horrified now. How can someone write down something like this? I would rather ask: how can we educate people about it? Because that is what Hollywood action films do. Is not the script of such films all too familiar? In these films there is a very bad guy and, of course, a very good guy. The very bad guy does something very bad to the very good guy – he usually kills one of his close friends or relatives: it is necessary to make us hate the very bad guy. Then the very good guy teaches the very bad guy a lesson. And then comes the final clash when the so far tough very good guy suddenly becomes weak and the very bad guy almost defeats him but, at the very last minute, the very good guy revives and beats the very bad guy to a pulp. Attention: the very bad guy has to kick the bucket in the end. Why? So that viewers can enjoy it. The very bad guy certainly cannot pass away due to old age or hay fever, can he? A spectacular, horrible and spine-chilling death, big smoke and a lot of soot, that's what viewers want.

Or the other scenario is when the very bad guy beaten to a pulp gives up and the very good guy aims a gun at the very bad guy to riddle him with bullets. But then a voice says from the background: "Don't do it, it's not worth it." Then the very good guy lowers his gun, after long wavering, and walks away turning his back on the very bad guy, thus going to heaven morally. But being a really very bad guy, the very bad guy takes out a six-shooter water pistol from his waistband, and tries to shoot (squirt) the very good guy in the back. It is necessary to enable viewers to satisfy their inclination to aggression without feeling guilty because then, in self-defence, the very good guy can fill the very bad guy full of lead from the top of the moral Mount Parnassus with pleasure. Bang, bang, bang, bang - sounds the 50 calibre Desert Eagle (which is definitely not a toy gun). And while the viewers hear bang, bang, bang, bang, they can feel a pleasant feeling, and say something like "That's what the bastard deserved", rubbing their hands in satisfaction.

Attention – the murder committed by the very bad guy at the beginning of the film is just as much a murder as the one committed by the very good guy at the end of it. In both cases somebody was killed (that is the way murders are); however, we are outraged at one murder but enjoy the other one. Why? Because the director guides us through a whole chain of feelings set up in advance: during the first murder viewers feel pity, sympathy and non-physical pain, while the rest of the film is dedicated by the director to increasing hate more and more. When the second murder takes place, viewers are already outraged, full of the strategic feeling of hatred, which is then followed by the aggression committed by the main character. The difference between the two murders is anger, which is the strategic feeling of death and destruction. As the whole film is about what a bastard the very bad guy is, viewers do not need to feel guilty for enjoying the very bad guy's death. He got what he deserved.

What is the message of such a film? What does it teach us? That it is pleasant to kill someone. Of course, we are only allowed to relieve bad guys of the dismal hell of life on earth; then we can have a clear conscience. But who is a bad guy? The one who does not give his wallet voluntarily? The one who has different political views? The one who belongs to a different religion? Or the one whose skin colour is different? Why are we surprised then that violence is on the increase all over the world? We educate people to be violent. And we do it to make money. Congratulations.

Most people have a false idea about evil. A person who steps on others, and is ready to use any means to achieve their goals is an indifferent and selfish bumpkin at worst. An evil person, however, is someone who enjoys aggression, and who does what (s)he does out of joy, i.e. kills for pleasure. To cite classics, such a person has turned to "the dark side of the Force". All this may only happen because aggression evoked by anger and similar feelings generate the strategic feeling of joy, as well as pleasant orienting feelings (or else we would not commit aggression).

What type of aggression we resort to depends on the intensity of our anger, our senses, our relationship with the person in question, our habits and what impact the aggression we want to resort to will have on our need hierarchy. If we resort to aggression toward a person who is physically stronger than us, our need for safety may be in danger. If we are reviled in front of a lot of people, our need for meeting others' expectations, for being a member of a group and, finally, our need for safety may be endangered. Offensive words may evoke dislike in our environment, which may entail exclusion from the group we belong to, which may ultimately endanger our need for safety. To put it simply, if we give our boss a piece of our mind in public, we may quickly be fired, and will have nothing to live on.

Anger and hate are the self-strengthening feelings of destruction and death, and they both have a positive feedback. It is pleasant to hate as hate makes us strong. But be careful – if we hate someone, the other one will feel it and they will hate us too as we want the worst for them. So we will hate this person even more as they want our downfall. And that's not the end. Hatred leads to hatred. As ye sow, so shall ye reap. However, be careful not to swing to the other extreme either. Anger and hate are natural feelings. We need anger, hate and their weaker variations. Without these strategic feelings humanity would most probably have become extinct by now as we cannot always take to our heels and we cannot always avoid dangerous situations.

Besides the "appropriate" use of anger, i.e. meeting our need for safety, we resort to anger in other areas as well, often incorrectly. This incorrect use has two reasons. The first and maybe most frequent reason has to do with the fact that one of the feelings that signal the need for safety is pain. Our organism normally works as follows: whatever causes pain should be avoided and is dangerous as it endangers our existence; therefore, it is nothing but an attack against us that should be either avoided or followed by a counterattack.

Although non-physical pain is a strategic feeling, it hurts too. Though the two different types of pain are completely different regarding their functions, the reactions to them may be the same because of misinterpretation. Let's leave physical pain out of consideration now, as it is much easier to evaluate it correctly. What concrete cases may evoke non-physical pain? One of the manifestations of non-physical pain is the consequence of envy. An attribute of envy is that we only envy things we find desirable. Another important criterion is that we only feel envious of our close friends and acquaintances. We envy our neighbour for their car, but we would never even think of envying the richest man in the world for his private jet fleet. The third important characteristic is that we don't feel envious of a person to whom we would give the object we envy as a gift, i.e. our children, our spouses or our loved ones. The fourth trait is that we won't envy anybody if we also get the deeply desired object. Consequently, we can draw the conclusion that envy is the outcome of the misinterpretation of reality that the person we envy took the desired object away from us, as a result of which we feel strategic non-physical pain: don't let it go, hold on to it. The same is true for jealousy – it is also strategic non-physical pain, a cry to hold on to the other person, and not to let them go. Most probably some of my readers are morally upset by the well-known fact that some married couples have a sexual relationship with other married couples, but this fact only pinpoints the way jealousy works. If these people went to bed with a member of the other couple on their own, they could be jealous of each other. But not in this case.

The obstacle syndrome is when we aim at a goal, strive to achieve it, obeying the order of desire, and then suddenly an obstacle appears, which makes our objectives unachievable. The strategic feeling of non-physical pain tells us to hold on to our goals and not to let them go. We can have the same feeling day by day when driving, when another driver hinders us somehow. We can suffer because of our strong ego, our symbol of the 'Self,' suffers as well since the outer world continuously and impertinently attacks our strong egos. Yuck. No matter what, the outside world just doesn't want to believe that we are the most beautiful, the cleverest, the most ... And it hurts badly. Of course, our 'Self' symbols can be attacked really, directly, for example, when we are reprimanded, which also evokes non-physical pain. When discussing the need to meet other people's expectations later on, we will explain the way the ego works. Unfortunately, some people tend to interpret the above-mentioned sources of pain as attacks against them and, consequently, they commit a counterattack with some form of aggression.

Another frequent misapplication of anger is the consequence of a bad learning process, as well as the fixation of this consequence. If affectionate people face an obstacle caused by somebody else, it may be relatively difficult for them to overcome it. They should examine the situation, the other person's interests, the importance and weight of these interests as well as their impact on their and the other person's lives. They should analyse the data and make a decision whether to avoid the obstacle, help enforce the other person's interests or stand up for their interests and confront, or perhaps attack, the other person.

People full of hatred are in a much easier situation though – what they learnt was to step on everything and everybody. For such people anger and hatred are problem solving methods. If they come across someone who tries to hinder them, the two of them could sit down and discuss the problem. They could try to understand the other one, their reasons, and the motives of their actions. Or, if the situation of the other person required it, they might even help them. But no, that would be so awkward for them. They would have to think and all that stuff, so they would rather attack the other one, sweep them away and destroy them. These people are unintelligent as intelligence means being able to adapt to our environment but these people simply cannot adapt. Once they have learnt a problem-solving method, they are simply unwilling to apply any other means and that is why they remain unintelligent. They close their way to development by not trying to understand others. Such people do not accidentally get into the habit of applying anger as a problem-solving method. Anger evokes pleasant gut feelings as it mobilises our reserves and makes us stronger. It is natural, as hatred and anger are calls to fight. In such cases physiological changes take place in our bodies which prepare us for the imminent fight. Our pulse rate rises, blood pressure and breathing accelerate, pupils dilate, blood sugar and adrenaline levels increase, etc. It is a pleasant feeling if we don't need to be afraid of a counterattack: aggression makes us feel joy. Finally, the whole process makes the aggressor feel superior, which makes their ego even bigger and thus makes them even more desperate. But the aggressor doesn't know yet that soon they will have to pay the price. Hatred that cannot transform into aggression is harmful. It is like turning our car engine to full speed and braking at the same time – our car will break down sooner or later and so will we. What should we do then? Should we beat everybody up? We don't think it would be a very good idea.

As a matter of fact all that is left is to be sensible. Everybody should learn to differentiate between real and presumed aggression. If we feel non-physical pain, we should try to find and understand the reasons behind it. We should rationalise the reasons and explain them to ourselves. Dear reader, please do not expect to achieve 100% success immediately. It will take a while to learn these things. It is important not to resist hatred, however. Hatred is a natural feeling, an often useful one, and one of the basic cornerstones of human behaviour. We cannot eradicate or put an end to it. The objective is to tame the non-physical pain which originates from the unrealistic judgement of situations. If we can keep non-physical pain within healthy boundaries, hatred will disappear. But it's not an easy task. Taming our egos is especially difficult.

Although it doesn't fit into our story of the man and the roast chicken, there is one more strategic feeling left, which is a bit different from the others as – while the previous strategic feelings are, so to say, genetically inherent, i.e. that is the way we are "set up" – this one is something we are not born with, rather something we learn. Another important difference is that while we cannot live without the first five strategic feelings, i.e. desire, disgust, joy, non-physical pain and anger, adults can live without the sixth one. It is a learnt strategic feeling. We suppose our beloved readers must be curious to learn which feeling we are talking about. Well, it is love. Love originates from the need to reproduce. It is not enough to give birth to a baby; it must be fed, protected and raised. Nature ensures this care through the feeling of love. Love means to protect our babies, to keep them alive, to take care of them, to feed them and to protect them from all evil.

From a system technology perspective, the flagship feeling, i.e. the orienting feeling of love, is a system of strategic feelings that consists of a complex set of orienting, strategic, tactical and technological feelings. Love, although scientific research has so far been unable to prove it, is likely to be more than a single feeling. Most probably the feeling of love entails a flow of energy. A person who feels love gives energy to the other person. Love is a very pleasant, heart-warming feeling always connected to people or living beings. We feel love when the person or living being is present or when we think of them. The intensity of the feeling increases if we come into physical contact with our loved ones, i.e. when we hug them, hold their hands or arms or simply pat them on the back. The importance of physical contact and the fact that we can only love a living being suggest the likelihood of energy transmission.

Why is love an orienting feeling? Because we can long for it, i.e. we can feel the strategic feeling of desire related to it. But we cannot have a strategic feeling related to another strategic feeling. We cannot long to feel desire, disgust or non-physical pain and, unbelievable as it may sound, we cannot long for joy either (or at least we cannot long to feel joy ourselves); what we can long for is the orienting, tactical, technical and status-indicating feelings which either precede or follow joy.

How do we know we love someone? Yet another stupid question, the reader may think, though it is not always easy to answer it. If we love someone, we feel joy when the other one is happy and we feel pain when the other one is suffering. It means that we are in synchronisation with the strategic and status-indicating feelings of our loved ones. If they are happy, we are happy too; if they feel non-physical pain, we feel the same way too. Then we do practically nothing else but extend our boundaries to our loved ones. We become one a little bit with the person we love.

When interacting with our environment or a person to whom we are indifferent, we only use our internal coordinate systems, i.e. we are guided by the orienting, strategic, tactical, technological and status-indicating feelings evoked in us. However, when we come into contact with someone we love, our coordinate systems are supplemented with those of our loved one. We are guided not only by our feelings, which are part of our coordinate systems, but we also continuously monitor the strategic and status-indicating feelings of our loved ones and our actions are influenced by the strategic feelings evoked in the other person. The intensity of the influence is in direct proportion to the intensity of the love we feel towards the other person. It means that the more we love someone, the more we care about them; but there is more to it than just passively monitoring the strategic feelings of the beloved person. As the two coordinate systems are in synchronisation, i.e. we are happy or sad when the person we love feels that way too, we are forced to do our best to make the other person happy so that we can be happy too and we make efforts so that the other person does not grieve in order for us not to feel grief either.

While in the case of anger it is enough to superficially monitor the feelings of the person we hate, in the case of love we need thorough, creative and comprehensive monitoring. We do not need to be rocket scientists to destroy and ravage, but we definitely need to be smart to create and to foster others. This is why only affectionate people can feel sympathy, anxiety and pity as a certain level of intelligence as well as learning to pay attention to others are necessary to be able to feel these feelings. A boorish person with an unfeeling heart is incapable of it.

Orienting feelings also play an important role in the set of feelings where the flagship feeling is love. For example, caressing and hugging are accompanied by three-variable orienting feelings. A grandmother may hate the fiddling around involved in baking, i.e. she may dislike baking, but if she needs to bake her grandchild's favourite cake, she will do it with all her heart, she will literally put all her heart into it.

What it is like to feel love is something we should ask mothers about: what they feel when they hold their child in their arms or when they hug them and protect them. Yes, mothers know what love is. This is love at its best. There is no other love. None. That is it. As simple as that. It is very important so, dear reader, please remember it.

Unfortunately, not every child is lucky enough to grow up in a loving environment. Such children cannot learn to love nor learn how to use it, although they need it too. Why do you need to learn to love? On the one hand because, as we have mentioned before, the set of strategic feelings where the flagship feeling is love is rather complicated and complex. We should feel and grow fond of the feeling of love, we should learn to pay attention to the beloved person and monitor their reactions; we should discover, come to like and then get accustomed to the pleasant strategic and orienting feelings caring for another person entails. Affectionate people are those who have already discovered the "realm" of love, have got into the habit of loving, and enjoy the pleasant feelings evoked by love day by day.

On the other hand, love requires courage, openness and opening our hearts to the other person. If we love someone, we become vulnerable. To love we need to be open and to trust the other person. You can't love somebody and put a gun to their heads at the same time just to be on the safe side. Yet love is one of the most effective "weapons" as love is great power. Love is a feeling with a positive feedback, i.e. it is a self-strengthening feeling. It feels good to love. If we love someone, they will feel that we want the best for them and will return it, and when we feel that this person loves us, we will love them even more.

But love must not be fetishised. We can't love everybody.

It would be stupid to love Adolf Hitler as he caused the death of fifty million people. We should clearly understand that both anger and love fulfil an important role. We mustn't turn either anger or love into a moral issue. The root of the problem lies elsewhere. Some people are full of love, and some are full of hatred. It depends on what we learnt, and how and when we apply it. Although love is connected to reproductive needs, we feel it not only while meeting those needs but we also learn to feel love in other areas of life. It is not only our child we can love, but our parents, wives, husbands and friends as well.

Of course, love has all sorts of shades. There is a difference between holding a child or our beloved ones in our arms, holding a small bird in our hands or hugging a friend. It's like good cognac – Armenian, Georgian and French cognacs are all different, although they are all made of grapes. Love is always a little bit different but the message is the same: life. Well, dear reader, the choice is yours. We can decide to love people and receive lots of love, or hate people and be hated ourselves. Unfortunately, the problem is not so simple, but the final conclusion, the final outcome is. If we were not taught to love in our childhood, it's never too late. We can learn to love at any time. It feels good to love. Try it and get accustomed to it. Then we will love someone not because it is in our best interests, but because it is good to love.

Of course, it doesn't mean that we should fling ourselves into everybody's arms – not everybody in the world has good intentions. Besides, we know the saying: it is better to give than to receive. When we give somebody a gift, we feel the pleasant feeling of love, we feel pleasant orienting feelings while making or buying the present and we are also glad to see that the other person is delighted with the present, while the person who receives the gift only feels joy and this feeling will soon fade away.

While discussing strategic feelings, so far we have mainly

concentrated on quality-related and functional indicators and have not had a look at the problem from the perspective of intensity. The intensity of the initial feeling of the process, i.e. desire, depends highly on the satisfaction level of the given need as well as the strength of the orienting feeling. If, for whatever reason, there are no obstacles, yet the process slows down, the intensity of desire may increase or decrease. At the end of the process the joy we feel over achieving our desired outcome is usually in direct proportion to the intensity of our desire. Attention though – this is not the orienting feeling evoked by the object we got hold of. In case of an obstacle the non-physical pain evoked is in direct proportion to our desire. If we are deprived of something we long for, it is much more painful than if it is something we don't want that much. The feeling of anger following non-physical pain is in direct proportion to the intensity of the pain caused. The more painful it is, the angrier we are, which is fully understandable. The aggression committed, of course, depends on the intensity of our anger.

However, after overcoming the obstacle our joy is not necessarily proportionate to the misery we have been through. If we have achieved our goals too easily, the joy is not that big; it is biggest when we have to struggle hard for our objectives. If the struggle was too long and exhausting and we were pushed to our limits, we are moderately happy or our joy may fade away completely. And if we fail, we will feel non-physical pain. We need an optimum level of difficulty to feel joy.

Doesn't it sound all too familiar? Of course it does. This is what all games are based on. We enjoy games and sports because we enjoy the joy felt after overcoming an obstacle. If the reward is too small, the game is dead boring. If we choose the level of difficulty well and can overcome the obstacles, we will be rewarded by feeling joy. If the bar is set too high though, we will knock it off and non-physical pain is guaranteed. The secret of a good game is to choose the right level of difficulty. As we will see later on, games are played not only on the strategic feeling level; technological level feelings like tension and slackness are also involved.

4.4 Tactical feelings
(Do you need to be tactical?)

As we saw, the common feature of strategic feelings is that they do not give us instructions about the method of implementation. If we continue the military comparison, now is the time for the lower ranking officers. They have been given the command to occupy the town and they are responsible for finding out how to implement the manoeuver. They pass on the results of their planning in the form of tactical commands to the NCOs and soldiers. Tactical feelings are the counterparts of tactical commands in our case.

It is clear from Figure 12 that all the incoming feelings plus sight, orienting feelings representing needs, the orienting feeling and the strategic feeling all take part in the generation of the tactical feeling. We need to take into consideration, however, that part of the feelings listed below have skipped the attention of humankind so far and therefore they do not have names. I will describe these feelings, along with the analysis of their impact on the process. Such a feeling, for example, is the tactical feeling influencing data processing. This feeling does not have a name but its impact on data processing takes the form of carefulness or its direct opposite, carelessness. These feelings make us thoroughly examine all the available data and make a decision on the basis of this examination, or alternatively take only a few items of the available data into consideration and make a decision on this limited basis.

Tactical feelings related to energy management are laziness, comfort and zeal. We decide on the basis of these feelings how much energy to invest in the implementation of a given task.

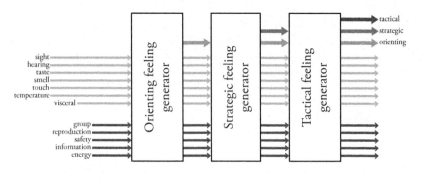

Figure 12

For example: let us suppose that on a hike we are walking to a rest house and there are two possible paths in front of us. One of them is shorter but it leads through a steep mountain, the other one is a comfortable path but it is a little longer. Which one will we choose? Time management is regulated by the feelings of hurry or leisureliness. Energy concentration is regulated by the feelings of tenderness and violence. The number of attempts is regulated by patience and impatience.

The next pair of feelings could be best described as a tank and water. The "tank" type of feeling urges us to get closer to our goal, crushing all kinds of obstacles, whereas the "water" type of feeling urges us to reach our goal cleverly, avoiding obstacles and confrontation on our way. It is important to note, however that, due to the function of strategic feelings, only one feeling, or command, can be active at any one time. So it is impossible to feel desire and disgust for the same thing at the same time just as it is impossible to long for and feel joy for the same thing at the same time. However, multiple tactical feelings can be activated at the same time thus ensuring that a need is satisfied. In our example, I can start climbing the mountain in a careless, zealous and impatient way instead of going around it cautiously, comfortably and in a leisurely manner. The only way this can happen is for each of the variants listed here to take a value. For example, since processes take place in time, the speed of a process will be somewhere between the extreme speed values determined by the feelings of hurry and leisureliness. At the worst, if a given parameter does not play an important role in the implementation of a task, it will take the medium or a random value between the two extremes. However, at the level of tactical feelings, we still do not find the feelings that are necessary for the specific implementation of a given task.

4.5 Technological feelings
(What do feelings have to do with technology?)

Finally, we have reached the level where the smallest details of human activities are decided upon. This is rather shaky ground where no serious scientific research has been carried out yet, the level of technological feelings. Getting back to our military comparison, we are now at the level of the soldier at the end of the series of commands. The soldier is aware that he must defend his homeland. This corresponds to the feeling of need. He can do that if he wins the war. That corresponds to orienting feelings. The strategic command is to occupy the town. According to the tactical command, a hard and concentrated attack is necessary. But it is up to the soldier to decide when he jumps out of the trenches, which bush he hides behind, which target he shoots at, how he holds his gun, which finger he uses to pull the trigger, how he bends his finger on the trigger etc.

If we go back now to our roast chicken story, our friend there was reminded of the need for energy supply by the feeling of hunger. Due to the orienting feeling related to the smell of the chicken, he is aware that he can satisfy his need with roast chicken. The strategic feeling of desire urges him to get the roast chicken. His tactical feelings tell him to act cautiously and quickly and spare no effort. And his technological feelings tell him how to climb over the fence, how to stretch out his arm, how strongly his fingers should grab the chicken, how to raise the chicken to his mouth, how to open his mouth, how to bite into the chicken, how to chew it, how to turn the food with his tongue and how to swallow it.

I know it looks pretty complicated for the first sight. And it is complicated, indeed! Somatic feelings play the most important role among technological feelings. These feelings come from the muscles and joints that move our body. Why are they so important? You may remember that at the beginning of the book, we listed the conditions of existence. In point 7, the last point of this list, we stated that it is not enough for a living creature to examine the internal and external factors threatening the integrity of its system but it also needs to evaluate the data it has collected and, at the end, it needs to act to preserve its integrity. And the emphasis is now on the word act. We need to act. But how? How can we act? Well, you can only act with your body. More specifically, by changing the position of the points of the surface of your body in relation to one another or/and to an external coordinate system (no one can wave with her blind gut).

Let us now list, without striving for completeness, our body parts whose position we can change in comparison to one another, i.e. the ones we can act with. See Figure 13.

BODY PARTS
eyes
facial muscles
muscles of the mouth
jaw
tongue
vocal chords
head
neck
upper torso
lower torso
upper arms
lower arms
hands
fingers
genitals
thighs
legs
feet
toes

Figure 13

Since we are discussing purposeful activities, accidental or non-intentional movements must be excluded to start with. Purposeful activities, on the other hand, can only be coordinated activities due to their nature. What is necessary for coordinated movements? Naturally, a coordinate system. In order to make this concept clearer to readers who are not familiar with technical terminology, let us examine the idea in a little more detail.

Let us imagine a dark room. We are given the task to enter the room and find an apple (this is the dessert after the roast chicken) in the darkness. In the first case we are given the instruction to walk ahead five steps, then turn 90° to the left and take two steps, then turn 90° to the right and take three steps and there we will find the apple. In the second case we are informed that a grid is placed in the room whose partition is 1 m x 1 m and the elements of the grid are at a 90° angle to one another. The task is the same. We should walk ahead along the grid until we find the fifth node, then turn to the left, walk ahead until we find the second node, then turn to right and walk ahead until we find the third node on the grid and that is where we will find the apple. You can see this on Figure 14.

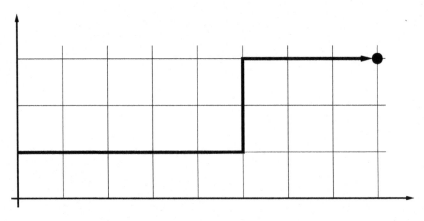

Figure 14

The two cases represent two different types of control. In the first case, the problem is that different people have different lengths of step and even one person might change the length of her steps and if the length changes even a little, such deviations can add up during the series of steps. The same applies to turns. If you only make a little mistake when turning, you are already in trouble. The errors of length and angle add up so that in the end, you may be in a completely different place from where you wanted to be. But the worst thing is that during the entire process you do not have the slightest idea where the heck you are in the room. In the second case however, you know exactly where you are all the time because the grid and its nodes give you accurate information about your current position and the direction and speed of your movement. The grid is nothing but a two-dimensional coordinate system where your exact position is given by the number of nodes you count ahead and across. If the apple is not put on the floor but on a shelf, the grid placed on the floor is no longer enough to find it because you also need to specify the height of the apple from the floor. So you need another grid in which you can define the position of the apple relative to the floor by counting the nodes from bottom to top. This is already a three-dimensional coordinate system (with length, width and height data).

Let us make things a little more difficult. The grid is made in such a way that the rods in it can be bent in relation to one another so the rods can only be not at right angles to one another but at any other angle without changing the length of the rods connecting the nodes. Take a look at Figure 15 below.

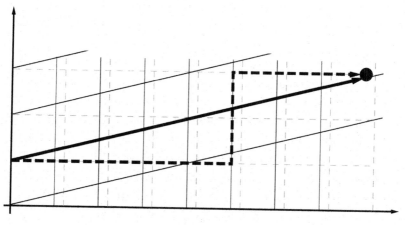

Figure 15

Can we now define the position of the apple? Yes, we can. We will find it in the same way in the darkness, only the instructions will say we should walk 7 ¾ nodes ahead instead of 5 nodes. If we want to define the place of the apple mathematically, we can easily calculate the new coordinates from the old ones by measuring the angle of the rods in the grid and counting the nodes.

So not only rigid coordinate systems can exist. A non-rigid coordinate system, for example, is the human body. Just as the length of the rods connecting the nodes in the grid does not change in the example above, the length of body parts does not change either in the human body; the only thing that changes is the angle of those body parts in relation to one another. So the coordinates of the tip of my index finger can be specified along with the angles between my torso and upper arm, upper arm and lower arm, lower arm and hand, hand and first finger bone, first finger bone and second finger bone, second finger bone and third finger bone and with the length of all these body parts.

Just think about it, my dear reader, how terrible it would be if we wanted to eat the apple in front of us and we had to take a folding ruler and a protractor and adjust each and every part of our body! We would definitely starve to death. Fortunately, nature has spared us this pain. We do not use a protractor (it had not even been invented when we started eating apples).

Yes, you may think that you can see the apple and the only thing you need to do is to pay attention to reducing the distance between the apple and your hand to zero. Yes, indeed, sight plays a very important role in coordinating movement but in order to ensure better intelligibility, let us disregard sight for the time being as we can eat in darkness and we can also touch any of our body parts in darkness. In other words, we know the exact coordinates of any of our body parts even in total darkness. Then what is it that can substitute for the folding rule and the protractor? Somatic feelings. Based on the feelings coming from our joints and muscles, we can accurately define the exact coordinates of all our body parts as well as our position in relation to the external world. We know even in darkness whether we are lying or standing, if our arm is bent or stretched out, what position the tip of our finger is in and how far it is from any of our other body parts. So we have an excellent somatic feedback system on the basis of which we know exactly where our body parts are at any moment in an imaginary coordinate system but we do not yet know where we need to move them. We do not have the target coordinates. It is exactly as if we gave a command to the gunners:

"Fire on the enemy!"
"Where's the enemy?"
"We don't know where the enemy is, we only know we're here. Shoot!"
"But where?"

There is nothing left to do but to give the target coordinates. How do we do this? Shall we take the folding rule and the protractor? Well, that did not work last time, so what shall we do then?

I suppose that not too many of my readers visit robotics exhibitions regularly. Let us then imagine that we are visiting one. The arms of the robots are moved by electric motors. Since robots do not have somatic feelings, different sensors are installed in the robot arms so the position, the coordinates, of the robot arms can always be defined on the basis of their signals. How can they program the robot arms? Well, with a folding rule and a protractor or... by learning! The operator of the machine switches the electric engines off and grabs the robot arm and simply leads it along the line the machine should follow until it reaches the goal. While he is doing so, the sensors installed in the robot arm continuously measure the exact coordinates of the arm and send them to the memory where they are recorded. When the electric engines are switched back on, the machine can carry out the movement on the basis of the coordinates stored in the memory. Or, not quite. If the machine only did this, we would repeat the scenario that happened to us in the dark room when we wanted to find the apple based only on the number of steps and we often made mistakes. The machine is designed in a much cleverer way. Although the machine follows the coordinates stored in its memory, it is also aware of the current position and the actual coordinates of its arm all the time on the basis of the data coming from the sensors. If the actual coordinates and the coordinates stored in the memory are different, the machine corrects the deviation. This is what the human organism copies. (Or is it the other way round?)

That reminds me of a joke in which somebody is asked: "Can you play the piano?" "I don't know. I've never tried." Well, playing the piano is something that you need to learn. In fact, not only playing the piano but any other coordinated movement also. When a baby is born, she cannot walk yet. Walk?! She cannot even turn to the other side while lying on her back, not to mention sitting or standing up! We need to learn how to move every single body part listed in the previous table separately. During our attempts, somatic feelings related to each body part are separately stored in a special compartment of our memory dedicated to the given body part. This is what we call learning. So the somatic feelings coming from the joint connecting the upper arm and the torso and the related muscles are stored in a memory compartment called 'upper arm', the somatic feelings coming from the joint connecting the upper arm and the lower arm and the related muscles are stored in a memory compartment called 'lower arm'. And this goes on and on with all the body parts listed in our table. Yes, but even this would not be enough! All we have achieved so far is that we have learnt how to move separate body parts but this is far too little for happiness. In order to take the apple in front of us, we need to coordinate the movements of the upper arm, the lower arm, the hand and the fingers. We learn this as well. We learn how to move different body parts, for example the upper arm and lower arm, together and we manage this knowledge as a subroutine, a small, independent programming unit. Then we organise subroutines into routines and this is how we store them. See Figure 16.

BODY PARTS	Somatic feelings	Subroutine	Routine
eyes			
facial muscles			
muscles of the mouth			
jaw			
tongue			
vocal chords			
head			
neck			
upper torso			
lower torso			
upper arms			
lower arms			
hands			
fingers			
genitals			
thighs			
legs			
feet			
toes			

Figure 16

So when I take the apple in front of me, I do not need to adjust all the joints and muscles between my upper arm and finger bones separately, I just take out from the appropriate "routine" compartment a nicely polished integral program suite that consists of a lot of sub-programs, subroutines or groups of somatic feelings that belong to each body part participating in the process.

Each need has its own set of activity routines. The need for energy supply has a different set of activity routines from those associated with the need for information, the need for safety or the need to reproduce. Naturally, since we can only act with the body parts listed above, these routines have similar grounds and partly overlap with one another. Food can be grabbed with the same movements as for a weapon, for example a pistol, only the rest of the series of movements is different (Never put a pistol into your mouth!).

The next group of feelings is the pair of tension and slack-ness, between the two extremes of which there are count-less intermediate states. The feeling of tension is closely re-lated to one of the groups of strategic feelings, namely the ones that start a process, i.e. the strategic feelings of desire, disgust, anger and love. We only feel tension if one of these strategic feelings has been activated before. The presence of only a need-indicating feeling or an orienting feeling is not enough to trigger tension and the slackness that follows it. So if you feel you are hungry, that alone will not generate the feeling of tension. If you feel the nice smell of some food, but you do not long for that food, tension will not appear. If the feeling of desire has already emerged and you would like to take steps to achieve the given goal but something does not let you do so or something stops the process; if the pro-cess of waiting and one of the strategic feelings mentioned above are present at the same time, that is when the feeling of tension appears. Waiting has a crucial role in the genera-tion of tension. If the obstacle is not there anymore and the wait is over, the feeling of tension discontinues and gives its place to the feeling of a pleasant slackness.

Functionally speaking, the feeling of tension always urges us to put an end to an intermediate state and finish the orig-inal process. The roles of tension and pleasant slackness are similar to the strategic functions of desire and joy, only they are at a lower, technological level. The notions of 'tension' and 'slackness' belong to one another and it is probable that they are elements of the same physiological process. Many do not know that these feelings play an important role in the sense of rhythm and in the fact that we enjoy rhythmic sounds, images or events. Rhythmic sounds are attractive to us because when we hear the sounds, the feelings of ten-sion and slackness keep alternating in us. After each and every rhythmic sound, we wait for the next rhythmic sound following the rhythmic interval with a growing tension, and when the next rhythmic sound arrives, tension immediate-ly disappears and gives its place to the pleasant slackness, then tension gradually takes over again, and so on and so forth. Since a certain amount of time is necessary for the generation and the fadeaway of these feelings and this time is limited by the capacity of the human nervous system, we do not enjoy rhythm above a certain frequency, or beat per minute, because feelings do not have the time to develop and fade away. The situation is similar if the tempo is too slow, only in that case feelings fade away before the new one can come to replace them.

So far we have seen that our decisions are prepared by paying attention to a great number of feelings. Naturally, these feelings will have to be compared and evaluated, and a good decision must be made. What specific groups of nerves participate in this process and what biological and chemical processes take place during decision-making, no one can tell today. But we can examine these processes at the level of feelings. The question arises of where and how the processing of the flow of feelings and the control of our activities take place. In order to clearly understand the situation, let us use our proven block diagram, shown here in Figure 17.

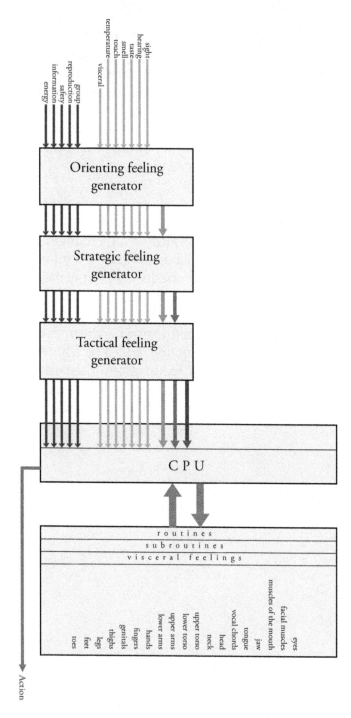

Figure 17

We can take the notion of the 'CPU', or 'Central Processing Unit', often used in information technology and add it to our diagram. The CPU is responsible for deciding if it is necessary to act, and if it is, what the goal of the action should be and how the action should be implemented with what and when. As the diagram shows, the CPU receives a great amount of data of many different kinds. The first thing the CPU has to do is to decide if it is necessary to act at all. The CPU analyses the level of satisfaction of the needs. If one or more needs are not satisfied, the CPU decides – on the basis of the data received through incoming feelings and sight, as well as the generated orienting, strategic and tactical feelings, and also taking the available set of activities into account – whether the given need or needs can be satisfied at the moment. This is when the technological feeling of decision-making appears.

However, we need to stop here for a moment. In the block diagram above there is no memory block in the direction of incoming feelings, that is to say the diagram does not take our experience from the past into account. Therefore, this diagram can only describe the process of a "first encounter", i.e. a situation where memory does not have a role to start with because this is the first time we have come across a certain phenomenon.

The feeling of decision-making is a dividing line. Some of the feelings participating in the formation of the decision cease or withdraw to the background. The decision, however, is not always followed by immediate action. The start of the activity may be postponed to a later time. The action itself is started by the short flash of the start feeling. Then the action itself starts and this action is characterised by the related somatic feelings coming into the forefront. The CPU loads the subroutines and routines necessary for the given activity and gives instructions to the muscles to carry out the task. At the same time, it checks the implementation of the series of activities with the help of the incoming somatic feelings and sight, and corrects the implementation of movements when necessary. The action is stopped by the flash of the stop feeling. The technological feeling of decision-making may be preceded by the technological feeling of choice. We often have to choose between two or more goals and the series of activities necessary for achieving them. Choosing may also take place at the level of needs, between the different demands related to the same orienting feeling of a given need. For example, at the level of the need for energy supply, in connection with the orienting feeling of hunger, I need to choose between the roast chicken and the apple. Choosing may also take place at the same level of needs but between the demands related to two different need-indicating feelings. For example, at the level of the need for energy supply, between the roast chicken related to the need-indicating feeling of hunger and a glass of water related to the need-indicating feeling of thirst. And finally, a choice can be made between demands related to different levels of needs. For example, shall I spend the night with my girlfriend or with my colleagues?

But of course, apart from choices made at the level of needs, we can also make choices in the case of actions controlled by simple orienting feelings. The technological feeling of choice can sometimes be followed by the technological feeling of doubt. Whereas the technological feelings of choice and decision-making close a series of feelings and, therefore, a phase of the entire process making possible the appearance of new series of feelings that represent a new phase of the process, the feeling of doubt opens up a loophole to reopen or revise processes that are already closed.

4.6 System status signals

(How can we find out what status we are in?
Why do we laugh at jokes?)

Those who we already had a car will know that you can drive a car without using the gauges. The gauges do not directly participate in the operation of the car as the engine or the wheels do. The gauges are very useful but, as a matter of fact, they are only there to give information to the driver about the current processes and statuses. One of the groups of feelings serves a similar purpose. In a car, gauges are organised in groups: a part of them monitors the status of the engine, for example the rev counter, the water temperature gauge or the oil pressure gauge; others, including the speedo or the inclination gauge of an SUV, show the characteristics of the movement of the car.

We can also classify system status signals into different groups. The first group may be the feelings indicating the status of the "engine", i.e. the CPU. This group includes the "rev counter". The "rev counter" is best characterised as the feelings ranging between excitement and "deep" tranquillity. For those who are familiar with information technology, these feelings are nothing but the indicators of the clock rate of the system. The clock rate coordinates the operation of the parts of a computer. Everything is adjusted to this clock rate. If we increase the frequency of the clock rate, the computer starts working faster; if we decrease the frequency of the clock rate, the system will slow down. Those who are not familiar with information technology, please imagine a pendulum clock. You can regulate the pendulum clock by raising or lowering the weight on the pendulum. If you raise the weight, the clockwork goes faster; if you lower the weight, the clockwork goes slower. We did not make any change to the clock mechanism itself, the only thing that happened was that we sped up or slowed down the operation of the system. Naturally, there is an optimum operation point also for human beings, where we can work the most effectively. If we "run" too fast, the cog wheels can get stuck or, in other words, we can make frequent mistakes; if we are too slow, we let the grass grow under our feet.

The next group of feelings is the one in which the feelings ranging between cheerfulness and sadness can be found. In order to better understand these feelings, it is best to compare them to the temperature of an object. If you want to change the temperature of an object, you need to transmit heat to it or extract heat from it and then, after a certain amount of time, the object takes the temperature of its environment. The time factor is defined by the heat inertia of the material of the given object. If the external temperature changes again, the temperature of the object will not change immediately, instead, it will try to keep its current temperature, due to its heat inertia.

There is a similar continuous transition between the extreme feelings of cheerfulness and sadness, which also change in a certain time typical for each person under the influence of the external circumstances we are exposed to. These states of feelings, just like the temperature of objects, have their own inertia. When we are cheerful, we do not like to deal with sad things and when we are sad we do not like to deal with cheerful things. More accurately, according to our current psychological state, the things of the world that would trigger sadness or cheerfulness almost rebound from us. But what is it that "heats up" or "cools down" people? Every unpleasant feeling moves us towards the extreme value of sadness, and every pleasant feeling moves us towards the other extreme value of cheerfulness in our imaginary scale.

Those who do not like technical comparisons, will suffer again for a few moments. We can better imagine the situation if we do not compare people to simple objects but rather to the heating and cooling type of air conditioner system (ladies are of course pink air conditioners, whereas gentlemen are electric blue ones) as an air conditioner does not only change its temperature on the basis of the influence of its environment, but can also heat and cool itself. It is important to introduce this comparison because people do not only change their mood under the influence of their environment, but their internal psychological processes will also have an impact on it. That is to say, the pleasant and unpleasant feelings generated by our own psychological processes also move us on the scale ranging between the feelings of cheerfulness and sadness. Our actual position on this imaginary scale will be defined by feelings triggered jointly by external and internal processes. This is a very important point as, to a certain extent, we ourselves can influence our own position on the cheerfulness-sadness scale at a given moment. Let us imagine that we are getting out of bed, hanging our head in a sombre mood on a foggy and rainy autumn morning. Suddenly we remember how much we laughed last night with friends, and we are already feeling better. Note that it is still autumn outside, it is still raining and our boss has not phoned to tell us that she has doubled our salary either. Everything is the same in the external world! But we have still moved upwards on the cheerfulness scale. However, you can also move down on the cheerfulness scale in the direction of sadness and depression even though nothing is changing in the external world! Only we push ourselves down in a deep-deep pit sometimes. We will address the mechanism of these pits in the chapter called *Feeling traps*.

The thermodynamics comparison also works well to describe how our thinking changes under the impact of sadness or cheerfulness. If you start heating water, you will see that the molecules forming it start "frolicking" more and more. Their range of movement in relation to one another gradually increases, whereas the connection between them gradually weakens and finally the boiling water evaporates, i.e. the connection between the molecules ceases to exist. Cheerfulness has a similar effect on us. The happier we are, the more scattered our thoughts become, the connections between the words of individual thoughts start weakening and finally, when we burst out laughing, our thoughts get completely disrupted and then disappear. Whereas sadness leads to our thoughts slowing down, thickening and freezing. Based on the above we can draw the conclusion that in order to ensure effective thinking, we need an optimum "room temperature", an optimum operating point somewhere between sadness and cheerfulness.

Although it is not too closely related to the topic, it will do no harm to say a few words about the "fuel", i.e. humour. Humour is the means by which we can move our mood in the direction of cheerfulness. Humour is always based on misunderstanding. There are two guys, each of them with their own coordinate system. In the beginning of their dialogue the two coordinate system is in synchronicity, i.e. both of them are talking about the same thing from the same aspect. However, at a given moment the two coordinate systems move slightly off in relation to one another. From this moment on, although they are talking about the same thing, they are talking about it from different aspects, each having a different series or chains of feelings. Both guys are having a good time in their own coordinate systems but they are "talking at cross purposes" and they do not realise that the coordinate system of the other one has slightly moved off. The person who is listening to the joke and looking at the event from outside, from an absolute coordinate system, immediately notices that the two guys are "talking at cross purposes". But he is not consciously aware of the situation, he only realises that the things the two guys say do not fit. When we get to the punchline of a joke, the coordinate systems having moved in parallel so far meet and cross one another and the mismatch, the fact that the coordinate systems have moved from one another, comes to light. This causes a moment of confusion in the listener who tries to find the answer. As a matter of fact, he wants to decide which of the two coordinate system is the valid one, which one he should choose and how to continue, i.e. which series of feelings he should follow. During the search for the answer, tension grows in him. After he realises the deviation between the two coordinate systems and understands the root causes, the tension suddenly drops and yields to the feeling of a pleasant slackness, the feeling of joy that the solution is found also flashes up for a moment and then laughing starts. And laughing is a very special process, a subroutine, if you like. All laughing does is it closes things down and 'deletes the data entering the CPU'. As if someone has pushed the delete button on a computer. The series of feelings related to the two different trains of thoughts crossing one another neutralise one another, the CPU gets reset and a completely new series of feelings is born. That is to say we do not deal with the solution of the problem anymore and the whole thing is deleted from the CPU. Laughing blocks further data input and processing, so to speak. If you laugh so much that you are literally rolling with laughter, the external world simply disappears for you. In such a case you do not feel needs, orienting, strategic, technological, technical or even incoming feelings.

Two friends meet. One of them sees that the other's arm is in a bandage.

"What happened to you?" she asks.

"Don't remind me! A dog bit me." answers the second one.

"And did you sterilise it?" his friend asks.

"No, I couldn't because it ran away!"

As a matter of fact, we like humour because of the pleasant slackness that follows the tension and because of the feeling of joy flashing up for the moment. The feeling of pleasant slackness can only be created if the tension, having built up in us, can discharge quickly. Therefore, too much deviation between the two coordinate systems is not allowed in humour: if you do not understand the punchline immediately, if you need to think about it for too long, the tension reduces and fades away and as a result the pleasant slackness will not be so much in contrast.

Based on the above, we can suppose that laughing heals. I remember once I participated in a Mind Control course where they offered 'laughter therapy' in the breaks. 20 or 30 people came together and started laughing, giggling and tittering violently. We, who were only observing the whole thing from far away, just smiled first but then we also burst out in wholehearted laughter. How can 'laughter therapy' work? It is simple! It erases the tensions accumulated in humans.

But it is not only humour that can help us to climb further up on the cheerfulness scale: we can also use other pleasant feelings. However, the law of maxima also stops the processes here, and we cannot feel happier beyond a certain level. To be on the safe side, nature sneaked a safety valve into the system. We can think of laughter as a kind of a safety valve that protects us from exaggerated storms of feelings by simply regulating pleasant feelings. But it is not only the happier end of the scale that has a safety valve: there is also one at the other end. This safety valve is nothing else but crying. Crying is also another delete button on the CPU. It deletes feelings that are too unpleasant. It is not a coincidence that they say you are relieved after having a good cry. The safety valve of crying can start operating in the case of 'storms of feelings' like getting moody, getting moved or being overjoyed.

Apart from the actual feeling of déjà vu, the group of déjà vu feelings also includes, in my opinion, feelings experienced when studying literary, musical or visual works of art: when we are 'touched' by art. These feelings are not in close connection with the theme of the works of art, we simply get goose bumps, or start choking on tears. There are not too many of these feelings and they are not too diverse so they can be isolated with a bit of care. (These feelings should not be confused with the orienting, strategic, technological and technical feelings works of art can trigger in us)

One of the groups of system feelings refer to the physical status of our body. This is the group of the feelings of 'general disposition'. When somebody asks you how you are, these are the feelings that you search among for an answer. Another group of system feelings gives information about our general psychological status. We may say we are unhappy after examining these feelings, but we quite rarely say we are happy.

5.

THE MEMORY

(How is our memory organised?)

Without memory, the higher level forms of existence would simply not be possible. Without memory, we would only have the knowledge we were born with and we would not be able to move on and develop. But what is the role of memory in the world of feelings?

As we have seen so far, the language of the external and internal information system of human beings is based, to a certain extent, on the system of feelings (apart from the chemically based internal information system). So we should presume that keeping and storing feelings plays an important role in this information system. Let us take an object and examine what we remember with regard to that object. Let us take a beautiful red apple for example. The image of the beautiful red apple has appeared in your mind's eye? Good. So we remember the nervous activation pattern generated in us when we saw the object. I use this phrase on purpose because I wanted to avoid the expression that we remember the image of the object. We also remember the feelings experienced when touching the object: how smooth the surface of the apple was, what size it was, what its shape was like, the weight of the apple, as well as its temperature and firmness. We also remember the feelings generated as we tasted the apple. We remember the feelings we had in our hearing system when we bit into the apple. So we can say we remember all the incoming feelings that we experienced during the interaction with the given object.

Not only the incoming feelings are recorded though! We also remember that the apple tasted 'delicious'. So we also remember our orienting feelings! And not only the orienting feelings but the related need-indicating, strategic, tactical and technological feelings, too. In fact, we remember the entire process of eating the apple. The feelings we store, however, are not all of the same importance so how we store each of them is not equally important either. As a consequence, some feelings are deleted earlier from the memory. For example, the tactical and technological feelings related to the apple are not that important because eating apples always takes place in different circumstances so these feelings are always different depending on the given circumstances. Therefore, it is useless to store these feelings, it would only result in overloading the system so we only remember these feelings in special circumstances. Storing need-indicating feelings, orienting feelings and strategic feelings, on the other hand, is very important. We will know on the basis of these feelings that we should not start chewing a piece of wood when we are hungry but we should start looking for the apple as the orienting feeling related to the apple is pleasant and we feel a craving for the apple.

These feelings are particularly important in the case of emergencies. For example, if I come across a tiger in the jungle, I should not start meditating about whether I should run away or not. In my memory, I already have the indicating feeling of the need for safety: fear, which is called up immediately as I see the tiger (the only prerequisite being that I have already met a tiger). To help understand this better, let us summarise what we have said so far in the small chart below (Figure 18).

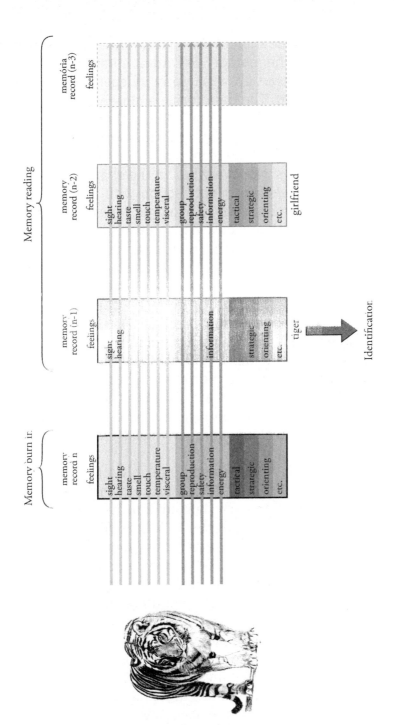

Figure 18

The left-hand column of the chart represents the burn in of the data into the memory. Record n represents the set of data collected about an apparently independent phenomenon of the world. The data forms a closely connected set which is present in the form of feelings. The dataset records the feelings provided by sight and the incoming channels of feelings, as well as the technological, strategic, orienting and other feelings. Not every box in the chart above necessarily contains feelings in connection with any given phenomenon. So in connection with a tiger, for example, simple mortals would probably have data only in the boxes of sight, hearing, safety, information, orienting and strategic feelings. If someone devotes his life to the observation of tigers, more boxes of the chart above will probably be filled in his case.

The second column shows record n-1. The earlier a record was created, the vaguer it is and the less we remember the feelings stored in it. A phenomenon is recognised by comparing the data arriving through sight and the incoming feeling channels with the data stored in the different datasets. If the match is close enough, the given dataset is selected and the other feelings stored in the dataset get activated.

So far so good, but we should probably offer a little clarification in the description of this process. One's head is not a computer where properly defined data are handled. As we will discuss later on in chapter 7.1, *The heterogeneous world*, incoming feelings provide rather inaccurate data about the world around us, and we need to survive an encounter with the tiger with the use of this inaccurate database. While in the case of data processed in computers an incoming dataset is identical with a dataset stored in the memory if each and every unit in it is completely identical, human data-processing, due to the inaccurate incoming feelings and the even more inaccurate feelings stored in the memory, cannot work in the same way. An inaccurate database can never be identical with an even more inaccurate database. Therefore, humans decide about the identity of incoming data and data stored in the memory with approximate matching. So if, let us say, 10% of the incoming inaccurate feelings correspond with the even more inaccurate feelings stored in our memory, then out, run, get out of here lest the tiger eats us.

The percentage limit at which we consider incoming feelings identical to feelings stored in the memory is a variable depending on our psychological status, the circumstances and the given situation. If I am peacefully sitting in a sweet shop in the company of an apple pie contemplating whether the waiter really brought an apple pie to me, I will say it is really an apple pie at a 90% match of the incoming feelings and the feelings stored in my memory. But if I am walking in the jungle in an excited state of mind, if my incoming feelings show only a 5% match with my feelings stored about a tiger, I will start the rocket engines in that instant.

If we do not have a sufficient amount of data to compare with the database, we cannot identify the given object. If we have abundant data about the given object but that does not show any match to the datasets we store, we will handle the given object as a new object and will open a new dataset for it. Let us now have a look how the data stored in our memory influences the processes outlined so far. Take a look at Figure 19.

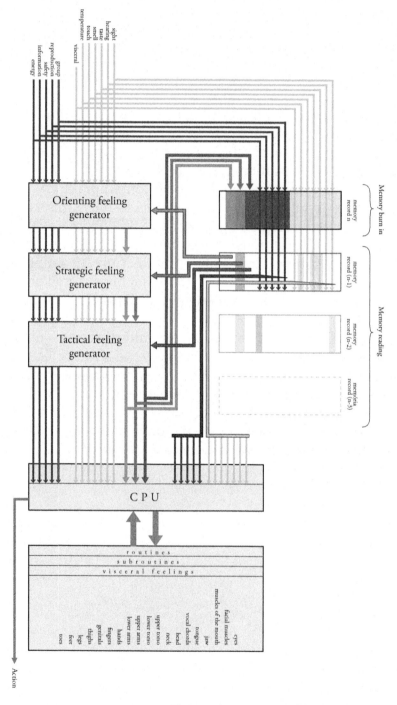

Figure 19

After being generated, the incoming feelings find their way to the units carrying out real-time data processing and also to the memory units. If we have never encountered the given phenomenon, the searches in the memory unit, naturally, cannot be successful and the real-time data processing units will play the decisive role. During their operation, real-time data processing units generate the orienting, strategic and tactical feelings that will be sent to the CPU and also to the memory units where, together with the incoming feelings, they will form a dataset related to the given phenomenon and will be stored. Technological feelings are also stored, but they are stored a little later, depending on the decisions made by the CPU. If we encounter a given phenomenon repeatedly, the events will run in two threads: at the level of the real-time processes and at the level of the memory units. In the memory, the orienting, strategic, tactical, technological etc. feelings related to the given phenomenon activate after the identification of the phenomenon. These activated feelings intervene in the generation of the orienting, strategic, tactical and technological feelings generated during the real-time processes, and modify those feelings. These processes are very significant! We do not need to discover the world around us again. We can immediately handle the phenomena we are already acquainted with appropriately. It is not necessary that the tiger bite me every time we meet in order to make me run. Already in our second encounter, I will know exactly what to do to avoid the bite (if I survive the first encounter, that is).

Before moving on, there are a few points to clarify here. It is not the sight of the tiger that will make me run in our second encounter but the need-indicating, strategic, tactical and technological feelings recorded in my memory in the past in connection with the sight of the tiger. Although this statement is now true, we need to do some further fine-tuning. If the sight of a tiger would be enough to make us run, we would fly in a panic if we saw the tiger behind bars in the zoo. But we do not do that. Rather, we compare the real-time incoming data to the dataset of the feelings coming from the entire situation of our first interaction with the tiger stored in our memory. That is to say, we examine the similarities between the complete interaction situation. So married people, for example, do not loathe their spouses. What they loathe is the rows because of the unpleasant feelings of the rows they have had with them in the past. This is particularly true for newly married couples. Of course, if one of them goes to extremes, the feeling of loathing may indeed be extended to him or her as time goes on.

The comparison of real-time data and the data stored in the memory, however, is carried out in a very interesting way, in our own best interests. For example, if a tiger jumps towards us, we do not start meditating that last time the tiger had three dark stripes on its right paw and now this one only has two, and last time its tail slanted to the right and now it slants to the left, its right canine was 5 mm longer and, in general, this is a much younger specimen. By the time we have thought all this over, we would be done for.

Of course, if we were sitting in a quiet and peaceful room, we might possibly recall all these fine details about the tiger, but this is definitely not the way to stay alive in the jungle. We solve this problem by weighting every single bit of data experienced in our interaction situations when we record them. Weighting is done by need-indicating, strategic, tactical and technological feelings. This, however, would not by itself make quick reactions possible so we distil from the dataset recording the interaction situation an essence of the feelings which reflects the main thread of feelings of the given situation. Due to its small size, this essence of feelings now makes quick reactions possible so, if the tiger chased me through the jungle for 10 minutes the first time we met, it is not necessary for me to watch all the feelings I experienced in a 10-minute movie in my mind's eye, and be paralysed for 10 minutes, I can make a decision in a fraction of a second instead. If the feelings appearing in the real-time processes show any similarities with the essences of feelings, a fast track script takes over, and saves lives sometimes.

Naturally, these essences of feelings are not only activated in real-time processes, they also appear when we are recalling events of the past and when we make plans for the future, and they divert our thoughts from unwanted directions. So if you, my dear reader, are planning your summer holiday hesitating between Mexico and India, you might have an unpleasant feeling cross your mind when considering India followed by the train of thought: "I'm not going there! I don't want to be eaten by a tiger!"

You may be asking now if we should give a name to this kind of essence of feelings. Do not bother with that. Someone has already done it. Namely, Prof Antonio R. Damasio, in his book *Descartes's Error* published in 1994. After elaborate reasoning in his book, Prof Damasio reaches the conclusion that, as a result of the interactions with our environment throughout our life, 'somatic markers' are created in us. In his view, these are special 'body feelings' and that is why he uses the term 'somatic'; and since they serve signalling or marking functions, that is why he uses the term 'markers'. He explains in detail how these feelings speed up our decision-making processes, sometimes making them fast as lightning.

During his research Prof Damasio found that certain patients, whose frontal lobe had been injured, produced very interesting symptoms. In the case of patients he examined thoroughly, he observed that although the ability for logical thinking remained intact, they nevertheless suffered from puzzling problems in decision-making. In Damasio's opinion, the patients he examined had decision-making problems because, due to their injuries, they had lost the 'somatic marker' database they had built up throughout their lives or they had become incapable of creating, learning and keeping these kinds of markers. Although their incoming feelings were connected to need-indicating, strategic, technological and technical feelings during the real-time processes, they were not able to distil them into an essence and connect these essences to the interactions they had experienced in their long-term memory any more. That is, if they met a tiger in jungle, they would not start running immediately without any contemplation just like anybody else, but would start thinking, for example: "Oh my God, this tiger's going to eat me right away. Probably it'd be a good idea to start running." And only then would they have start running.

Naturally, there are cases when inappropriate or too strong memories are recorded in our memory in connection with a certain event. In these cases, you can modify your memories. If you repeat the event in new circumstances, the newly generated orienting, strategic, tactical, technological etc. feelings will overwrite the old feelings stored in the memory. Naturally, the CPU has access to all the feelings related to a given phenomenon. Except in some special cases.

The processes described so far can probably also be found in more developed animals with the difference that their level of need does not exceed that of the need for belonging to a group. The most important conclusion we need to draw from this fact is that animals are also creatures with feelings. Animals also suffer pain and, above a certain level of development, animals can love as well.

6.

SYNCHRONIZATION

(Isn't it only computers that you need to synchronize?)

So far, we have got acquainted with the different types of feelings and their functions and, with the help of block diagrams, we have seen how these feelings are organised into a uniform system. Now let us try to follow the processes of need satisfaction. But before we do so, we need to pay attention to an important phenomenon. What happens if a process is hindered by an obstacle?

Well, a very interesting thing happens in these cases. At the moment when the primary process runs into difficulties, a secondary process starts, whose goal is not the original goal any more but rather to get over these difficulties. Until we get over the difficulties, the strategic feelings of the primary goal are hibernated and tactical and technological feelings related to the secondary process appear. After we have solved the secondary process, the feelings which instigated the implementation of the secondary process disappear and the feelings which instigated the implementation of the primary process get de-hibernated and the process continues. A complete hierarchy of processes can be built up in this way. The important bit, however, is that a given process can appear as a primary process or as a secondary or subordinate process. The characteristic feature of a primary process is that it is controlled at the level of strategic feelings. The control of the same process as a subordinate process is carried out by lower level tactical and technological feelings.

For example, if we want to find the cure for cancer, this is going to be our primary process. But in order to do so we need to get to our workplace in the morning. This is the secondary process. Now, in order to get to our workplace, we need to get dressed first (it would be awkward to find the cure for cancer naked, wouldn't it). This is the tertiary process. In order to get dressed, first we must find our socks. This is the quaternary process. See Figure 20.

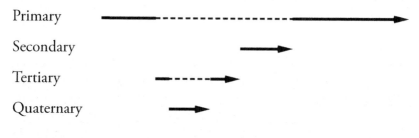

Figure 20

In the quest to find the cure for cancer, the main driving force is the strategic feeling of desire, which will be followed by the strategic feeling of joy (hopefully). Getting into the workplace, however, is not controlled by the feeling of desire but by the technological feeling of tension, which – after successfully getting to our workplace – is followed by the technological feeling of slackness.

Getting to our workplace is a secondary process in our example but we can imagine a situation where it is the main process. For example, I have worked a lot abroad and I have not met my colleagues for a long time so it would feel good to have a chat with them. In this case, the strategic feeling of desire starts the action and the strategic feeling of joy closes it.

After closing subordinate processes, we must make sure

that we get back to the primary process. Subordinate processes cannot be controlled by feelings of the same importance as the primary process because then we would never get back to the primary process. That is, the strategic feeling of joy felt after finding our socks would not make us interested in continuing our search for the cure for cancer (it would be easier to turn the flat upside down searching socks).

Classifying the processes taking place in us as primary or secondary processes is not the only way to do it though, we can also classify them on the basis of the feelings controlling them as fully controlled and partly controlled processes. We call processes controlled by need-indicating and orienting feelings fully controlled processes. For a better understanding, let us now follow a fully controlled process and let us pay attention to the chronological progress of feelings, as well as their synchronicity and timing. In Figure 21, we will try to do the impossible. From the ocean of feelings existing in us, we will try to pick the feelings that influence our behaviour the most and, at the same time, we will try to monitor their progress in time. In reality, these processes are incredibly complicated and complex so let us consider the figure below a humble attempt that serves better understanding.

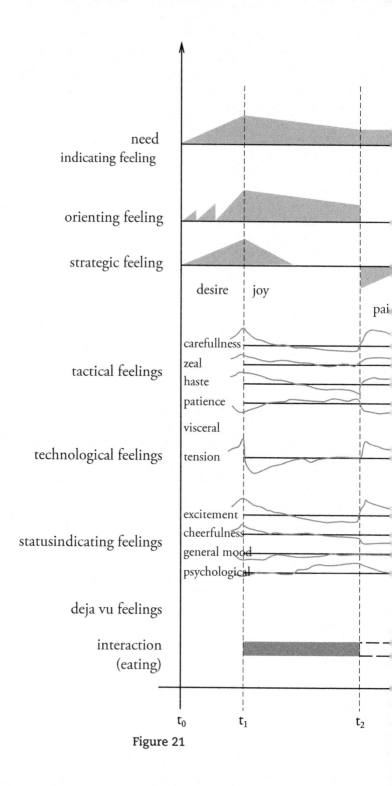

Figure 21

134

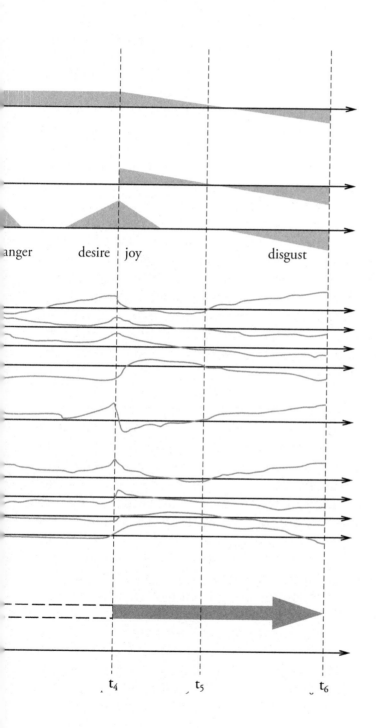

anger   desire │ joy   disgust

t₄   t₅   t₆

For the sake of simplicity, let us take our favourite example of the roast chicken again and let us assume that we have eaten roast chicken previously in our life so we have feelings related to the roast chicken stored in our memory. The vertical axis on the left-hand side of the chart shows the intensity of the feelings participating in the process on an imaginary scale, whereas the horizontal axis represents time. The process starts at the t0 point with the appearance of the need-indicating feeling of hunger which intensifies with time. At the same time memories of orienting feelings related to the roast chicken are recalled from memory. These are not as strong as the orienting feelings coming from actually eating roast chicken but they are real feelings you can experience. The orienting feelings recalled from memory activate the strategic feeling of desire which gradually intensifies. In the meantime, tactical, technical and status-indicating feelings take values as appropriate in the given situation. Naturally, we do not even try to show the visceral, somatic and déjà vu feelings, we only make a note of their existence.

Point t1 shows the moment when we get the roast chicken. From this point on the intensity of the need-indicating feeling, i.e. hunger, decreases. The orienting feeling reaches its maximum within seconds and then it starts gradually falling. The strategic feeling of joy appears and disappears relatively fast. Tactical, technical and status-indicating feelings take values as appropriate in the given situation. The tactical feelings of carefulness, zeal and hurry show a weakening trend, whereas patience grows. The technical feeling of tension melts within seconds and gives way to a pleasant slackness. The status-indicating feeling of excitement falls, whereas cheerfulness grows and our general mood gradually improves just like our psychological status.

At point t2, the neighbour rings the doorbell and we need to open the door, so the process of eating is interrupted and a secondary process is started. We will not, however, discuss the diagram of the feelings controlling the secondary process for the time being. The decrease of the need-indicating feeling of the primary process, hunger, stops and it remains at the same level (as we can quickly get rid of the neighbour, let us disregard the fact that the feeling of hunger must increase with time). The orienting feeling drops to zero. With the interruption of eating the strategic feeling of non-physical pain appears. The tactical feelings of carefulness, zeal and hurry increase, whereas patience is on the decrease. The technical feeling of tension suddenly grows due to the fact that a secondary sub-process has started with the appearance of the neighbour.

At point t3, the strategic feeling of anger appears: "What the heck does this neighbour want now?" If our anger is strong enough, it can even trigger aggression, which could be classified as a tertiary process but let us disregard this possibility for the moment. After talking to the neighbour, the feeling of desire for the roast chicken may emerge again. The tactical feelings of carefulness and patience will decrease, while zeal and hurry will grow. The tension that urges us to close subordinate processes will also grow. The status-indicating feeling of excitement increases, whereas the indicators of cheerfulness, general mood and psychological state deteriorate.

At point t4, we can finally resume eating. The need-indicating feeling of hunger starts decreasing further until it disappears completely. The intensity of the orienting feeling drops and the feeling discontinues. The strategic feeling of joy, which we feel about getting the chicken again, quickly expires. The tactical feelings of carefulness, zeal and hurry decrease and patience starts growing. The technical feeling of tension suddenly shifts into the feeling of a pleasant slackness which will gradually disappear later on. The status-indicating feelings of excitement and cheerfulness start continuously decreasing. Our general mood and psychological state are continuously improving.

At point t5, the need-indicating feeling of hunger disappears to be gradually replaced by another need-indicating feeling, the feeling of fullness. The pleasant orienting feeling is gradually replaced by an unpleasant orienting feeling, which means we will not want the food any more. The gradually increasing strategic feeling of disgust appears. The tactical feeling of carefulness is growing, whereas zeal, hurry and patience start decreasing. The technical feeling of tension gradually grows. The status-indicating feeling of excitement also grows, whereas cheerfulness, general mood and psychological status deteriorate.

Many readers might think at this point that they do not have so many feelings while they eat their roast chicken. These readers are right and wrong at the same time. Because these feelings, and millions of others, are present in us, only we do not pay attention to them. We can discover each of these feelings in ourselves one by one. And the emphasis is on the "one by one". Although these feelings exist simultaneously, we can only follow one of them at a time with our attention. This feeling, however, can also be a composite feeling which we cannot break down to its components any more.

Next, let us examine a partly controlled process, the control of which is carried out by orienting feelings. The special feature of these processes is that need-indicating feelings do not participate in them. These partly controlled processes are well represented by the example of the apple pie. If you walk into a sweet shop, you do not usually go there because you are hungry but because you long for the orienting feeling triggered by the apple pie. The goal of the processes is to experience the pleasant orienting feeling so the process is controlled by the orienting feeling. The situation is similar with sex. As we age, the need-indicating feeling of the need to reproduce does not appear that often but we still long for the pleasant orienting feelings related to sex. We can use the previous chart also for processes controlled by orienting feelings, only we need to disregard the top line representing need-indicating feelings.

Depending on their genetic code, education and age, as well as the given situation, people experience different feelings during the same event. There are strong feelings that appear in a given period of life of a given person and can sometimes dominate the feelings of the given person. A typical example is a desire trap.

7.

THE THINKING HUMAN BEING

7.1 The fragmented world

(Why do not we see the world homogenous?)

Let us now set out on an imaginary journey to visit a fabulous beach with silky smooth sand. Walking on the beach, we suddenly notice a box the waves must have washed to the shore. We open the box and wow! There is a pair of magic glasses in it. And they are none other but the famous all-seeing magic glasses! Let us try them on! It is an incredible change. If we raise our eyes to the sky again, we see that the atmosphere is not only infiltrated with the electromagnetic radiation visible to the human eye, i.e. light, but also by other electromagnetic rays that are invisible without the magic glasses. These rays reach the Earth. Some of them are reflected from the surface of the sea but others run into the water. These rays also reach us and some of them are reflected from the body, while others enter into it and get absorbed, with others again simply passing straight through our body. We notice that our body also emits electromagnetic rays, mostly heat-rays, but the human nervous system also radiates because electric impulses run through our nerves and accelerating electric charges do radiate.

Molecules of air form small bubbles in the foam of the

sea water and get absorbed in the water making it possible for the living creatures of the sea to get access to oxygen. We also inhale air into our lungs but we breathe through our skin as well. Who can tell whether the oxygen molecule on the surface of our skin belongs to us or to the external world? Or whether the heat-ray that is leaving our skin was generated in our body or is the reflected heat of the sun? The visible rays of the sun penetrate our body to a depth of several centimetres. What does this light belong to? To us? To the sun? Or to some of the twinkling stars?

The Earth attracts our body but our body also attracts the Earth, as well as the Moon and the Sun and the entire Universe! The invisible threads of the field of gravity entangle everything. Through our magic glasses we can see that everything is connected to everything.

Now let us take off the magic glasses. What do we see? That there you are, dear reader, there I am, there is the sea, the moon the sun and the stars. All of them in separation. And none of them has anything to do with the other. Although nothing has changed since we took off the glasses. The lack of magic glasses has left a trace on the way humans think. Due to the imperfection of their optical and incoming feeling channels, humans break up the world into units apparently independent from one another. We scan these supposedly independent units (objects, persons or phenomena) and process the signals we receive in a way that creates the representations of these supposedly independent objects in our mind. What is a representation? A very lacking dataset received through our optical and incoming feeling channels and processed in our brain that creates a specific system of neurological stimulus states in the central nervous system that is only typical of the given phenomenon. The dataset is lacking because it only carries very few of the properties of the given object. Through our sight, we only have limited ideas about the form and the colour of the given object. The ideas are limited because our eyes only perceive certain wavelengths of the electromagnetic radiation so we do not see the entire spectrum. So, with the help of our sight, we cannot tell the temperature of the given object, how temperature is distributed on its surface, in what spectrum the given object emits radiation, what radiation it absorbs and how it reflects the incoming electromagnetic radiation throughout the entire spectrum. But even if we saw the entire spectrum, the resolution of our eyes is relatively modest so we still could not see each and every small detail of the given object. The situation is pretty similar with hearing, taste and touch as well. Each of these data channels can only process a small fraction of reality and therefore the mapped and stored data is rather lacking.

Everything that has been said so far is true but...! We should not forget about a fairly important circumstance. For the sake of simplicity, let us start with heat sensation. Let us suppose that we need to walk out onto the street in Siberia in wintertime for some reason (to buy a bottle of vodka in the convenience store at the corner). We will feel that it is biting cold out there. Let us imagine that, in the desert of Sahara, we also need to walk out from a hotel onto the street for some reason (to buy a cold drink in the convenience store at the corner). We will feel that is incredibly hot out there. Note that nothing has changed in us. Talking about the air, it is of the same chemical composition. The only thing that has changed is that the molecules of the air move and zigzag much more vehemently in Africa. The kinetic energy of the molecules of the air has increased. As a result, or rather as a result our interaction with the air, the feeling of hotness appears in us. Be careful! The feeling of hotness appears in us and not in the air. The feeling of hotness belongs to us and not to the air. The air is as it is with all its dancing molecules. So we cannot say the air is hot or cold. The only thing we can say is, due to our interaction with the air, a feeling of hot or cold has been generated in us.

Let us continue with smell. If we smell a rose, we say

what a nice smell it has. However, as a matter of fact, the rose has no smell at all. The only thing the rose does is that it evaporates complicated chemicals. These chemicals are nothing else but complex molecules. Molecules do not have a smell, they are only molecules. The feeling of smell is only generated in us as a result of our interaction with them. So the smell of a rose is created in us and not in the rose. The same applies to tastes. Foods do not have taste. Foods are only complicated heaps of molecules. The feeling of taste is something that only appears and exists in us, humans. "And what about hearing?" you may be asking. I have bad news for you. The song of the lark is another thing that only exists in us. Beyond the outside surface of our eardrum, there is nothing else but the dancing molecules of the ocean of air. There is no lark song there. It is the vibrating air that creates the feelings of sounds in us that only exist in us.

And finally we arrived at sight. Usually it is the most difficult for humans to digest that everything we see also only exists in us. So the beautiful red rose does not look the way we see it in the least. If I want to be accurate, I need to say it does not look like anything at all, it only exists. The sobering reality is that electromagnetic radiation does not have a colour. Just like x-rays, radio waves and heatwaves do not have any. "And what is the case with the visible range of electromagnetic radiation?" you may ask. In terms of its physical properties, the visible range is not any different from the nonvisible range: the only difference is that its frequency, and therefore its wavelength, are different. All that happens is that our nervous system can interact with this range of electromagnetic radiation. The feeling of colour is only created IN US after we have interacted with electromagnetic radiation. Only in us. So the beautiful world we see only exists in us!

After I have managed to have sufficiently sadden my readers, let us see what follows from the statements above is. It clearly follows from the statements above that the external world appears in us, humans, through our feelings. So when we think we are examining the external world, in fact, we are not doing anything else but examining our own feelings. And since these feelings do not cover the entire available spectrum, our feelings are fragmented. But the world is not fragmented.

Why was it important to mention the apparent fragmentation of the world? Because the fragments of feelings created in the process form the basis of word creation – we attach words to these fragments of feelings – and thinking in words, i.e. symbols, is the most important method of human thinking. This thought is worth a little consideration. As I explained earlier, sounds are feelings. As a consequence, words are nothing else but series of feelings of sound. So our thoughts are nothing else but chains of series of feelings of sounds. When we create words, all we do is we assign series of feelings of sounds to feelings generated in us through our interactions with the external world. But how does it work then?

1. The external world shows itself to us through our feelings.
2. Words are nothing else but series of feelings, or more accurately, series of feelings of sound. Our thoughts in turn are chains of series of feelings of sound.
3. Our internal world shows itself to us in the form of feelings.

What is the consequence of all this? "Only" that the ONLY world that exists for the individual human being is the WORLD OF FEELINGS itself. This is the only world that exists for any individual. For a better understanding, please consult Figure 22.

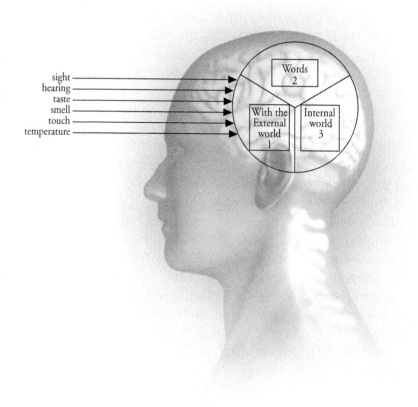

sight
hearing
taste
smell
touch
temperature

Words
2

With the
External
world
1

Internal
world
3

Figure 22

So the definition of feelings used at the beginning of this book "Feeling is what we feel" I would modify as follows: Everything that exists in the internal world of human beings is feelings. That is to say: FEELING = EVERYTHING. Naturally, this equation is only true for the internal world of humans. Poor Descartes, if he was alive, would definitely be sad because his famous saying "Cogito ergo sum", i.e. "I think, therefore I am" should be modified to "Sentio ergo sum", i.e. "I feel, therefore I am". With this little twist, I think I have caused a bit of a headache to a few philosophers, too.

7.2 Ways of thinking
(Is it not only possible to think with words?)

As we know, people can also think in images. When I say I go down to the shop I can replace this thought with imagining my way down to the shop, as I am walking in the street and at the end I enter the shop. The drawback of this way of thinking is that it is cumbersome and slow. Slow because images, although they provide data that may be lacking about the world, are fairly large databases that occupy a large space in the memory and, due to their size, handling them is rather difficult.

IT experts faced a similar problem in modern information technology. They had their problems with managing images. What was the solution they found to their problems? They invented compression. In order to avoid image data occupying so much space, they did not store images in their full size but, with the help of complicated algorithms, they converted them on the basis of their characteristic points into symbols that occupy much less space and that are much easier to handle than the original ones and that can be converted back to the original ones in case of need. Almost. As with everything else, compression has its advantages and disadvantages. One of the main disadvantages is the loss of data. The images cannot actually be restored to their original form: quality will always deteriorate a little.

Unfortunately, I have bad news for my IT specialist readers: they did not invent compression. We humans have been using data compression through our development although we did not know about it. The key of data compression is that we further compress the originally lacking data sets representing the data acquired about certain images through sight and replace them with patterns of nervous stimulus states representing series of feelings of sound. We call the series of feelings of sounds words. If I wanted to be less accurate and more easy to understand, I would say we replace the images of objects appearing in our mind with words. Due to their size, words are much easier to handle. They occupy much less space in the memory and searching them in the memory takes much less time than recalling each and every detail of an image. However, since we are talking about compression, we also face the risk of the loss of data here. If you read the word 'apple', you are fully aware of the meaning of the word – or at least that is what we think – but as a matter of fact each and every person will think about a different apple. Some of them will think about a red one, some of them a yellow one; some of them will think about a small one, some of them a big one etc. Although if I showed them the photograph of the apple, all of them would be thinking about exactly the same apple. So the word 'apple', due to the compression process, did not preserve all the data. Though thinking in words or symbols has its undoubted advantages, the loss of data due to the compression might give rise to misinterpretations.

Thinking in images and thinking in symbols are isolated from one another: they take place at different levels. There is, however, no sharp or impassable barrier between the two levels. We can switch levels and change from one way of thinking to the other as we please. It is an indisputable fact that all humans prefer thinking in symbols. At the level of thinking in symbols, thinking is only possible with the use of symbols. If there is no symbol for something, we cannot operate with it at this level.

To give a comprehensive overview, we need to mention another way of 'thinking'. I put the word 'thinking' in inverted commas because this way of data processing does not actually have a name and we know very little about it. The shared feature of thinking in images and thinking in symbols is that the process can be monitored and reproduced. The process of the third thinking (shall we call it 'third thinking') however cannot be monitored and cannot be reproduced, in fact, we only have indirect evidence of its existence. We often see that, when we do not find a solution for a problem, the solution just 'clicks in,' sometimes after hours, sometimes only after days have gone by: we are given an answer or we dream the right way to proceed. And we do this without analysing the situation at the level of either image-based or symbol-based thinking directly before the answer arrives.

7.3 The database
(According to what rules is the database of humans organised?)

Apart from being able to create words, you also need to be able to use them. From our words, we need to build a manageable and organised database: a network where bits of data are connected to one another in a predefined order. What defines the order or the structure of the database? The order of the world. If the goal is to map reality, symbols cannot connect into one another at will, they can only connect on the basis of a definite order. In forming the connection of the symbols, our goal should be that these connections reflect as much as possible the relations of the apparently independent units represented by the symbols. Although, without the magic glasses, we have formed an image of the world that suggests the world is made up of apparently independent units, paradoxically we strive to find out the connections between these apparently independent units throughout our entire life.

The connections of the world are defined by the properties of the units we consider independent. We can build houses from stone because the properties of stone make it possible. We can make a raft from wood because the properties of wood make it possible. We cannot build a raft from stone as the properties of stone do not make it possible. The apparently independent units cannot connect with one another at will. They can only organise into the kinds of systems their properties permit. But what is a property? A property is nothing else but interaction. For example, the property of objects that they have a certain weight cannot be interpreted without the field of gravity. The weight of objects comes from the interaction of objects and the field of gravity. Properties do not make sense on their own, only in comparison to, or interaction with, something else.

Words in the data network are organised on the basis of the properties of the units represented by those words. The data network is a multilevel network. The levels are formed on the basis of the different properties of the apparently independent units. There are levels of physics, chemistry, biology, sociology, politics, philosophy etc. At these different levels, the apparently independent units of the world connect to one another on the basis of different properties.

Words shown in Figure 23 can be connected to one another at multiple levels. Based on the property of being easily workable, the word 'wood' can connect in our mind to the words 'furniture', 'door' and 'cart'; based on the physical property that its specific weight is lower than that of water, the word can connect to the word 'raft'; based on the chemical property that it easily oxidises, i.e. burns, it can connect to the word 'fuel'. But the word 'wood' does not directly connect to the words 'steel' and 'plastic'. The words 'plastic' and 'crude oil' can connect to one another based on their chemical properties, whereas the words 'steel' and 'crude oil' can connect at the level of politics.

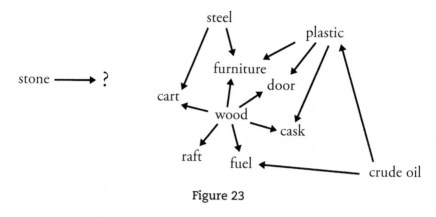

Figure 23

Thinking at these levels is simply logical manipulation with symbols. The basis of logical manipulations is that we suppose that if there is a certain type of connection between apparently independent units A and B at a given point of time, t1, this connection may also exist or may be valid at another point of time, t2; or another, more extended version of the same thing is that if there is a certain type of connection between A and B as well as between B and C, then there must be, as a consequence, some kind of relationship between A and C, and if it is true at a given point of time, t1, then it may be true at another point of time, t2, as well. This way, theoretically, we can get from any point of the data network to any other point of the data network and we can not only examine the present on this basis but we can also make conclusions about the future.

Since words represent data packages that are highly compressed and subjectively defined, manipulation with symbols is rather inaccurate. Consequently, in the parts of the data network that were not created by direct experience or measurement but by logical deduction or with data acquired from others, the map of the connections between the apparently independent units often does not correspond with the actual connections between the apparently independent units in the real world. In more simple language: misconceptions may be created.

The data network is gradually built up in individuals. Only a few elements and their connections exist in the individual's mind at the start and then new elements connect to the already existing ones. Elements can only connect if they fit one another. Individuals asses the connectibility of elements at multiple levels. Individuals do not incorporate elements into their knowledge network that are not compatible with, i.e. do not fit, the already existing data network.

I suspect that the data network plays an important part in the case of 'third thinking'. When we do not understand something we want to get an answer to, we do nothing but try to fit the given phenomenon into our existing data network or check how the already fitted phenomenon connects with the other elements of our network. We always try to do it by looking at the problem from the point of view of the element to be fitted and not from the point of view of the uniform data network. If we do not see the exact modes of connecting, the piece to be fitted will not fit in the big picture, i.e. we do not find a solution for the problem. Then one or two days pass and, with our thoughts wandering about other parts of the data network, we are suddenly faced with our unsolved problem but now we are not looking at it from the point of view of the problem but from the point of view of the data network, i.e. from outside or from above. Looking at the problem from the point of view of the data network we can discover new connection options and then suddenly the solution clicks in. The missing piece finds its place, we have added a new piece to the data network and we have found a solution for the problem. This scenario would also explain the fact that 'third thinking' cannot be reproduced and monitored.

Naturally, as we are humans, we can make mistakes while building our data network and database. The earlier we make these mistakes in building up our data network, the larger the bit of faulty network we create. The larger the faulty network is, the more difficult it is to fix it and the more work it takes to partly or completely dismantle it and rebuild it again. So in terms of convenience, individuals are interested in preserving their data network. Another motivation for preserving the data network of individuals can be that dismantling the old database and building up a new one may also threaten some of the needs of the individual. For example, changing your political conviction may have an impact on your need for a group as you may become outcast, or it may even have an impact on your need for safety if you have to face persecution for your political views. Theoretically the construction of the data network and movements between its points would only be possible on the basis of logical considerations but actually this is not the case.

7.4 The role of feelings
(How do feelings influence our thoughts? Do we surely think of what we want to? What can we want to think of?)

The use of words has made thinking easier and faster but also less accurate. Sometimes the accuracy ensured by one single word is enough but if not, we use more words. We try to clarify the picture and make it more accurate with these extra words. So I do not just say apple but I also say red, the size of a fist, fragrant, sweet, tasty, delicious, juicy, crunchy Jonathan apple. But how do these extra words fulfil their function? What happens actually? In the previous chapter we could see that while we are recording phenomena in our memory, we also store various feelings apart from the data acquired through our sight. However, we do not only record data acquired through our sight and incoming feelings in connection with the given phenomenon but we also record the words describing them and we record all this information in a uniform, discrete dataset. Please take a look at Figure 24.

Apple

Feelings	Words
sight	red
hearing	crunchy
taste	weet
smell	sweet-smelling
touch	smooth
temperature	
visceral	
group	
reproduction	
safety	
information	
energy	
orienting	delicious
strategic	
tactical	
technological	
etc.	

Figure 24

So the dataset representing the apple does not only contain the "image" of the apple but also the related words: 'round', 'red', 'shiny'. With the typical feeling of taste, we store the word 'sweet' and with the typical smell, we store the word 'fragrant'. Or, more accurately, the nervous pattern of stimulus states representing the sound of these words is assigned to the corresponding need-indicating, orienting, strategic, tactical and technological feelings. Naturally there may be empty boxes here if the given feeling was not stored, did not become conscious or does not yet have a name or we simply have not tried to describe the given feeling with words. When we use these extra words we are trying to describe with them the feelings we experienced to the extent, and in detail, made necessary by the given circumstances. We are trying to convert our feelings into a compressed form. We do compression! This is natural because this is the only thing we can do. In the previous chapter we said that at the level of thinking in symbols we can only operate with symbols. So we could not think about the apple at this level if we did not have the appropriate symbols, i.e. words. Therefore, we must simply compress the data acquired through sight and the incoming feeling channels as well as the need-indicating, orienting, strategic, tactical and technological feelings related to the apple, and create symbols, or words, with which we can operate at the level of symbol-based control as we please.

Figure 18, which we created in Chapter 5 when we were discussing the memory, will be modified in reality as the words describing different feelings will also be added as shown in Figure 25.

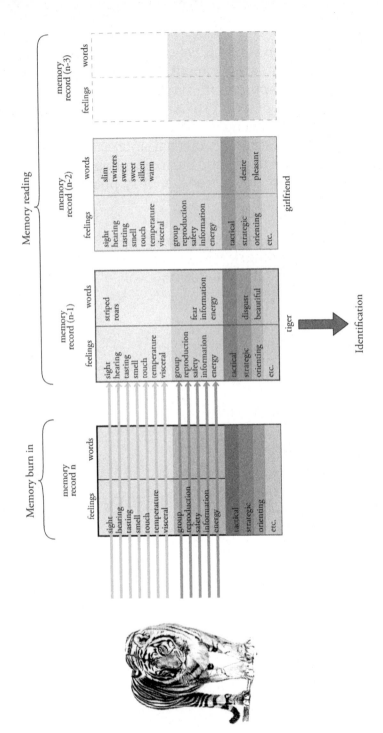

Figure 25

Naturally, we also have the problem of data loss here. No matter if we say the apple is red, round, fragrant, sweet and delicious, the other person will never understand it accurately and feel the same feelings as the person who made the statements even if he also tastes the same apple because different orienting feelings will be generated in him.

Another form of data loss derives from the use of notion. Notions are meant to denote several similar but apparently independent units. The word 'apple' is also a notion because we denote several types of apples with this word. The human brain is incapable of the remembering the exact shape, size and other properties of all the apples we have seen and the endless amount of feelings connected to the hundreds of apples. From all the apples we have seen, our mind creates an average apple but, due to the nature of things, the image of the average apple is going to be vague and will only cover the most important data unlike the original individual phenomena. There is, however, a very important fact to remember! The table above works in two directions. Not only do certain words belong to certain feelings but also certain feelings belong to certain words. The word 'fragrant' might make me think of apples. Also the word 'red' might recall the image of the apple in my mind's eye. This is what poets and writers use. Just think about it, my dear reader, what feelings talented writers or poets can present their readers with. And all that with the help of words! And this phenomenon also plays a significant role in the process of learning. Because there are two basic ways to get to know new apparently independent units. The primary way is when we map the given unit with our own optical and incoming feeling channels, i.e. we fill in the boxes of the table with visual data and the feelings we ourselves acquire through our incoming feeling channels and we ourselves assign words to these feelings. The secondary or indirect way is when we ourselves do not have visual data about the apparently independent unit and our incoming channels do not provide us with feelings about it either. This is the case when another person describes in words or in writing the properties of an apparently independent unit unknown to us. In this case the table is filled the other way round. First we learn the words and then, with the help of the words, we try to evoke the feelings that are generated in the person who came into direct contact with the given phenomenon. This is an efficient but rather inaccurate way of passing data on. In this case passing on orienting feelings and strategic feelings as well might be of crucial importance. When we want to introduce somebody to the fly agaric, apart from the physical description of the mushroom, we also need to tell him that although fly agaric tastes nice, i.e. produces pleasant orienting feelings, it is fatally poisonous, which statement is meant to influence the strategic feelings of listener. What happens in reality? It is simply impossible to convey orienting, strategic, tactical or technological feelings with words. Although it may be more or less possible in cases of phenomena that can be directly experienced by humans, it is absolutely out of question in the case of notions.

Let us take the science of wine tasting for example. Yes, as an ex-vine grower, I can confidently say that, although anyone can drink wine, not everybody can appreciate and assess it. In order to have a "wine tour" you need at least two people. A wine tourist, i.e. the person who tastes the wine and who is still inexperienced in the science of wine, and the guide, or the professor, who is the expert in the science of wine. Wine tasting – and I will save the reader the details of the whole ceremonious choreography – starts with both the tourist and the guide taking a glass of the heavenly nectar in their hands – naturally, as the author is Hungarian, we are talking about Hungarian wines – and taste it. Then the professor starts explaining to the student step-by-step, with the help of words, what types of tastes, orienting, strategic etc. feelings she is experiencing. Obviously, the two people cannot experience the same feelings in reality, but their feelings can still correlate somewhat. But the method described above cannot be used for notions. It is impossible, for example, to completely convey the feelings one person has experienced in connection with words like 'freedom' or 'homeland' to another person. However, we must admit that great poets and writers of world literature have done much in this respect.

But what actually happens here? If we hear or read the explanation of a phenomenon we cannot directly experience, then, for want of a better option, we assign 'marker feelings' to the given phenomenon. Marker feelings are nothing but the compressed and general forms, or essences, of orienting, strategic, tactical, technological etc. feelings. My dear reader might rightfully ask now what's new in that. What is the difference between somatic markers and marker feelings? Both of them are essences of feelings distilled from similar feelings. The most important difference is that while we assign somatic markers primarily to interactions, we assign marker feelings usually to symbols or words. So whereas some of the somatic markers emerge when we are in situations of interactions we find familiar, marker feelings are usually recalled when we hear familiar words.

Marker feelings are assigned to every word. As we will see later on, these marker feelings range from negative through neutral to positive (It is a different issue that these marker feelings get further modified or sometimes deformed later on.) So if I have never eaten papaya in my life, no orienting feeling can connect to the word 'papaya' in my mind. But if I read somewhere that papaya is a good, delicious fruit, then the marker feeling connected to the words 'good' and 'delicious' will get connected to the word 'papaya' in my mind and next time when I have a chance to taste papaya, I will act according to these marker feelings. Or, for example, murder, rape or brutality are probably connected with strong negative marker feelings in most of my readers' minds. Fortunately, they are only marker feelings and not orienting, strategic or other feelings acquired through actual experience.

We have been being programmed since our early child-hood: we are told what is good and what is bad, what we need to do and what we need to avoid. And if we actually meet these phenomena in our life, we will automatically act according the marker feelings taught to us earlier. And during our life, the marker feelings we were taught gradually get connected to feelings acquired through real-life experience and form a joint database. In the meantime, naturally, marker feelings can be modified through our experience. These modified marker feelings accompany us in our life and give us great help in speeding up our thinking and, as we will see later on, may also define its direction.

As we have already seen, phenomena in the world, and in our mind, are in close or more distant connection with each other. When we encounter a phenomenon, we extend and connect some of the feelings connected to the given phenomenon to other phenomena directly connected to the original phenomenon. This is what we call the law of the extension of feelings. For example, the most dangerous part of the snake for us is its head but we know that it is better not to tamper with its tail either: the best thing is to be at a safe distance from the entire snake.

Later on we will see that the extension, or more accurately the connection, matching or association of feelings is incredibly important! This is what human thinking, and even the entire human existence is based on. In life, discovering and avoiding dangerous things has much more significance than discovering nice things. If we accidentally bump into something nice, what can happen? No problem. We had a lucky encounter, at the worst! Our encounter with bad things, however, may be our last encounter in the world. That is why feelings related to bad or unpleasant phenomena usually extend more intensively into a wider range of other phenomena connected to them.

Since feelings have a crucial role in life or, more accurately, they are the only thing that have a role at all, we classify the phenomena of life very carefully according to the bad, neutral and pleasant feelings assigned to them. The accuracy of the classification is very important because our life might depend on it. We put phenomena triggering good and pleasant feelings into one box and phenomena triggering bad or unpleasant feelings into another box and never mix the two. We meticulously keep order instead. Let us have a look at the following example. We have positive orienting, strategic, marker etc. feelings stored in our database in connection with the old lady next door. These feelings fundamentally define our behaviour and attitude towards the old lady. This set of feelings is also represented at the level of symbol-based thinking. The lady next door is very nice, kind and helpful: these are the words that represent our feelings towards the lady next door at the feelings level. However, the old lady next door suddenly dies. From the logical point of view, I can use any of the words 'depart', 'decease', 'pass away' or 'die' to describe this event. All these words mean the same: the life functions of the old lady stopped working. But what do you think about the expression the 'old lady kicked the bucket'? I suppose you feel upset and outraged. But do not forget: from the logical point of view, the phrase 'kick the bucket' is completely equal to the words listed above. Well, yes, logically it is equal but the related marker feelings are completely different. When we use the word 'die' or 'decease', no negative marker feelings are connected to them. But if we use the expression 'kick the bucket' it is connected with negative marker feelings. We simply cannot use this phrase for the old lady next door and even if we think about using it, it triggers a negative feeling in us because the feelings connected to this expression do not fit the pleasant feelings that are stored in our database in connection with the old lady. But if I say Hitler kicked the bucket, it will not trigger any objection in most of my readers. Why? The reason is the same. Although the feelings connected to the expression 'kick the bucket' are the same in both cases, most probably the feelings connected to Hitler's name in my readers' database are not in opposition with the feelings connected to the expression 'kick the bucket'.

Based on the above, we can draw a very important conclusion. We cannot move in the direction we want to in the data network available to us at the level of symbol-based thinking even when we observe the rules of logic because states at the feeling-based control level may overwrite our decisions. It does not only mean that we do not want and cannot use certain words because of the feelings connected to them but it also leaves its mark on the entire process of our thinking. Certain trains of thoughts and certain databases simply get blocked. Let us take an example. Two women are talking:

"And what does your husband do?"
"He's a doctor. He's a brilliant and respected surgeon. He saves the lives of people every day. I'm really proud of him! And what does your husband do?"
"Oh, my husband's a qualified mass murderer. He's very good at it! Last week he killed 12 people. But he has done better: there was a case where he massacred 122 people! It was a premeditated action. He was praised and given a pay-rise for it."

Well, my dear reader, I think this dialogue is a little shocking. Although the dialogue may take place in reality with the same logical content, it is not very likely that the speakers would use the same words. As a woman who loves her husband, i.e. feels positive feelings towards him, she does not want to be faced with the fact that her husband is a mass murderer because of the negative marker feelings connected to this word. The two groups of feelings exclude one another in her mind: the opposing feelings connected to the two symbols, the husband and the mass murderer, do not let the two units connect in the data network. This is a forbidden connection. In reality, the dialogue would sound something like this: "Oh, my husband's a professional soldier. He's very brave and clever! Last week, he removed 12 enemy soldiers.

But he's performed even more heroic deeds. All alone, he successfully stopped the advance of a 122-strong enemy troop when he blew up a bridge under their marching column. He'd worked out the plan of the action accurately in advance. He was awarded for it and his pay was even raised as a result."

Without consciously realising it, the wife replaces the words that carry negative feelings for her with words carrying neutral or even positive marker feelings. The words 'kill' and 'murder', which are clearly associated with negative marker feelings, she replaces with the word 'remove' which is associated with neutral marker feelings. The marker feelings connected to the expression 'enemy soldiers' are completely different from the ones connected to the word 'people'. You can slaughter and massacre the enemy because they have no fathers and no mothers and no wives and children are waiting for them at home. Let the devil take the hindmost! And a soldier is not a woman, not a child and not an elderly person. He is a strong man. Why did he come here? You need to remove them, that's it. The only problem with this train of thought is that this is the claptrap they have been feeding soldiers and their relatives with for thousands of years on both sides of every war. How lucky that people are not hurt, only the enemy is killed.

And now we have arrived at the discussion of the difference between Antonio R. Damasio's 'somatic markers' and my 'marker feelings'. As a matter of fact, these two expressions symbolise the same phenomenon only two different sides of it or two different approaches to it. If I wanted to summarise Prof Damasio's thoughts in a nutshell, I could describe his theory by saying that human thinking becomes very effective by attaching small packages of feelings, i.e. somatic markers, to the possible thought scenarios, which will immediately divert our thoughts from scenarios, and their possible outcomes, carrying negative somatic markers towards scenarios with packages of positive feelings, i.e. positive somatic markers. This way our brain is not overloaded with thinking over useless scenarios with unfavourable outcomes because the somatic markers divert our thoughts in the bud.

For example, if someone is heterosexual, she will not think about finding partners from the same sex. This train of thought does not even appear in her mind or, more accurately, this train of thought cannot even start because right at the onset a very unpleasant somatic marker appears (and of course the same is true about homosexual people, only the other way round). But why did Prof Damasio's patients have problems with making decisions? Why couldn't they make decisions even in the simplest cases? Because, due to their brain injuries, they lost their somatic markers. They could not "weight" their thoughts. For them, the outcomes of their trains of thoughts were equally (in)significant.

Prof Damasio's findings described above are incredibly important, although they only shed light on one side of the coin. They only give an answer to the question of why the patients could not make decisions but they do not answer the question of why Phineas P. Gage used "foul language". This man, mentioned in Prof Damasio's book not only became unable to make decisions but also started to use vulgar words after his brain injury.

So what are we talking about? We are talking about the fact that we humans are controlled by two levels of control: feeling-based control and symbol-based control (although we know that the latter is also based on feelings, i.e. series of feelings of sound). Prof Damasio approached the question from the level of feeling-based control, whereas I approached it from the level of symbol-based control. The feelings he calls somatic markers primarily belong to the feeling-based control level and are not directly connected to words so they only have an indirect influence on the symbol-based control level. Although the somatic markers he discovered are also marker feelings, they are not feelings that directly postulate the existence of thinking. These feelings can also be present if somebody is not thinking or cannot think at all. For example, they can also be present in more developed animals. Although the somatic markers have an impact on thinking, they do not have an impact on the selection of words. They have an influence on the general direction of our thoughts and they exert this influence at the level of strategic feelings. Since these feelings are essences or concentrates, they are not as elaborate or detailed as the original feelings we distil them from. We could best describe them with the words 'yes/no' or 'want/don't' want.

Getting back to the sexual example we mentioned previously, somatic markers will define the primary direction, the main line of our thoughts: so men will have thoughts about women. But it will be marker feelings that will define what words they will use to think about the representatives of the female sex: 'slut', 'bitch', 'babe', 'chick', 'girl', 'miss', 'young lady'. And, my dear female readers, please do not get offended: I just wanted to demonstrate the repertoire of the available marker feelings.

And now we have arrived at the explanation of the use of vulgar words produced by Phineas P. Gage. As a matter of fact, the unfortunate invalid did not at all mean to be vulgar, all that happened was that, besides losing his somatic markers, he had also lost his marker feelings connected to the words, i.e. series of feelings of sound, as a result of his injuries. So he formed sentences from words only on a logical basis and he did not pay attention to the connected marker feelings, only the meanings of the words. The words 'slut' and 'young lady' both denote female individuals but, let us face it, it would be disastrous if we stripped them of from the related marker feelings and used them interchangeably, or on a random basis, for example in a speech for International Women's Day. Marker feelings permeate our entire life. Just remember the story of the soldier's wife. They leave their mark on our thinking wherever you look and in ways and fields you would not even think of!

I suggest that we examine the differences between somatic markers and marker feelings further. Somatic markers are partly based on the set of feelings we are born with, such as sexual orientation, and are partly built and distilled from fragments and sets of feelings that we have experienced during the interactions with our environment throughout our life. While a part of our somatic markers are already with us when we are born and new ones are added to them continuously, a natural precondition of the existence of marker feelings is that we have words and can speak. Because if the individual has not yet reached the status in her ontogeny where she is able to use words, there is simply nothing in her mind to connect the marker feelings to.

Marker feelings can be generated in two ways. One of them happens when we interact with an apparently independent phenomenon and "distil" the feelings generated in us during the interaction and assign the created essences of feelings to the given series of feelings of sound, i.e. words. For example, we take a papaya in our hands, touch it, smell it and taste it, and we assign the essence of feelings generated in us in the meantime to the word 'papaya'. But wait a minute! My dear reader must have noticed that the way marker feelings are generated is uncannily similar to the way the acquired somatic markers are formed. That is right. There is an overlap here. That means marker feelings can also be generated from somatic markers! But while somatic markers cover the entire spectrum of feelings continuously, in an analogue way so to speak, and can also connect to interactions and scenarios that do not have a name, marker feelings do not continuously cover the entire spectrum of feelings. They produce breaks, they are digital so to speak, as they can only connect to specific words and, therefore, they are inaccessible and impossible to interpret for phenomena that do not have a name or which we do not denote with words.

The other way of generating marker feelings is when we assign marker feelings to a given word through learning with the help of another person. That is, if we have never seen, touched, smelled or tasted papaya in our entire life, we need to rely on other people's accounts. After we have been told what a papaya looks, feels, smells and tastes like, that it is really delicious, contains a lot of vitamins and is very healthy, the marker feelings representing the information acquired this way will generate the marker feelings connected to the word 'papaya' in our mind. That is to say, the marker feelings of the words 'vitamin' and 'health' will be extended to the word 'papaya'. Since the marker feelings generated in this way do not rest on feelings acquired through direct interactions with the given phenomenon, no somatic markers can be formed from this kind of marker feeling. So this is a one-way street. While marker feelings can be formed from somatic markers, somatic markers cannot be formed from "sterile" marker feelings.

At first sight, this fact does not look that important. However, it most certainly is. Because we cannot touch, smell and taste everything in the world. There are words that denote things we cannot interact directly with. Therefore, somatic markers cannot be connected to these words. These words are notions. As a consequence of the above, in turn, it is clearly marker feelings that control the process of thinking in notions. When thinking in notions, the role of marker feelings in symbol-based control is uncannily similar to the role somatic markers play in feeling-based control. Just as somatic markers can influence the direction of our trains of feelings within split seconds at the feeling-based control level, marker feelings can also define the direction of our thinking, or what words we should use or avoid, at the same speed. An interesting consequence of this fact is that in the field of social sciences, which operate primarily with notions, marker feelings will primarily define the direction of our thoughts, as opposed to the field of natural sciences where somatic markers are often formed as a result of the experiments so, apart from the marker feelings connected to the notions also existing in this field, somatic markers will often play a role here. Neither the topic nor the size of this book allows for a discussion of the differences between the ways of thinking about social and natural sciences in detail. If any of my readers are interested in this topic, I suggest that you read my book *Words* (© 2015 Győző Margóczi, Budapest, ISBN 978 963 12 1585 4).

In order to better understand human thinking, let us ask a silly question: "How do our feelings influence our thoughts?" Why, this question is silly, I am sure you have already realised. If we want to just quickly answer why this question makes no sense, the answer is quite short. It is because there is only one world that exists in us humans, and that is the world of feelings. A slightly more complicated answer would be that the question makes no sense because our thoughts are nothing else but chains of series of feelings of sound. How could we then transform the question "How do our feelings influence our thoughts?" into a meaningful question? Like this, for example: "How do the processes taking place at the level of feeling-based control influence the processes taking place at the level of symbol-based control?" To make the question even more interesting, we could add "and vice versa" to it like this: "How do the processes taking place at the level of feeling-based control influence the processes taking place at the level of symbol-based control, and vice versa?" All we have to do now is to answer this question.

The most important thing to take into consideration is that, apart from a few special cases, our thoughts are not generated randomly in us. Our thoughts are organised into two main groups:
   – thoughts related to our needs hierarchy as a whole and to the individual needs in the hierarchy separately, and

- thoughts related to looking for pleasant orienting, strategic and status-indicating feelings and avoiding unpleasant orienting, strategic and status-indicating feelings.

Although the feelings in the second group also participate in the implementation of the satisfaction of needs mentioned in the first group, we often strive to experience or avoid them irrespective of need satisfaction, just for the sake of experiencing pleasant feelings and avoiding unpleasant feelings. That is why it is important to classify them into two different groups.

Of course, we may encounter difficulties during the realisation of the goals mentioned above and have to cope with secondary, tertiary etc. sub-processes. Naturally, in these cases, our thoughts are absorbed in these lower level processes. For example, where I should park my car when I go to the store to do the shopping. But after having parked the car, my thoughts related to buying food come to the forefront again. And, as a matter of fact, if we take the entire process into consideration, my thoughts related to parking the car also served the purpose of satisfying the need for energy supply as a whole.

Examining the interaction between symbol-based and feeling-based control, it makes sense to have a look at the impact of feeling-based control on the processes taking place at the level of symbol-based control. It makes sense to examine things in this order because the feeling-based control level is the primary level as it was formed earlier than the symbol-based control level both in phylogeny and in ontogeny. With this we have arrived at one of the most fundamental and most understandable cases, when the need-indicating feelings appearing at the feeling-based control level define the thoughts appearing at the symbol-based control level. If the need-indicating feeling of hunger is torturing us, we will have thoughts related to getting food; if the need-indicating feeling of getting information is bothering us, we will be thinking about how to get more information; if the need-indicating feeling of safety, i.e. fear, is harassing us, we will try to find out how to escape from the dangerous situation etc. Naturally, we can sometimes overturn the order of the hierarchy of needs. For example, if we are head over heels in love, it is not always certain that we will think about our stomach. Instead we will have thoughts related to the satisfaction of the need to reproduce.

Since the satisfaction of our needs, as discussed earlier, is achieved with the help of the system of our feelings, I suggest that we take another look at Figure 17. As a matter of fact, the processes taking place at the feeling-based control level, as shown in the figure, define the processes taking place at the symbol-based control level. If one of our needs is not satisfied, the unpleasant need-indicating feelings will start our thoughts, as we observed earlier. For example, the thought "Dammit, how hungry I am!" may arise in us. If the orienting feeling generator comes up with a pleasant orienting feeling while we are eating a certain food, we will put the emerging orienting feeling into words: "How lovely this roast chicken is!" or if we see Julia, we might say: "How beautiful Julia is!". If on the basis of the pleasant orienting feeling our strategic generator generates the feeling of desire in us, we will say: "How much I want that roast chicken!" or "How much I want Julia!" (It is not advisable to mention to Julia that we want her as strongly as we want the roast chicken. ☺). The feeling of impatience generated by the tactical feeling generator may trigger the following sentence in us: "That waiter could be a bit faster!" Or the feeling of tenderness appearing in the case of Julia might make us say: "Can I hold your hand?"

In the cases listed above, our thoughts only commented on or diagnosed the feelings emerging in us. In this mode of operation, the two levels of control are present as equal partners: they work nicely alongside one another and nei-

172

ther of them wants to dominate, suppress, control, manipulate or rule the other one. This peace, however, does not last forever. Sometimes there are coups. Either one level or the other takes control and tries to achieve "its own" goals. Let us look at a couple of examples where the feeling-based control level takes power.

The simplest example of a coup carried out by the feeling-based control level is the case of smokers, alcohol addicts, drug addicts or those on a slimming diet. The person in question controls the situation for weeks, or sometimes even for months with the help of her symbol-based control but suddenly the coup takes place. Then the person jumps on the forbidden things and gobbles up the "pleasures", i.e. pleasant orienting feelings. For us, it is exactly this period of gobbling which is the most interesting. During this period, the given person simply cannot find a single thought in her brain that would stop the process of gobbling. Her brain is simply empty without a trace of a single thought. The first thought that appears might be the exclamation "Oh my God, that was delicious!" at the end of the gobbling. It is an entirely separate issue that after finishing the gobbling, when the symbol-based control has recovered its strength, a feeling of bad conscience will usually appear: "What an idiot I am! What have I done?" But the feeling of a bad conscience does not always come. In order to avoid non-physical pain appearing as a consequence of the feeling of a bad conscience, the feeling-based control level deletes the events and "unhappens" them. The person will simply not think about what she has done. As if it has not happened at all. And that means that while we only saw the simple suppression of thoughts during the period of the "gobbling", this time we see a much more serious, qualified case of deleting the memory.

The feeling-based control level can also take control in other cases. A typical case would be quick actions. For example, we are skiing and speeding down a slope very fast and we do not have time to think over what we need to do at the symbol-based control level because in the meantime a huge tree may jump in front of us. So we do not have time to think "it would probably be better to turn to the left sharply and go around the tree and then ski on the right-hand side of that small heap of snow" because by the time we have thought all this over, we will need somebody to scrape us off the tree. In such a case, we just automatically do what we need to do and enjoy the speed.

The cases above were relatively easy to understand. But there are also trickier ones. When I was a young lad, I used to court a girl rather vehemently. As usually happens, when we were left alone in private, I immediately started lusting after her in the natural way. Due to her good manners, she did not want to say yes immediately and I had to use all my "eloquence" to satisfy my desire. At one point I realised that I had said something untrue. "Oh my God! I have lied!" the thought flashed up in my head "She is not the most beautiful girl in the world!" What happened in reality? All that happened was that the feeling-based control level took me over. "Okay, Okay," you may think "there is nothing special in this so far." The special thing is that, controlled by the strategic feeling of desire, the level of feeling-based control assumed power over the level of symbol-based control and used words as means or tools, to achieve its goal. Just like a joiner uses his plane or chisel. The sentence that she was the most beautiful girl in the world was not preceded by any kind of conscious planning or logical plotting, it just slipped out of my mouth even though the girl in question was not exactly the beauty queen type and I was fully aware of that.

But it is not only when driven by the strategic feeling of desire that the level of feeling-based control can assume power: the strategic feeling of anger produces similar situations also. When we make a verbal attack against someone or, more simply, we reprimand somebody, we attack our victim led by the strategic feeling of anger at the level of feeling-based control, while at the level of symbol-based control we are using the words as tools or weapons. We do not engage in complicated reasoning beforehand and do not make an elaborate plan about what we are going to say. We simply shout at our victim: "You idiot! You swine!"

But it still not only the feelings of desire and anger that can make the feeling-based control level use the words coming from the symbol-based control level as tools but all the other strategic feelings, i.e. love, non-physical pain, disgust and joy as well. And all this happens without the symbol-based control level having the slightest idea: we just simply do not know what we are doing and why we are doing it.

Boasting people usually do not prepare "strategies" covering each and every move of theirs, they just drop a sentence or two like this in a very laid-back manner: "Oh, darling! Imagine, last time in Dubai they had the cheek to book a miserable five-star hotel for us. What is more, after our plane had stopped at the place reserved for private jets, they sent the previous model of Rolls-Royce to collect us." It took me 10 minutes to sweat out these two sentences. For someone with a little more cunning, it would not take a second. As we will see later on, boasting is a misshapen way of satisfying the need of meeting others' expectations which the boaster experiences as a relative exaltation of him or herself and feels joy about, while the person listening to the boasting experiences it as a relative put-down and feels non-physical pain as a result. That is, the boasting person feels a little better at the expense of the other person's suffering. Very nice... There are schemers who are masters of manipulation with words. Using the words as weapons, they can stab a "knife" into the heart of their victim with their series of elaborate manoeuvres. Why do they do that? Because they enjoy it.

The cases listed in the book *Games People Play* by Eric Berne properly demonstrate the dominant role of feeling-based control over symbol-based control. In the cases observed by Eric Berne, the patients were not aware that they were playing games, what is more they had never heard of these games in their entire life but this fact did not prevent them from playing them. This could only happen to them in a way that the feeling-based control level assumed direction over the symbol-based control level and manipulated it, using the words found there as their tools, so that at the end of the game the given person – as Eric Berne put it – got 'gains'. With this word Eric Berne reached his limits and the limits of the science of psychology. No matter how clever he was and no matter how extensive his knowledge, he could not move on without an important discovery. And the missing discovery was that the word 'gains' he used actually means feelings, or a specific combination of them. And this is the point where the science of psychology must hand over the problem to the science of sensology. This is the border where the traditional means and methods of psychology are no longer suitable for the investigation. If someone is willing to spend the money and the time, and takes the effort, she can describe the train of feelings in the games listed in Eric Berne's book and can find out their "secret".

But let us move on. Another, much less harmful and much more pleasurable example of games we play is co-quetry: when women and men use very sophisticated methods, sometimes almost artistic phrases to help each other experience pleasant feelings. Of course, no script like "I will say this, and then he will say that, and then I will answer like this..." is written in this case either. How is it possible? We do not think over in advance what we will say! Who is controlling what we should say? The answer to this question is complicated and simple at the same time. Let us first examine how we learn to skate or ski. I did not mention the example of walking because, supposedly, each and every one of my readers will have already learned how to walk but not all of them will have learnt how to skate or ski. I recommend that those among my dear readers who can already skate or ski think of tightrope walking. So how do we learn these activities? All we do is we give all our attention to the somatic feelings emerging in our body. We monitor at what angle our feet, legs and thighs are, in which direction and how much our body leans, how we are holding our hands etc. How do we monitor these things? Naturally, with the help of our feelings. We try to memorise what feelings should and should not be generated in which of our body parts. After falling down several times, when we are all black and blue, we learn which are the feelings that we should beware of in order to avoid falling down and which are the ones that we need to experience in order to avoid the painful feeling of landing on our bums and to experience the pleasant orienting feelings triggered by speeding. After a certain amount of time, the whole process becomes automated and if we run onto a rough patch, we will know immediately how to correct and how to avoid falling down just as we also "know" what movements we should do to make our speeding even more exciting. So we learn which feelings we should experience one after the other in order to enjoy the speed. And we do it all without a single train of thought crossing our brain.

The situation is exactly the same when the feeling-based control level learns which feelings should be experienced and used after which other feelings – i.e. series of feelings of sound in the given case – in order to be able to use them as tools to express our love, attack others, fulfil our wishes or only experience small and pleasant feelings by boasting or by "stabbing someone through the heart" with scheming or games. And we do all this without any kind of thinking, i.e. without deliberate involvement at the level of the symbol-based control.

The dominance of the symbol-based control level over the level of feeling-based control is also an everyday phenomenon. This is what the conventions of our society expect from us. The great thinkers of humankind have been preaching for thousands of years that reason and sense should control the chaotic, dirty, dark and sinful realm of feelings. Phooey! Well, they were mistaken... Because it is our feelings that always and exclusively control us. Of course, we can ask the question of ourselves: "What is better? Should we listen to the feeling-based control level or to the symbol-based control level while we are making decisions?" It depends. If the symbol-based control level is filled with nonsense, then we are in trouble if we listen to it. Just think of our theories connected to the word 'übermensch'.

The next group is when the feeling-based control level and the symbol-based control level become independent of one another and both do their own stuff. For a clearer understanding of this, let us start with machines or, more precisely, computers. In computers, the speed of 'thinking', i.e. completing operations, is approximately constant. Machines can work continuously at an approximately constant speed. We humans, however, cannot. Our thoughts sometimes speed up and sometimes stop to have a little rest. Our thoughts oscillate. A clear example of this is that we phrase our thoughts into sentences and sometimes pause between our sentences for quite a long time. Let us see why it is so important. Let us have a look at the following sentences: "At the weekend, I'll go down to the sea and do some scuba-diving. Then I'll visit my favourite restaurant where I'll have a pint of good beer after a healthy portion of squid." While we are saying or thinking over the sentence "At the weekend, I'll go down to the sea and do some scuba-diving." we will see that the feelings connected to the individual words have fallen off or broken off somehow. That is to say, in the one or two seconds we need to say or think over this sentence, the feelings related to travelling and scuba-diving do not arise in us. So we will not feel that we are sitting in the car, holding the steering wheel and changing gears, the landscape gliding past the car will not appear in our mind's eye either, just as we will not feel how the goggles are pushing our face or how the water surrounds us etc. And this is perfectly natural. The capacity of our brains is not enough to recall all the feelings related to the words while we are saying our sentences. The feelings I mentioned above appear in us before or after saying the sentence, i.e. in the breaks between the sentences. From this, we can draw the conclusion that the feeling-based control and the symbol-based control levels are in a looser connection with one another while we are saying or thinking over the sentences. The strength of this connection is not constant. It is continuously changing and adjusting to the given situation instead. While we are driving a car, for example, our mind can be wandering and we can drive kilometres without remembering anything of what we have seen on the way.

Now I suggest that, with the help of the things we have learned so far, we try to follow the process of the interaction of the two levels on a few trains of thoughts. Let us assume that we are walking on a street experiencing the unpleasant indicating feeling of the need to reproduce. First, we do not understand why, we just feel uncomfortable somehow. This feeling will only appear at the symbol-based control level if we attach a word to it, as we can only operate at the symbol-based control level with symbols, i.e. words. If we have a look at Figure 26, we can see that the symbol-based control centre is not directly connected with either the feelings arriving through sight and other incoming feeling channels or the feeling generators and the feelings produced by them. While the CPU in real-time mode receives the signal of the incoming feeling channels and the feeling generators directly, the symbol-based control is connected to the system through memory. This cannot be done in any other way because the incoming data must be identified and must be connected to the appropriate symbol or word that is, naturally, stored in our memory. So if we are feeling the unpleasant need-indicating feeling of the need to reproduce, we are simply not capable of thinking of 'horny' until the unpleasant need-indicating feeling of the need to reproduce reaches our memory and connects with the appropriate symbol, i.e. the word 'horny', which then reaches the control centre where I can already take action on it. (I must apologise but there are not too many words in English to describe the unpleasant need-indicating feeling of the need to reproduce: lustful, randy, horny).

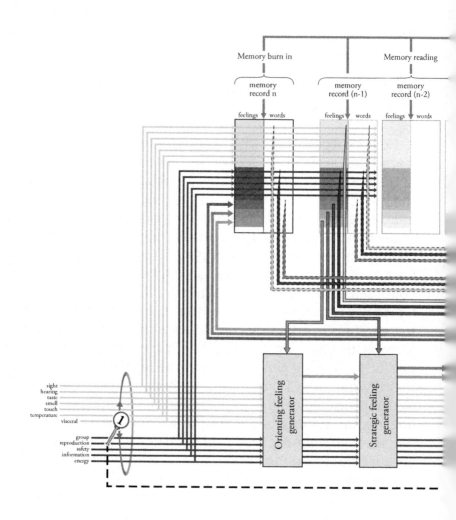

Figure 26

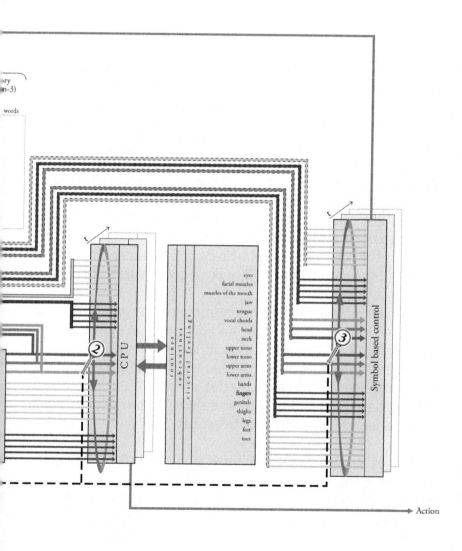

Once the word 'horny' has appeared in our thoughts, we can start thinking about how to get rid of this uncomfortable feeling. And this is the point where somatic markers start to appear. We will decide in a split second which sex we are interested in and who are the ones among them who give us a thrill. Thanks to the somatic markers, we will only scan that section of humankind that we find attractive.

If we continue thinking about the solution of the problem, we will see that the role of marker feelings will dramatically increase. Yes, marker feelings can assume power over the control of our thoughts. It is an undeniable fact that positive marker feelings attached to words such as 'doctor', 'lawyer' or 'banker' can often play a really strong role in the selection of our partner. But so can marker feelings attached to words such as 'Buddhist', 'Christian', 'Moslem', 'Jew' or 'democrat', 'communist', 'republican', 'social democrat' etc. Sometimes it does not matter if people who are very attractive to us, both sexually and as human beings, are standing in front of us, if they are not doctors, lawyers or bankers, we dump them all the same. They will make a good lover at best.

Marker feelings, just like somatic markers, can influence the direction of our thoughts and decisions in split seconds. This is a rather strange situation. We might think that the symbol-based control level makes the decisions because we are using words but, as a matter of fact, it is the level of feeling-based control that makes them with the help of the marker feelings attached to the words.

The examples above demonstrated the process of selection. Let us now look at another example of how marker feelings influence our actions. Since the human being is a thinking creature, we not only react to interactions with the external world, we also have our own independent thoughts. In the symbol-based control centre, we carry out operations with words and as a result we usually get a derived output symbol: a word. Let us suppose that this word is 'sin' this time. This word is sent to the memory where the feelings related to it, including marker feelings, are recorded. Then these feelings are sent to the corresponding feeling generators where they influence the current processes.

If we see someone who is attractive to us in terms of the need to reproduce, a pleasant orienting feeling may be generated in us and the strategic feeling of desire might also appear. Then, driven by our tactical and technological feelings, we may even take steps to bring about a sexual relationship. The strategic feeling of sexual desire reaches our memory which deciphers this feeling with the words 'I want her sexually'. But at the symbol-based control level, the word 'sin' – if, due to our upbringing, it is attached to the word 'sex' in our data network – will recall negative strategic and marker feelings when it is brought to mind. Having reached the strategic feeling generator, these negative strategic feelings will influence the operation of the generator and can overwrite and block the original process of need satisfaction.

7.5 Attention
(Are there different types of attention?)

You can see three magnifying glasses in Figure 26. These magnifying glasses symbolise attention. Because attention resembles a magnifying glass the most. Huge amounts of data reach our mind and it is impossible to process all the data completely: our brain simply does not have the capacity for it. We can solve the problem by processing the incoming signal of only one incoming feeling channel or the optical channel at a time in full resolution and full detail and switch between channels. But this way, idle time would be created in some of the channels. So we would not hear, would not be able to smell, taste or use our sense of touch while we are seeing. Then, when we switch over to hearing, all the other data channels would be blocked. This is obviously nonsense. It would be very difficult to stay alive like that. The solution is to run all the incoming data channels in parallel at the same time but in low resolution or low detail mode. This way only as much data enters into our mind as we can process. If we notice something unusual, the resolution of the process of the given incoming data channel suddenly increases and we have more high-resolution data available but the other channels are not blocked at the same time, only their resolution decreases a little at the worst.

When we focus our attention on something, this is pretty similar to looking at things with a magnifying glass. Everything we are looking at through the magnifying glass shows in much more detail and in a much higher resolution than its surroundings. There are three lenses in the table. One of them is watching data coming from the external world. This lens, however, cannot function alone, it can only work together with, and under the control of, the second one. The first lens is nothing else but the front lens of the second one because in order to operate it you need an active action. If something appears in the scope of our peripheral vision, we need to turn our eyes towards it so the light falls on the fovea, the highest resolution part of our retina. If we notice some noise, we need to turn our head in its direction to be able to hear it with both of our ears. If we smell something, we try to localise the source of the smell by turning our head and so on. So in order to operate the first lens, we need to monitor our somatic feelings, and this is done by the second lens. The second lens monitors the feelings coming from the internal and external incoming feeling channels, from the feeling generators and from the memory, and also the data coming through our sight. The third lens, in turn, monitors the processes taking place in the symbol-based control unit. The third lens can only get data about the external world in cooperation with the second and the first lenses. When we decide at the symbol-based control level that we will examine something in the external world in more detail, we need the first lens, which is controlled by the second lens. When we decide at the symbol-based control level that we will examine our feelings in the present and the past because, let us say, we are attracted to somebody, we use our second and third lenses and the first lens is out of operation. When we are sitting in an armchair thinking about mathematical problems, we only use the third lens that is monitoring the symbol-based control level in the memory and we do not care about the external world. When we think about mathematical problems while we are driving a car, the third lens focuses only on the symbol-based control level in the memory and the first and the second lenses are monitoring the external world. In these cases, the feeling-based and the symbol-based control levels separate from one another and work in parallel on their own tasks, independently from one another. It is important, however, to point out that, both when we are awake or asleep, all lenses are operating only at a level that is appropriate for the given state. When we are dreaming, the first lens shows a lower level of activity, whereas the second and third lenses may be actively working.

8.

FEELING TRAPS

A shared property of feeling traps is that our feelings, due to their being used differently from their original function, urge us to carry out mental processes and actions that might be painful or explicitly harmful for us.

8.1 The desire trap
(How can we become the slaves of our desires?)

Although the desire trap may look harmless at the first sight, this is the trap the most people suffer from around the world. Another reason for discussing the desire trap first is because it often connects to other traps to form trap systems with them. In order to understand the essence of traps, let us take an example. Let me invite my dear reader for a pint of beer in the local pub (or the more sensitive ones for a tea in a tea shop). We are sitting there peacefully with our beer at the counter when the rhetorical question arises: Do I desire a beer? The answer is: No way. The man who has been wandering around the desert for two days: yes, he desires a beer. He'll almost die to get a beer, that is how strong his desire is! As a matter of fact, you can also desire a beer when you are sitting at the counter but you cannot fall into a desire trap. You only need to stretch out your arm and the beer is yours. Due to its function, desire can only exist for a few seconds until we get the object of desire. The two criteria of a desire trap though are: the desire itself and the fact that you cannot get the object of your desire.

Two friends are walking in the desert and they have long run out of water. One of them is thinking like this: "I have not drunk anything for two days. The next oasis is still 30 km off. It is not beyond reach, but I must walk in the night so that my strength lasts." The thoughts of the other friend are going like this: "I have not drunk anything for two days. How good a pint of cold beer would feel now! Just imagine how the mist is glimmering on the cold glass and how thick the foam head is on the top! I am now raising the mug to my mouth and tasting the cold nectar. The taste of the beer fills my mouth and I just drink and drink and drink..." And then suddenly back to the hot reality! What processes take place in the second friend? First, there is the need-indicating feeling of thirst that warns of the strong need for energy supply. So far so good. But the only available water is 30 km away in the watering trough of the oasis and even that is stale. So no positive orienting feelings could be triggered in our friend by the water. And this is the point of no return. This is where our friend could have turned back on the path of his feelings with a relatively small loss. And, as a matter of fact, he did recall the positive orienting feeling triggered by the water from his memory but, since one might as well be hung for a sheep as a lamb, he opted for the orienting feeling of beer instead. The orienting feeling of beer did its job and started the strategic feeling of desire. And, since the feeling of desire is rather unpleasant and our friend was a relatively less patient type, he decided that he would not wait until the next pub (200 km). What did he do? He travelled in time! He simply projected himself into the future. What happened during his time travel? While he was in the "future", all he did was recall in minute detail the visual data and other feelings such as smell, taste, temperature, touch and so on, and the related orienting feelings experienced during his beer drinking in the past. Although these feelings are not as intensive or strong as those experienced in actual beer drinking, you can still feel them and they have a very special feature.

The changes of the orienting feeling during normal need satisfaction is shown on the graph in Figure 27. One of the axes show the intensity and quality of the orienting feelings, the other one shows time. An intensive orienting feeling accompanies need satisfaction, which dies relatively fast and transforms into a neutral orienting feeling which, after a while, may transform into a negative orienting feeling.

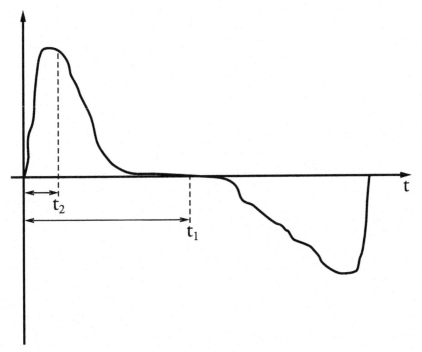

Figure 27

In a normal case, need satisfaction stops at the point where the orienting feeling becomes neutral, that is before the negative orienting feeling appears. So normally, we save the average value of the set of feelings experienced between points 0 and t1 in our memory. But if we indulge in time travel, the curve of the orienting feeling does not have time to run down, or rather it cannot run down, because no real need satisfaction takes place. Therefore, the average value of the feelings between points 0 and t2 is what gets added to the content of the memory. But that is very positive! We need to take into consideration here that we are not talking about a computer. That means that the average value of feelings experienced between points 0 and t2 does not completely overwrite the prior content of the memory but the contents of the old and the new record will be averaged. However, due to the repeated time travel, this average gradually moves in the positive direction and can result in an extremely strong positive orienting feeling. An extremely strong positive orienting feeling, in turn, will bring about an extremely strong desire which is a very unpleasant feeling. Another factor that helps the formation of the previous process is that, due to the nature of things, we only like to remember pleasant orienting feelings. No one will travel in time in order to experience unpleasant orienting feelings. However, sometimes it might help, in order to bring the scales back to balance.

When our friend drinks real beer and then, for some reason, he needs to stop drinking it, he will have been able to satisfy his need at least to a certain extent, and the intensity of the orienting feeling, and therefore also the feeling of desire, will decrease so our friend will be in a better position than he was when he started to drink the beer. But when he comes back from his time travel, he will be in a worse position than before. Before he started travelling in time, he was only thirsty, but recalling the orienting feeling of the beer also triggered the feeling of desire. He completed his time travel and had a pleasant orienting feeling in the "future" but that orienting feeling wasn't able to die down so it moved the average of the orienting feeling stored in his memory in a positive direction. The more positive an orienting feeling is, the stronger the desire that belongs to it. So when our protagonist arrives back in the present, he will already be tormented by a stronger desire. His desire may also be joined by some non-physical pain due to the loss of the imaginary beer. The need-indicating feeling of thirst may also intensify in an attempt to warn the guy to drink more and not to stop drinking. On the one hand, he has his worsened position, while on the other hand, he has the possibility of another period of time travel where a pleasant orienting feeling will be waiting for him. Therefore, our friend projects himself again and again into the future, and as a result, he moves the average of the orienting feeling more and more in the positive direction, creating an increasingly unpleasant desire in himself while his feeling of thirst also grows. This is a recurring vicious circle which is not only very difficult to get out of, it's impossible to get out of without non-physical pain.

If we leave the example of the beer behind, the indicating and orienting feelings, and the related desire, of other needs can also cause desire traps. Similar desire traps related to the need to reproduce are sometimes mislabelled as love. The operating mechanism is the same, only the orienting feelings involved are different. The stronger the orienting feelings we experience during our time travel, the more we suffer and the more difficult it is to get out of the trap.

The desire trap has a less dangerous version. In this version, instead of projecting herself out into the future, the time traveller projects herself back into the past. This is something you tend to see more with elderly people. They recall pleasant orienting feelings experienced in the past again and again. Due to being recalled again and again, the pleasant orienting feelings strengthen in the memory, while the unpleasant ones slowly fade: "Remember the good times". Since, however, these events happened in the past, you do not see much chance to repeat them in the future so you can control your desire more easily.

You need to learn to recognise desire traps in time. When

you notice that you go time travelling too often, you must bring yourself back to the present deliberately before it is too late.

8.2 The tension trap
(Is there such a thing at all?)

As a matter of fact, tension traps do not exist on their own, they can only appear as result of a desire trap. In our investigation of strategic feelings, we saw that primary processes may be broken down into subordinate processes. While the driving force of the primary processes is desire, the driving force of the subordinate processes – which are generated as a consequence of the temporary interruption of the primary processes – is tension. If we set a goal for ourselves and something blocks us from achieving this goal, tension is created in us which urges us to overcome the difficulty. There are difficulties, however, that are beyond our abilities. Let us take the example that we have a strong desire for something, it could be anything, for example, a partner, an apartment, our university degree, happiness and so on, and it just does not happen. It is delayed for days, months or years. It often happens that we spend these days, months and years in continuous tension. We keep constantly asking: when? When will my time arrive? When will I be happy? When? When? Or we keep repeating to ourselves that we will be happy when we have a partner, an apartment, a university degree and so on and so forth. These thoughts are all born when the process started by a desire either stops for a reason or does not even start. And we are wearing ourselves away in continuous tension waiting for happiness while we are living in the hell we made for ourselves.

If the difficulty is something we can overcome, we should overcome it and move on towards our goal but if we run into difficulties that cannot be overcome – time, luck etc. – we will be better off if we try to control our desires, otherwise we'll sentence ourselves to suffering. The combination of the desire trap and the tension trap can be very painful and devastating.

8.3 The fear trap
(How does the fear trap work?)

Fear traps are created when we think that something threatens our need for safety. In this case, the indicating feeling of the need for safety, i.e. fear, is activated. In order to get rid of the fear, we need to avoid the expected danger. In such a situation, our mind strives to find a way out. If we find a simple and certain way out and we can easily implement it, we are in the winning position. If not, we may be faced with a trap. One of the preconditions of the creation of a fear trap is that the situation is uncertain. The other precondition is that we do not have the opportunity to act immediately and we must wait for some reason. If we can act immediately, the implementation of the action will hold our attention, and the trap cannot form. Because the essence of the fear trap is that, driven by our fear, we start feverishly thinking about how we can get out of the difficult situation. While we are thinking about the way out, we experience a decrease of our fear because our attention is diverted or scenarios appear in our mind's eye, and thinking through the scenarios apparently ensures that we can break free from our difficulty. While we are recalling these scenarios, we actually travel in time to the future just as in the case of the desire trap. While we are spending our time in the future watching the movie about our pseudo-solutions, our fear decreases. But then we come back to the present again. Our attention is diverted, but it is not diverted enough because we are still thinking about the solution of the emergency, which we do not find in the end. When we stop thinking about the solution of the problem, we immediately start to have the fear again. In order to avoid fear, we start thinking about the solution again, we project ourselves into the future again and we are back in the vicious circle. If we are running the umpteenth unproductive circle of thoughts, we must draw the conclusion that we do not have enough data to find a way out in the given moment and we must try to overcome our fear. When we have more data, it may be worth thinking about a potential way out again but otherwise our thoughts will simply be running around fruitlessly.

8.4 The game trap
(Is it not a pleasant one?)

The easiest way to examine the working mechanism of this trap is to look at different games. It may be a simple video game, a slot machine, cards, horseracing and so on. When the game starts, the player feels the need to win and to achieve the goal of the game. During the game, excitingly tense and pleasantly slack moments keep changing place with one another. If the player wins, his reward is the strategic feeling of joy followed by a pleasant slackness. These are the pleasant feelings he would like to experience again and again and that is why he starts playing another game. If he loses, he is tormented by the strategic feeling of non-physical pain and the unpleasant feeling of accumulated tension which he would like to get rid of. If he starts a new game, his attention is diverted from the non-physical pain and he can experience the dynamic changes of excitingly tense and pleasantly slack moments and he can win as well. Whether he wins or loses, he will restart the game for one of the reasons, and he goes around and around again.

8.5 The pain trap

The operation of the pain trap is also cyclical. If we experience a certain non-physical pain, it is often very difficult for us to get rid of it, no matter whether it is caused by the loss of a beloved person, infidelity or by someone simply "trampling over" our soul. As we know, non-physical pain is a strategic feeling that sends us the message "Don't let it go!" (In the case of attacks against our ego, the message of the non-physical pain is the same as you will see in Chapter 9.6, in the discussion of meeting others' expectations.) Our thoughts typically return again and again to events causing non-physical pain when we cannot fulfil the strategic command of the non-physical pain or we need to let something go or perish. In these cases, we relive the situation again and again, it hurts again and again and we still cannot solve the problem: we need to say farewell to somebody or something anyway.

The first step in these cases is to recognise that we have fallen into a pain trap. The second step is to assess whether we can get rid of the event triggering the non-physical pain. If we can, we must take the necessary steps. If we cannot, we must give up the thing that torments our heart and we should divert our thoughts from the event. If we do not do that, our mind will keep sending the same message: non-physical pain saying "Don't let it go! Don't let it go!" until the end of time.

A consequence of the pain trap is the hatred trap. If somebody has caused us non-physical pain, the feeling of hatred may appear and we may want to strike back at the person triggering our non-physical pain with some form of aggression. This is revenge. This is something, however, we often cannot do. This is when we can fall into the hatred trap, if we keep recalling the event triggering our non-physical pain again and again. The non-physical pain will also keep reappearing in us giving birth to anger again and again. Anger, as we know, is a strategic feeling whose message is "Destroy it!" Since, due to external circumstances, we cannot fulfil the command of our strategic feeling – i.e. we cannot show aggression, this means we have a process started by a strategic feeling and stopped by external circumstances, and the feeling of tension appears in us. And this can go on this way from now to eternity if we keep thinking about the event causing us non-physical pain. The Bible urges us to forgive them that trespass against us. Do we have to forgive? Well, it is not a statutory obligation so we will not be held liable for it but this is recommended anyway. Recommended because the psychological processes mentioned above will torment our soul and not the soul of the person who triggered the entire process in us. What is more, sometimes the person who hurt us is downright happy to see us suffer. Okay, I know it is nice to make our fellow human beings happy but this is not the way. I mean, I would not do that. Instead, we need to draw the conclusions of the story and try to avoid similar situations in the future.

The hatred trap mentioned above is a good example of how sometimes entire systems of traps can be formed starting with pain, hatred and tension traps. The remaining feeling traps are not actual traps. As a matter of fact, they are about enjoying some of the pleasant feelings so much that the feeling-based control level causes us again and again to experience the same feeling even though the symbol-based control level prohibits us from experiencing that feeling for some reason. We simply cannot resist temptation and the rational part of our mind helplessly watches what the feeling-based control does. Examples of these trap-like scenarios include feelings coming from natural sources, related to gluttony, sex, aggression and so on, or feelings coming from artificial sources such as drugs, alcohol, smoking and so on. It is important to point out that the games described in Eric Berne's *Games People Play* also belong to this group. Naturally, these pseudo-traps often connect to real traps, like the desire, the tension, the fear or the game trap.

9.

ONCE MORE ABOUT NEEDS

After having successfully classified our feelings and having taken a closer look at them, I think it is time to get back to needs and have another look, with the help of our newly acquired knowledge.

9.1 Need for energy supply
(What do commercials have to do with eating?)

There are two threats to humanity in this respect. One of them is starvation, while the other one is obesity. This is a seemingly absurd and grotesque situation but it is a fact that one part of humankind is still starving, while the other part suffers from problems related to obesity. I am not going to discuss the economic and political reasons for famine now. As for obesity, thousands of books have been written about the topic. I suggest that we have a look at the issue from the point of view of our newly acquired knowledge.

Prehistoric humans, with their food-gathering lifestyle, did not have reserves. The odd prey, the scarcity of food and their frequent hunger urged them to eat anything they could get hold of because "no one knows what the future may bring". These habits became a part of us, developed over thousands of years. Today, when most of humankind do not do tiring and calorie-consuming physical work and, at the same time, have all sorts of food in abundance, it is difficult to break the habits we inherited. But this is only one of the reasons that we already know. Another reason that we have not yet discovered is that "they" want to lure us into a trap. I am sure now you are thinking: "Oh no! Another guy who suffers from a persecution complex!" To make it easier to understand what I think, I will clarify my point a little. They want us to fall into a desire trap. They want to make our feeling-based control take power over our symbol-based control. Okay, I know I was a little blunt. But this is exactly the goal and the principle of operation of commercials. The goal of commercials is to convince us to buy things, i.e. to generate desire in us. Commercials do not influence the symbol-based control. Commercials will not describe in detail the advantages of buying a particular product to convince our symbol-based control. Commercials generate desire in us in 5 seconds. And this is exactly the goal! Don't think! Why should you? It will only give you a headache. Buy something instead! Or don't even bother with buying anything, just give us your money and get the heck out of here!

The role of food commercials in gaining weight, I think, is obvious. But what is the case with other commercials? "Oh, c'mon! Don't try to tell me that I'll put on weight because of a commercial for a car!" you may be thinking. Yes, indeed, not because of one and not everybody will. However, a huge number of commercials are bombarding people in today's modern societies. There are countries where commercials are more sophisticated and there are others where they are more aggressive. Just think of commercials starting like this: "Real men drive this and that car!" So if I do not drive that particular make of a car, I am not a real man!? (Just imagine all those unfortunate guys whose manliness depends on a certain brand of car. What will happen to them if their car gets stolen?) Or for example: "Everybody who matters buys a house by the riverside!" Do you have a house on the riverside? Because if not, you have screwed your life up for ever.

Commercials generate unsatisfiable desires in most of the people and this can lead to the tension traps discussed in the previous chapter. Most of the people in these cases, in order to reduce the feeling of unpleasant tension, start unconscious activities to distract their attention that, apart from helping them get rid of the unpleasant tension, also reward them with pleasant orienting feelings. Activities like this may include eating, drinking or using drugs. It is a well-known fact that some women, when they are upset, go to the closest sweet shop. But I personally also prefer eating something nice instead of getting pissed off because of some crap. Who does not?

9.2 Need for information

(Is that a real need? What is information?)

The question may arise of whether the need for information is a real need. Isn't it a little exaggerated? Because everyone knows that you need to eat and you need to take breath but is information a vital need? And what is information to start with? Information has many definitions: philosophical, mathematical, technical and so on. We should not forget, however, that the word 'information' is a symbol and, what is more, it is also a notion, so it is the collective symbol of other symbols. Using other symbols to describe a symbol gives a rather inaccurate result due to the nature of symbols (compression). Naturally, we cannot do without symbols because then this book would only be a set of empty pages. But if we still want to make the word 'information' more understandable, it would make sense to examine the process itself and describe that with symbols so we can understand things better.

One thing we need to clarify at the beginning is that information is a notion or symbol that only exists for human beings. Things in the world only exist, happen or interact with one another. The sun is shining, the water evaporates under the effect of the sun and becomes a cloud which, in turn, will become rain and so on and so forth. But no information anywhere! Things just happen in their own way. It is the human being who arbitrarily picks one or two of the processes taking place in the world and tries to draw conclusions about the way things work by examining them. It is the human being that starts investigating the spectral composition of the sunlight and finding out which wavelengths of the electromagnetic radiation make more water evaporate. But water can evaporate perfectly well without the human being all the same. If we still insist on using the symbol of information we could best describe it as the image at the symbol-based control level of the cross-section of an observed interaction between an apparently independent phenomenon and us at a given point in time, t_1. The word 'observed' is important because there may be many different types of interactions between an apparently independent phenomenon and us but we do not observe every one of them. Only the ones the optical and incoming feeling channels of the human being can collect can appear as information. So although the ultraviolet radiation of the sun interacts with our body so that our skin peels off as a result, it cannot appear as information because our optical channel cannot collect and register it and therefore its existence does not appear at the symbol-based control level. Or rather its existence cannot appear there until we can broaden our optical channels with the help of instruments and discover the ultraviolet radiation and we name it, i.e. we make it appear at the level of symbol-based control.

For example, a tiger is walking calmly in the jungle and his body interacts with the electromagnetic radiation it is exposed to. It absorbs a part of it and reflects another part, and it also emits its own electromagnetic radiation. It just happens, this is a process. Information is only created when we expose our eyes to the effect of the electromagnetic radiation having been involved in the interaction with the body of the tiger and we succeed in converting the nervous impulses created in this process into the level of symbol-based control. If we do not expose ourselves to the effect of the light reflected from the tiger, i.e. we do not look at the tiger, or if we do not do the analysis at the symbol-based control level, we cannot talk about information, only a series of interactions following one another.

You may ask what I want with the symbol-based control level again. Couldn't information simply exist without appearing at the level of symbol-based control? No. The word 'information' is itself a symbol that only exists at the symbol-based control level of human beings. So if I see that the tiger is approaching and I start fleeing, this is nothing else but a chain of connected interactions or a series of processes. If I see that the tiger is approaching and I think "it is approaching": that is information.

So when we are discussing the issue of the need for information, the question to ask is whether there is a need to interact with our environment; whether it is necessary that our optical and incoming feeling channels interact with the environment; and whether it is necessary that these interactions are also represented at the symbol-based control level. It is easy to answer the first part of the question. This is no request programme. Like it or not, we are in a tangled network of interactions with our environment. The same thing happens to a stone that is passively lying at the side of the road: it is also in interaction with its environment. It is more difficult, however, to answer the second part of the question. The stone I just mentioned only exists passively: it does not adjust to its environment. But living creatures do adjust to their environment. Adjusting assumes activity that takes interactions with the external world into account. It avoids some interactions and seeks others. Avoiding and seeking assumes manoeuvring among interactions where the perception of a given status is not the only important thing, the direction of the movement is equally important. So it is not enough to "know" that we want to maintain or avoid a certain interaction at a given moment, we also need to "know" in which direction we should move in order to maintain or avoid it. Sometimes it is relatively easy. For example, when we feel that the campfire is warming one side of our body, whereas the other side is cooled down by the cold wind, we can make decisions about the direction of our movement at our own discretion. Or if some food has an unpleasant taste, we can simply remove it from our mouth. In the case of some interactions, however, it is not enough if you try to avoid an interaction when it has already happened. For example, if the tiger is already licking your bones with relish, it is a little too late.

Therefore, it is better to prevent the interaction in the first place. But what can we do? We use some medium. The light rays coming from the sun start interacting with the fur of the tiger. As a result of the interaction, the sun's rays change in a special way that is typical of tiger fur. Then our eyes start interacting with the light modified or transformed by the tiger fur. In this case, we do not interaction with the tiger directly but with the same medium the tiger interacted with, and modified previously. While it is roaring, the tiger also interacts with the air and changes it in a special way only typical of tigers and we then only interact with this modified intermediary medium.

In the case of a stone, it is all the same what interactions it has with its environment, but for a living creature it makes a world of difference. So the living creatures form special and very selective and sensitive interfaces for the best possible outcomes from the interactions that occur the most often and that are the most important for their survival. Do not only think about the optical and feeling channels but also about the combination of the mouth and the stomach, the lungs, the legs, or, in the case of humans, the hands.

It is beyond doubt that the role of the optical and incoming feeling channels culminates in manoeuvring among external interactions. We can also reduce the throughput of the optical and incoming feeling channels or we can even close them down, for example by closing our eyes or covering our ears. Can we do it without negative consequences? For a short time, yes, but for a longer time, no.

Let us do an imaginary experiment. Let us imagine that we put someone into a pool of water at 36°C. Let us dissolve so much salt in the water that the given person starts floating in it. Let us put an oxygen mask on her face, let us cover her eyes and ears and let us put some clothes on her that make any movement impossible. This way will deprive her of the possibility of using her optical and feeling channels. She will not know where up and down is or whether it is night or day so we have completely isolated her from the external world. How long will she be able to stand it? Not too long. She may even go mad. Even if her reaction is not that drastic, one of the most unbearable things for convicts is a dark cell where they must spend days alone in a low stimulus environment. You can try it. Lock yourself in a dark room and monitor what kinds of feelings will overcome you and how soon.

So far, we have only checked the functional and psychological side of the issue. Looking at the issue from the biological and physiological point of view, we will see that, if we do not use them for some reason, the optical and the incoming feeling channels will be damaged and will degenerate sooner or later. So in order to prevent their degeneration and to preserve our health, we need to use our optical and incoming feeling channels. Thus, our answer to the second question, whether it is necessary to use the optical and incoming feeling channels, is a clear yes: it is indeed a real need. But as a matter of fact, we also answered the third question: the interactions of the optical and incoming feeling channels do not necessarily need to be represented at the symbol-based control level. I can go around the armchair in the living room even if I do not think about the word 'armchair'. Or I can eat without continuously repeating the words 'knife', 'fork', 'plate' or 'meat' in my mind, according to which one I am looking at or interacting with at the moment.

During the discussion of our needs we have seen that these needs have their own special indicating feelings that are only typical of one particular need. What is the indicating feeling of the need to use our optical and incoming feeling channels? Boredom, you might say. But this is not the case. Boredom is the result of the lack of activity at the symbol-based control level. When we are just rubbing along with our symbol-based control level in idle speed, we experience the feeling of boredom. And it is enough to focus on any task to be done at the symbol-based control level, and we stop being bored immediately, although we might be lying with our eyes closed in a quiet room minimally using our optical and incoming feeling channels.

The indicating feeling of the need to use our optical and incoming feeling channels does not yet have a name. This is an unpleasant and tense feeling. We often feel it when we need to stay in a low stimulus, closed room and we can hardly wait until we get out. The indicating feeling that prevents the overcharge of this need is apathy. When we are flooded with so many and so diverse interactions that we cannot process them anymore, the state of confusion appears first. That means the capacity of our brain is not enough to process the amount of incoming data. Then we usually try to select a given field and concentrate our attention on it. But if too large and too diverse a dataset is poured over us through our incoming feeling channels, then, after a while, we give up and close down and that is when the feeling of apathy appears.

If we have not yet sufficiently mapped an interaction between an apparently independent phenomenon and ourselves with the help of our optical and incoming feeling channels or we have not yet managed to convert the created image to the symbol-based control level, we might experience the strategic feeling of desire, which is, in the case of the need for information, nothing else but curiosity.

But it is not only the strategic feeling of desire but also that of disgust that might appear in the case described above. This is the case when we really do not want to know about something. But we need to be careful here as well. Because it might also be the case that we do not want to experience the unpleasant orienting, strategic or marker feelings triggered by an apparently independent phenomenon at the feeling-based control level or by the word representing the same phenomenon at the symbol-based control level. For example, I do not want to know where my spouse was last night because it may turn out that I was cheated on and it would trigger the strategic feeling of non-physical pain in me. This is simply the ostrich policy. What you do not know cannot hurt you. In this case it is the strategic feeling connected to the content of the interaction that puts you off, i.e. deters your thoughts. But I may also want to avoid being seen as a "cuckold". In this case, what I was trying to avoid is the negative marker feeling.

The strategic feeling of disgust in connection with the interactions appearing through the optical and incoming feeling channels emerges when we are forced to map an interaction that is not interesting for us, that we are indifferent to or that is complicated and burdensome. In this case, it is not the content of the interaction that we find unpleasant (because we do not even know it yet) but the mere fact of the interaction. For example, you are given the task to measure the distance in relation to one another of 2000 trees in a forest. Who cares how far tree 254 is from tree 1872? Does it matter at all?

9.3 Need for safety

(Do we need fear? Is self-humiliation a pleasant thing?)

It makes sense to start the discussion of the need for safety right away with the interpretation of the word 'safety'. Safety, as a thing, does not exist. Safety does not exist just as the hole in the cheese, a shadow or silence do not exist either. The hole in the cheese is created because there is no cheese there. A shadow is created because there is no light there, and silence happens because there is no sound there. The case of safety is pretty similar: you are in safety when there is no danger around you. So we should more accurately call the need for safety the need for the lack of danger.

What does the word 'danger' mean? For the appropriate interpretation of the word 'danger' I suggest that we take the processes taking place at the feeling-based control level as our starting point. At the level of feeling-based control, a dangerous situation is not represented by the word 'danger' but by two need-indicating feelings. One of them is the feeling of physical pain and the other one is fear. Physical pain is created when our body is exposed to an impact that may cause harm to its tissues. We could live without being able to feel the feeling of physical pain but probably not for too long. Because the feeling of physical pain is the need-indicating feeling that warns us that the physical health of our body, and our existence as a consequence, is under threat. There are people who are born without the ability to feel physical pain but they usually die prematurely exactly because they suffer fatal injuries that could have been avoided if the need-indicating feeling of physical pain had warned them in time.

The other indicating feeling of the need for safety, fear, is not generated without prior events. We feel fear if our external environment or we, ourselves, activate in our memory the optical and incoming feeling channel imprints of phenomena to which unpleasant feelings are connected and which we have a real or imaginary chance to experience again. Fear is nothing but an unpleasant feeling that is meant to prevent us from experiencing even more unpleasant feelings. That is to say fear is the herald of a harmful interaction and its task is to urge us by its unpleasant nature to avoid the harmful interaction connected to it before the harmful interaction actually occurs. Memory plays an important role in forming fear because fears are heavily influenced by our previous experiences. A phenomenon that is unknown to us can be either good or bad. Until we have entered into an interaction of a certain depth with the given phenomenon, we cannot decide if we should go close to it, treat it neutrally or try to avoid it. We classify unpleasant feelings according to their strength and this is how the strength of our fear in connection with them is defined. If we are threatened by the possibility of experiencing several unpleasant feelings at the same time, we always start fighting against the occurrence of the phenomenon that is connected to the most unpleasant feeling at the level of the feelings, and that triggers the strongest fear. This is what we focus our energy on.

The situation is a little bit different at the symbol-based control level. The word 'danger' symbolises the possibility of an interaction at the symbol-based control level that might damage our current state. Animals only react to their environment at the feeling-based control level. They are not capable of travelling in time. They do not know about the future, the only thing that exists for them is the present. They operate in real-time mode. The feelings their environment activates in their memory trigger fears that correspond to real emergencies. Human beings, on the other hand, are capable of travelling in time both into the future and into the past. Therefore, humans can relive the fears of past events again and again and can also be afraid of events that have not happened yet and may not ever happen at all. A possible consequence of travelling in time may be the fear trap.

Another important difference between how animals and humans react to a given emergency comes from the fact that humans can draw conclusions about the future with the help of logical operations taking place at the symbol-based control level, whereas animals cannot. The consequence of this is that, while an emergency is always a 100% emergency for animals, humans can assess the likelihood of the occurrence of a certain event.

Another consequence of the operations carried out at the symbol-based control level is that, while at the feeling-based control level we are trying to avoid the interaction that triggers the strongest pain and that is associated with the most intense unpleasant feeling, at the symbol-based control level we are trying to avoid the unpleasant feeling with the strongest impact when we experience fear. The word 'impact' in the given case could probably be best described as the product of the intensity and duration of the given feeling. So if we suppose that the intensity of a given feeling scores -10 on an imaginary scale and we feel it for 2 seconds, the impact index of the given feeling would be -20 units. The intensity of another unpleasant feeling is -2 on our imaginary scale but we feel it for 15 seconds so its impact index is -30 units. From two evils, we usually choose the lesser one, i.e. the first unpleasant feeling in our case, even though its intensity is higher. A good example of this is toothache. If our tooth aches, we know that the relatively weak pain might well last four weeks. But if we have our tooth pulled, something we are really afraid of because it hurts much more, the pain stops relatively quickly. In these cases, we usually choose the dentist even if we are afraid. Naturally, it may take some time until we decide whether we should listen to the signal from the feeling-based control level or the reasoning from the symbol-based control level.

The next factor that is worth paying attention to is the law of subjective reality. Although interactions that are harmful to us may objectively occur in the future, we are not nec-

212

essarily aware of them so, subjectively, we do not calculate with them, i.e. they do not exist for us. Let us suppose that the main beam above our bed is cracked and the crack is gradually growing day by day. The change objectively exists but since we do not know about it, it does not exist subjectively for us so we sleep peacefully every night. The opposite of this scenario can also happen. We have a fixed idea that the main beam above our bed is cracked and may break and fall upon us at any moment, whereas, as a matter of fact, the beam is solid and, therefore, the given process objectively does not exist, it only exists subjectively in us. Naturally, the healthiest solution is if subjective reality corresponds to objective reality. We need to recognise, however, that subjective reality is what each of us goes by. It is subjective reality that defines our reactions.

Subjective reality has two levels: the level of feelings and the level of symbols. Thus, I can be afraid of something even if it is not articulated at the symbol level. The feeling of fear is a necessary evil that is one of the keys to the survival of higher level forms of existence. "Then why is it important to have no fears?" you may ask. Because, due to its natural function, fear channels our attention and efforts primarily into avoiding the phenomenon triggering the fear and, therefore, it takes energy from other useful activities and the satisfaction of other, higher level needs. When we are afraid, we simply cannot concentrate on anything else but the phenomenon triggering the fear and we do everything to avoid the interaction that is unpleasant for us. And that is as it should be! On the other hand, depending on its intensity, fear is accompanied by a number of physiological changes. Our heart rate and blood pressure increase, our breathing accelerates, our pupils dilate, our perspiration intensifies, our blood sugar level increases and our blood flows from the stomach and the intestines to the brain and the skeletal muscles and so on. Among other reasons, this is why it is impossible to live in constant fear: because the constant emergency mode of operation damages our organism.

Therefore, the need for safety or, more accurately, the need for the lack of danger, is a real need.

The indicating feeling of the need for safety is fear which, just like any other unpleasant indicating feelings associated with other needs, we try to get rid of. During the satisfaction of the need for safety, or rather the need for the lack of danger, we usually encounter three-variable orienting feelings and, less often, floating orienting feelings. Feelings that do not trigger orienting feelings, or trigger them in negligible quantities, in our everyday life may produce pleasant three-variable orienting feelings in the case of danger. If, for example, we do not usually lock the door, turning the key in the case of danger may produce a pleasant orienting feeling. Or carrying everyday objects in our hand in the case of danger, for example, a knife, an axe or a baseball bat, may also trigger pleasant three-variable orienting feelings.

But it is not only physical movements or activities that can be accompanied by the appearance of pleasant orienting feelings. We can experience a similar pleasant orienting feeling, if we surrender and show respect to an obviously stronger power with overwhelming supremacy because this way we can avoid the anger of the superior power and we can ensure and strengthen our position. It is not by accident that people become traitors. On the one hand they get rid of their unpleasant fear and can enjoy the feeling of self-humiliation and, on the other hand, they can also benefit financially from their move (so many people suffer from backbone problems these days).

Since the feeling of fear automatically presupposes a process of waiting, the technological feeling of tension is also connected to fear, and since it is an emergency and we change into a higher gear in emergencies, the status-indicating feeling of excitement can also be observed. These feelings cease when the unwanted event occurs or, in some cases, fails to occur. This is also the case with the student waiting for an exam. He is full of a mix of fear, excitement and tension while he is waiting but when he has picked his question, the feelings of fear and tension stop and he feels relieved. Naturally, the situation is the same if the exam is cancelled for good, only then the feeling of excitement also ceases.

9.4 The need to reproduce
(What feelings control our mating? Who controls who?
Does love exist at all?)

My dear reader, we have arrived at the first level of needs that individuals cannot satisfy alone and where the cooperation of another person is necessary to satisfy it just as in the case of the need for a group or the need to meet expectations. Since people do not live in isolation, they can interact with one another while satisfying their needs. The interaction may take place just at the level of one need or possibly even at the level of all needs at the same time. During the interactions, we can help or we can hinder one another in satisfying our needs. The relationship between a man and a woman, however, is a very special one. As a matter of fact, this is the only relationship where the partners can satisfy each other's needs at every possible level or, at least, they can significantly promote their satisfaction. That is why we have a chance to experience real happiness in a well-functioning man-woman relationship.

A well-functioning relationship can further the satisfaction of the need for energy supply. The exchange of views between two people and the chance to encounter different views can also promote the satisfaction of the need for information. Two people can be more successful in their fight against the threats of the external world. They can reproduce. They can also satisfy their need for a group. The need to meet expectations may force them to adapt to one another. During their relationship, they may also develop and help one another to meet their own expectations and they can also support each other on the bumpy road of self-realisation. They practically create a mini-universe, a closed micro-cosmos. No other relationship can do so. At the same time, this is only a chance we either can or cannot take. Because, while on the one hand, we can help the satisfaction of each other's needs, on the other hand, we may also hinder, or even block it in our relationship. Therefore, it makes sense to walk hand-in-hand, helping and encouraging each other in the satisfaction of our needs. The ideal case is when we reach the different levels of needs at the same time and we work together on reaching the next level. At the basic levels of needs – for example the levels of energy supply, information and safety – this is relatively easy to do. At the levels, however, where you need to fine-tune the cooperation of several people and you need sophisticated thinking, achieving harmony is much more difficult or may even be impossible. It also makes a great deal of difference who you choose as your life partner. It is the privilege of a few to reach the top of the needs hierarchy but, just as in many other walks of life, what matters here is not necessarily the outcome but the struggle itself. But it is important to have a partner in this struggle who does not hold you back but can keep up with you and help you.

Due to its nature, the satisfaction of the need to reproduce takes place primarily at the feeling-based control level, although the symbol-based control level can also intervene in the processes. But since there are passionate and intense feelings involved, the symbol level usually cannot take control over the feelings level. It is sometimes good and sometimes bad as there is a lot of confusion in relation to this issue in our mind. I suggest that we examine things from the point of view of feelings and we may be able to put some of the things, if not everything, in their rightful place.

The indicating feelings of the need to reproduce and the related orienting feelings

The need to reproduce is defined basically by a pair of need-indicating feelings. The first one of them is the unpleasant indicating feeling related to the lack of sexual intercourse which is commonly described by the phrase 'I'm horny'. This phrase is probably a little more difficult to interpret in the case of ladies but the corresponding feeling definitely exists in a female version. This unpleasant indicating feeling urges us to have sexual intercourse with a representative of the sex we find attractive to get rid of the feeling.

Talking about the orienting feelings of sexual intercourse, we can observe two groups. The orienting feelings of the first group play an important role in the selection of our partner, whereas the ones in the second group give us clues about the intercourse itself and the "appropriate" implementation thereof. Both optical and incoming feeling channels participate in the selection of the partner. During the assessment of the data coming in through the optical channel, orienting feelings are primarily generated on the basis of the shape, sizes and proportions of the body of our partner. But interactions acquired through our hearing, smell, taste and touch also play a role in the generation of orienting feelings. It is not a mere coincidence that physical parameters play a role in the selection of our partner because people, though unconsciously, strive to create the offspring with the best possible genome and, therefore, the best possible properties, the ones that will be the most fit for life. And since the DNA test was not in fashion in the prehistoric age, we could do nothing but select the best partner on the basis of physical characteristics.

The other group of orienting feelings, as I already mentioned, helps the implementation of the intercourse. These pleasant feelings only appear when certain body parts are stimulated and, even then, only as a reaction to certain series of movements, thus helping us create the conditions for conception. I will not spend much time discussing the details of these feelings because the shelves of bookstores are full of related literature. But these books fail to dispel one myth: the orienting feelings experienced before and during intercourse have nothing to do with the strategic feeling of love! If we experience pleasant feelings around our genitals while having sex with somebody, that is not the strategic feeling of love, that is only a pleasant orienting feeling. You do not need to love somebody in order to have a pleasant sexual experience together. It is another issue that sex feels much better if you not only want but also love somebody. Therefore, we should not use the phrase 'making love' instead of 'having sex' as the two types of feelings are completely different both in terms of quality and in terms of function! But why do we still talk about 'making love' when we should talk about 'having sex'? Because, in most people, positive marker feelings are attached to the expression 'making love', whereas less positive, or even downright negative, marker feelings are attached to the expression 'having sex'. The need-indicating feeling marking the lack of sex naturally has its counterpart. This is the feeling of being tired of sex, at least for a while.

The justification of the second pair of need indicating feelings is given by the fact that the active contribution of two parents is desirable to raise a child. In the animal kingdom, especially in the case of lower level forms of existence, the male and the female only stay together until the moment of the fertilisation and the descendants often grow up alone without any parental help. In the case of more developed forms of existence, the offspring to be born is not yet fully developed and is incapable of finding food, protecting itself or stay alive alone. The case is similar with human beings. After it is born, a child needs to be fed, protected, educated and helped for years, indeed for decades. This is one of the functions of the institution of marriage. But as we all know, the institution of marriage is a relatively new one compared to the history of humankind. What was it that kept families together without the institution of marriage. Of course, nature did not leave it to chance.

Looking out of my window, I see a pair of pigeons on the roof of the next building. They usually sit on a huge antenna. They are always together. If one of them flies one metre away, the other one immediately takes wing to get close to its partner. I suppose it is not the institution of marriage that keeps them together. It is rather a feeling. Well, a very unpleasant indicating feeling related to the need to reproduce also exists in us, humans. This one does not have a name yet. I could use the word 'loneliness' but we also use it when we do not have friends. The appropriate word might be something like 'partnerlessness' or 'the lack of the other parent'. No one knows. Life will decide.

The orienting feelings related to the indicating feeling of partnerlessness often blend with the indicating feelings related to sex. As we get older, however, our priorities change and this change can help us separate these orienting feelings. In older age, when the indicating feeling of sexuality declines, it easier to separate orienting feelings. We notice that, at a given moment, we do not sexually want the other person but it feels good to hold her hand or simply to be with her or to listen to her breath as she is sleeping next to us. In these cases, the feeling of "how good it is that I have you" fills us. Just as with any other need-indicating feeling, the indicating feeling of partnerlessness also has its counterpart whose task it is to prevent overcharging the need. Sometimes we feel that we are fed up with our partner and we would like to stay alone for a while.

The orienting feelings related to the indicating feeling of partnerlessness can also be classified into two groups. The orienting feelings of the first group give us help in the selection of our partner. Data arriving through the optical and incoming feeling channels also play an important role here.

Since humans map the world primarily through their sight, sight also dominates here. But it is not so much the shape, sizes and proportions of the body that are important here but, for some mystical reason, the orienting feelings triggered by the sight of the face are the ones that play the most significant role in the selection of our partner. This is when we say somebody is beautiful. But make no mistake: beauty is one of the typical cases of orienting feelings. Beauty, as a thing, does not objectively exist! If we find somebody beautiful, we can only say that the given person has triggered pleasant orienting feelings in us. So the word 'beauty', in reality, expresses the fact that, due to his or her geometrical properties, the given person can trigger pleasant orienting feelings in some other humans. Although there is only one word for 'beauty', that single word covers millions of feelings. We experience different orienting feelings when we see a beautiful young woman, a beautiful painting or a beautiful car, even though we use the same word to describe them. Naturally, the data provided by the incoming feeling channels (smell, voice and so on) also play an important role in the selection of our life partner.

The other group of orienting feelings related to the indicating feeling of partnerlessness helps to ensure that the parents stay together. Touch has a particularly important role here. It feels good to hold his hand, to hug him or to snuggle up to him. And we can do that without even thinking about the feeling of sexual desire. And this is perfectly logical because you need to be close to somebody or together with somebody in order to be able to touch him so these feelings hold us physically together. Sometimes it is also enough if we know that the other person is around. We do not even need to see her, it is enough to hear that she is in the next room fidgeting with something and we immediately calm down. And it feels very bad when she is not with us.

There is another group of orienting feelings that also helps parents stay together. These are floating orienting feelings such as intimacy, affection, trust or warmth. These orienting feelings, however, are fairly special because they can last for a really long time. A general characteristic of orienting feelings is that they disappear after they have completed their mission. These orienting feelings, on the contrary, may last for years or even for decades. One of the reasons might be that raising a child takes years and another could be that we may have more than one child. Due to their functions, these orienting feelings play a very important role in keeping parents and partners together. These orienting feelings are not necessary in synchronicity with the orienting feelings related to sexual desire. This may mean that we do not necessarily want to live with somebody who is sexually attractive to us or that the person we find suitable to live our life with may not be as sexually attractive to us as Miss or Mr Universe.

Last but not least, there is another orienting feeling. This is commonly known as a person radiating charisma. As a matter of fact, the feeling of charisma is generated in us. Let us try to clarify it. As for radiation, there is indeed something in it. According to various estimates, we humans have as many as 10,000,000,000-1,000,000,000,000 nerve cells with electric charges running through them. If you paid attention in the physics lessons in school, you may remember that accelerating charges can generate an electromagnetic field around themselves. So, we have the same number of miniature radio stations operating in us at a very low power as we have nerve cells. "Then why don't scientists receive the signal?" you may ask. The answer is the same as the answer to the question of why cannot you receive TV signals with a lightbulb. In order to receive TV signals, you need a receiver of the same magnitude of complexity as the transmitter. You cannot receive TV signals with a lightbulb just as you cannot with a stone axe. Then how should we get a receiver of the same magnitude of complexity as the human nervous system? The answer is simple: let us find another human being! These "receivers" are called clairvoyants, mind readers or mediums. "Phew! This is unscientific!" Yes, I know, but it still works. If you do not believe it, go and check it out! Of course, you need a bit of openness because if negative marker feelings are connected to the symbols of the 'clairvoyant' or the 'mind reader' in somebody's mind, they will not modify their data network or overwrite their database, come what may. But this is perfectly natural, because the given person cannot do anything else.

Getting back to the radiation, you do not need to be a clairvoyant or a mind reader in order to be able to receive the signals, or at least a part of them, of other people. But the case is similar here to TV transmission: it does make a difference who radiates what and how powerful that radiation is. The phenomenon of 'radiating charisma' is not only experienced between individuals of opposite sexes. You can feel the radiation, or aura, of others if they are the same sex as you. The feeling is really difficult to describe but most of us can usually experience it in the company of wise and pure hearted people. The personality of the other one simply captivates you even when no word yet has been spoken.

We have basically covered the indicating feelings of the need to reproduce and the related orienting feelings. However, these are not the only orienting feelings participating in the selection of our partner. Imagine that you are walking down the street and you suddenly notice that a vendor is selling fresh steak. They give you a paper plate with the meat on it and you can eat the mouth-watering steak standing in the street and holding the plate in your hand. But you also notice that an elegant restaurant is inviting you in on the other side of the road. You enter. There is a soft carpet on the floor, you feel the air conditioning and see the elegant antique furniture around you and notice the comfortable armchairs and hear the nice music. Then you see the beautiful china and the silver cutlery on the table. As you check the menu, you find the same steak on it but as you look around, you see on the plates of the people sitting at the tables that the meat doesn't look very fresh: it looks as if it has been reheated and its colour is also suspicious. Which steak would you choose? The one at the street vendor or the one at the posh restaurant? Let me give you a little bit of help. It is not the china or the silver cutlery that you need to eat. Not at all! You need to eat the meat. And if you eat the reheated, greenish looking steak, you will have a stomach-ache if you are lucky, but in a worse case you may need to visit the toilet frequently and, in the worst case, you may even be taken to the hospital or directly to the mortuary.

What is the mistake that we make if we choose the steak in the elegant restaurant? We do not actually pay attention to the steak itself but to the environment and to our pleasant orienting feelings. The problem is that the orienting feelings, after fulfilling their function, die away but your upset stomach stays with you. Many people make the same mistake when they select their partner. They do not concentrate on the partner they choose but on the accompaniments. The beautiful villa, the luxury car, the yacht and the private jet. These things all generate pleasant orienting feelings in us which will fade away the moment we get these objects. The unpleasant orienting feelings experienced because of the bad choice of partner, however, will stay for ever or, at least until they complete their mission, i.e. until the partners bid farewell to one another. Naturally, you may think that the solution is to have a lover. And this is what we often do in such a case but, apart from the fact that deceiving our partner and ourselves is not very ethical, it usually brings its result also. The other partner is not a fool and will find out what is going on sooner or later.

Now, before we condemn people who are selecting their partners on the basis of money and wealth, we need to differentiate between two groups of people. Those in the first group consciously give priority to money, wealth and financial advantages when they choose their partners. Those in the second group, however, do not act consciously. We could probably best describe the behaviour of these people with the expression they 'buy a package'. You must have seen products in shops which do not really sell and in order to make them sell better, the shopkeeper adds some knicknacks to them. Actually, it is the knicknacks that sell these products. The buyer cannot be blamed for a kind of "base" scheming, he is only concentrating on the knicknack and makes his "bargain". The knicknacks might be a castle, a yacht, a private jet and so on. In these cases, the victims only concentrate on feeling nice with their future partner but do not look for the reasons for their nice feelings. Either because they do not care or because they do not want to face the facts. In the case of famous actors, you can also observe that the positive feelings related to the roles played by them are extended to the actors themselves, though their personalities may not be that big a deal at all. And still millions of people become mellow because of the knicknacks.

We need to recognise the fact that it is impossible to assess the potential candidates in hermetic isolation from their environment when we are selecting our partner. There will always be environmental elements attached to our future partner that will trigger additional orienting feelings in us. It is important, however, that we can separate the orienting feelings triggered by the environment from the orienting feelings triggered by the person. This is not only crucial because of ethical principles but also because of our own interest. The grounds for selecting our partner on the basis of wealth and social status are that we concentrate on the positive orienting feelings triggered by the environment so these feelings will slowly but surely disappear. But it is not only the external orienting feelings connected to the chosen person that can mislead us: the orienting feelings triggered by the personality traits and the mentality of the given person can also be dangerous.

I am sure you have encountered the phenomenon of 'love

at first sight'. In these cases, the partner is chosen within seconds. That's right! Only the selection is done at the feeling-based control level with a total neglect of the symbol-based control level. Instead of being made from one moment to the next, the image of the ideal partner develops in us slowly and gradually under the influence of our environment. This is proven by the fact that every era had its own beauty idols. When we are walking down the street, going to the theatre, to the beach or to any other place where we can meet people, we do nothing else but continuously scan for potential partners in our environment and if the scanned image strongly corresponds with the image of the ideal partner stored in our memory, our knees start shaking and we will experience the bolt of lightning effect. What does it mean? Nothing, as a matter of fact. It only means that our feeling-based control level got the hots for the other person (I am sure you noticed how scientific I was). But we still do not know anything about the chosen person. We do not know what her favourite book is, what sort of music she likes to listen to, what her religion is, what her mental capacities are like, what political views she holds, whether she is a nice person or a puffed up fool, whether she is generous or mean, selfish or unselfish or whether she likes Shepherd's Pie or not. Nothing at all!

For begetting and raising a child alone, these processes will be perfectly sufficient. This is actually more or less what happens in the animal kingdom. The human being, however, is a thinking creature and, as a result, the symbol-based control level intervenes in the process described above whether you like it or not. The symbol-based control level in humans is programmed: on the one hand it has fixed ideas about what you may and what you may not do and, on the other hand, it can draw conclusions about the future on the basis of logical operations. Feelings and marker feelings are connected to the pre-programmed content and to the output of the logical operations. And these feelings do they job: influence our decisions and choices.

As for orienting feelings, if these feelings connected to our partner are positive, they will disappear; but if they are negative, they will stay according to the law of orienting feelings. Yes, I know this is unjust! But that is what we have. So if our partner is a hard-working, clean and nice person, then our orienting feelings related to these characteristics will disappear after we move together, i.e. after we've got him or her, because they have lost their function. The fact that our chosen one snores, plays cards and drinks will, however, trigger negative orienting feelings in us which will not disappear since their function is to urge us to avoid our partner but we do not obey because we have just moved in together. It doesn't sound too promising, does it?

The entire process of the need to reproduce starts at the feeling-based control level and is also characterised by the dominance of this level. If the symbol-based control level reveals a negative feature to which extremely negative feelings or marker feelings are attached, there is a chance that the symbol-based control level can intervene in the process which is otherwise primarily controlled by the feelings level. If, however, the symbol-based control reveals a feature to which only weak negative feelings or marker feelings are attached, it cannot shout down the storm of pleasant orienting feelings coming from the feeling-based control level. The "matrimony" is concluded: the positive orienting feelings that were raging at the feeling-based control level disappear, the negative orienting feelings stay, and the relatively weak negative marker feelings connected to the symbol-based control level now come to the surface and never disappear, but cause constant inflammation just like a nasty thorn under the nail. This is when the attempts to re-educate your partner start. And the process of re-education often generates negative orienting feelings in the partner.

Most of these negative orienting feelings can be resolved through compromise. But there is a huge emphasis on the word 'compromise'. In a relationship, both partners should be equally important to each other. If it is not like that, this is not a good thing because the relationship becomes unstable. The partner who finds the other one more important will give up more. But the more they give up, the more negative orienting feelings will be generated in them, which will reduce the importance of the other partner. The many small negative effects will add up, until one day the dominant partner will notice that they are alone.

Another typical scenario is the triangle. The couple comes together, the positive orienting feelings are gone and a third person appears. The positive orienting feelings revive but now they are connected to this third person. The funny thing is that no matter how beautiful our original partners are, the orienting feelings related to them will disappear just the same – because beauty is not something that exists objectively, it is only a pleasant orienting feeling – as if they were less beautiful. Men often say when they see a beautiful woman: "Somebody's bored with her too!" That is why it may happen that we choose the third person even if they are not as beautiful as our original partner. Another factor is that while the negative orienting feelings related to the faults of our old partner are pushing us away, the positive orienting feelings related to our new partner are attracting us, the negative orienting feelings generated by the new partner are still suppressed and have not yet appeared. Therefore, it can easily happen that we jump out of the frying pan into the fire. Because if we leave our old partner, although we have got rid of the negative orienting feelings related to him or her, the positive orienting feelings related to our new partner will also disappear and the unpleasant orienting feelings related to the new person will appear. The situation of our old partner further deteriorates due to the fact that we may see them as an obstacle between us and our new partner, which can trigger anger and hatred in us towards our old partner making matters worse between us. If we cannot get rid of our old partner, we might be forced to live in tension and hatred for years. What is the solution?

Of course, there is no hundred percent solution. How long a relationship lasts primarily depends on the amount of negative orienting feelings. Therefore, it is advisable to examine our future partner-to-be from the of symbol-based control level before the feeling-based control level takes over. Because many problems come from differences in habits, traditions, ethical principles, upbringing, religion, political views or education that exist at the symbol-based control level. The rest of the problems come from the differences in our personality traits. So it makes sense to choose a partner who is as close to us as possible. Naturally, this is only true with a grain of salt. Imagine what a nice couple an aggressive, neurotic person would make with another aggressive, neurotic person! You need harmony for a good relationship and in order to achieve harmony, you should sweep in front of your own door first. And when everything is clean in front of your own door, then you can look for a partner whose house is also clean and orderly.

There is one very special orienting feeling among the those related to the need to reproduce that is worth mentioning. This is an "art for art's sake" type of feeling, a three-variable orienting feeling originating in the need to reproduce, which I call the Casanova feeling. This feeling is the pleasant orienting feeling connected to the art of conquest which is generated as a result of the perfect implementation of the masterly manoeuvres applied during the process of conquest. To put it more simply I would say this is the art of flirtation. The satisfaction of the need to reproduce is not the goal of the process of flirtation but the means and opportunity of experiencing the pleasant orienting feelings related to flirtation. There is no problem with it as long as both partners have a pleasant intellectual fight at the level of flirtation. Problems start when one of them starts acting out of character and falls down to the level of the need to reproduce, i.e. starts taking the game seriously. That is why it is important to understand the driving forces behind this orienting feeling, because then we can save a lot of complications both for ourselves and for others too. This way we will not confuse flirting with true attraction and can save ourselves and others the disappointment. Due to the nature of flirtation, other feelings also appear during the process of flirting. These feelings, however, are not related to the satisfaction of the need to reproduce. One of these pleasant feelings can be when we feel that somebody else finds us attractive. This feeling is related to the need for meeting others' and our own expectations, and it swells our ego.

So far in the investigation of the need to reproduce, we have focused our attention on the feeling-based control level, but what is the case with the role of symbol-based control here? If we start questioning people looking for a partner about what kind of partner they have in mind, instead of personality traits – like nice, good-humoured, honest, loving – we are often faced with a list of jobs as an answer. Physician, lawyer, economist. What is the reason? Do these people want their partners to operate on them every day or do they want to listen to interesting legal stories in bed? Not very likely, is it? For the answer, you need to have a look at fairly-tales. I suppose you have noticed that in fairy-tales, the reward of the poor boy is always a princess; or that Cinderella is saved by a prince and not by the peasant boy from the mud hut next door; that the heroes are almost always princes or princesses or sons and daughters of kings. Although history is full of degenerate, stupid, mean and tyrannical monarchs! And this is very often due to the fact that, in order to keep the purity of the bloodline, they have married within a very narrow circle. That's right! Brainwashing starts in our childhood. Positive marker feelings simply get programmed in our mind in connection with the symbols of the 'princess', 'prince', 'king', 'physician', 'lawyer' and 'economist'. And the program works properly ever after: "Yes, I know you are an honest person but what did you say your job was? A builder? Thank you very much, but then I would rather not." "Are you a corrupt lawyer? I love you, darling!"

In the early phase of meeting somebody, marker feelings play a very important role. Potential candidates drop out in the first screening unless a good fat marker feeling is connected to their person. If the given people are not rich, not well-known, not actors or popstars, they are done for. Women often say that they want to have somebody who they can "look up to". And when they say that, they usually do not mean they want a very tall lover. As a matter of fact, they want a man to whom you can attach big, fat positive marker feelings, no matter what he is (a prince, a football player or a bank robber). The only problem with this method is that they do not concentrate on the person but on the marker feeling. But the marker feeling is nothing else but an uncertain essence of feelings attached to a vague notion, or a collection of symbols, which keeps changing in each and every person and in each and every society, culture and era.

Naturally, as usual, other layers of needs, such as the need for safety and the need to meet others' and our own expectations, are also involved in these cases. That is to say, we can feel much safer, at least financially, as the partner of a physician, a lawyer or an economist. We can get other people's appreciation more easily and we can feel "more" or "superior" if our partner is a prestigious person. As a matter of fact, we are trying to spread the marker feelings we find positive related to our partner to ourselves.

The asymmetric nature of male-female relationships

In order to beget offspring, you always need the contribution of two parents. The advantage of this setup is that the genome of the offspring is always refreshed. However, only one parent can bear children. Another important circumstance is that only the parent that has breasts can take care of the feeding of the child after it is born. Nature "naturally" arranged these matters in a way that the parent that gives birth to the child also has the breasts. These facts create an asymmetric situation in the male-female relationship which gives asymmetric tasks to the male and to the female partners and you need asymmetric feelings to complete these tasks. The woman has an enormous responsibility because her contribution is not only necessary for the conception and for the birth of the child but she is also primarily responsible for raising the child, at least in the first period. In order to make sure that she can cope with her responsibilities, nature did not distribute the indicating feeling of sex and partnerlessness in the same proportions between men and women. While the indicating feeling of sex is dominant in relation to the indicating feeling of partnerlessness in men, the indicating feeling of partnerlessness dominates in women over the indicating feeling of sex so they can ensure that the child is raised. So while men suffer more from the lack of sex, women suffer more from the lack of a partner. Now, before anyone would describe men as lustful sex machines, let me call your attention to the fact that the disproportion of these feelings is not to be interpreted in absolute terms but in relation to one another.

As a result of the asymmetry described above, men are willing to make more sacrifices for sex, whereas women are willing to make more sacrifices to put an end to their partnerlessness. This is often shown in the phenomenon that men are more willing to tolerate a relationship – which is also their need, for that matter – in order to have sex, whereas women are more willing to tolerate sex – which is also their need, for that matter – in order to have a relationship. To make the asymmetric situation even more asymmetric, nature arranged things in a way that while nothing prevents men, who are primarily motivated by the unpleasant need-indicating feeling triggered by the lack of sex, from maintaining sexual relationships with several women, women, who are primarily motivated by the unpleasant indicating feeling of partnerlessness, can only live with one man at the same time, due to the nature of things. As a consequence, women sometimes have to choose between available candidates. Which one should they choose and which one should they live with? In these cases, the burden of proof, to use a legal term, falls on the men. They need to convince women that they should choose them and not their competitors.

After the father is selected on the basis of his physical properties (see the part on sexual orienting feelings), women need to strive to examine the future father from the point of view of whether he is going to make a faithful and devoted partner in raising their child. Accordingly, his actions that suggest that he will stay with her for a long time and will be supporting her in raising their child and in the other difficulties of life will trigger pleasant orienting feelings in her. And his actions that ensure that she will choose him as the father of her children and her partner for life will trigger pleasant orienting feelings in him. So men will experience pleasant orienting feelings when acting in ways that trigger pleasant orienting feelings in women. And vice versa. So men will experience unpleasant orienting feelings when acting in ways that trigger unpleasant orienting feelings in women. So in order to ensure fertilisation and cohabitation, the behaviour of men adapts to the expectations of women. This is what we commonly call courting. The processes of courting are nothing else but the efforts of men to prove to women that they are the ones who will be their devoted and reliable partners in raising their child and in the other difficulties of life. Courting is the demonstration of their willingness to sacrifice.

But there is a very important element here which we must not neglect. The entire process of courting is driven by orienting feelings. And due to their function, orienting feelings as such disappear when they have completed their mission. Women, once married, often experience that the behaviour of their husband changes after a shorter or longer period. This is when women start asking the famous question: "Don't you love me anymore?" Well, ladies, I have to disappoint you: it is possible that you have never been loved at all. Both men and women tend to confuse the orienting feelings felt and demonstrated during courting with the strategic feeling of true love. Before passing a harsh judgement on men and blaming them with premeditated "heart-breaking", let me, as a man, protect ourselves. Dear ladies, I can reassure you that it fills us men with very good and pleasant feelings if we can please our chosen ones. And we do this without any hidden agenda (at least, most of us because there are naughty ones among us also). It feels good to indulge every whim of our sweethearts and pamper them. It fills us with joy if you are happy and it makes us sad if you are suffering.

Oops! Let us get back for a moment to the definition of the strategic feeling of love. How do you know if you love someone? "If you love someone, you feel joy when the other one is happy and you feel non-physical pain when the other one is suffering." Is it not the same thing? Well, the orienting feeling experienced during courting and the strategic feeling of love are very similar. But they are only similar. "How could you differentiate between the two in practice?" the question arises. Life gives us an answer to this question, too. What the difference between the orienting feeling experienced during courting and true love is we can only understand when a woman is trying to break up with her man. A man who feels true love, although he experiences strong non-physical pain because of losing his lover, would never become pushy or aggressive. While a man without love, who is only demonstrating commitment, may become aggressive. He gets angry, starts abusing or assaulting the woman, or even threatening her life, even though previously he bought her the most expensive presents. In this case, the man is selfish and actually he does not care about what the woman feels. There is only one thing he cares about and that is the satisfaction of his sexual desire to which the woman is only an essential aid. Driven by the pleasant orienting feelings experienced during his courting, this man simply carried out activities that generated pleasant orienting feelings in the chosen woman while, in the meantime, being under the impression that he loved the woman (except if he was acting on purpose). But actually love was never part of the equation here. If a man feels true love, no matter how much it hurts when his woman is breaking up with him, he still cannot hurt her, because the feeling of love prevents him from doing so. There are, of course, all sorts of intermediate states between the two extremes depending on how much true love there is in a given man.

And now you should pay really close attention because we have come to the innermost secrets of long-term male-female relationships! As a matter of fact, true love is the only force that can guarantee a long-term male-female relationship. True love never stops and indeed cannot stop! In the discussion of strategic feelings, I already mentioned that love is a feeling that reinforces itself. The person we love feels and returns our love and therefore we will love him or her even more. Many pleasant orienting feelings connect to the activities related to love and although these orienting feelings disappear, since they are pleasant, we strive to relive them again and again and thus, we feed our love. While love remains, the orienting feelings experienced during courting will become irrelevant and disappear sooner or later after the selection of our partner. These feelings may return temporarily, if the relationship is under threat but will disappear again after the situation has "returned to normal". At the same time, we should not forget that love is not something you just get automatically. Somebody's love is not your inalienable right. We cannot love everybody. Love must be deserved. On the other hand, not everybody has the same capacity to love. If you were raised in a loving environment, you were given more love and you can give more love to others. That is why it really matters how much love you give to your children. At the same time, you can take to love, you can get hooked on its taste. And I can tell you that it tastes very nice. Just try it!

Getting back to our original track, it is not quite sure, my dear ladies, that the man who brings the biggest bouquet of flowers loves you the most! There is another non-negligible consequence of the process of courting and this is that men start to dislike having any conflict with their chosen one. It does not mean that men do not have their own opinion or own will, simply that they do not like arguing or quarrelling with their sweetheart. This is perfectly reasonable because arguing and quarrelling is in marked contrast to the goal of convincing their chosen one that they are going to be their trustworthy, long-term companion in raising their child. You cannot please someone and always contradict that person at the same time. If men entered into conflicts with the women of their choice from the beginning, they would reduce their chance to start a family. This state can last relatively long. At least as long as the man finds maintaining the relationship important for some reason. Since the presence of both parents is necessary for raising the child and the mother has a decisive role in this process, nature arranged it so that the parents can stay together as long as possible by raising the willingness of men to compromise. "But then what is the case with the men that are arrogant, noisy and rude with their partners?" you may ask. The answer is simple: these men are not afraid of losing their partners. Either because they would already like to get rid of them, or because external circumstances (legal, economic, religious and so one) make it impossible that they separate, or because they themselves hold the woman back forcibly. One thing is for sure: the woman as a partner is not important for a man like that, only as someone who can satisfy his sexual desires.

Dominance

Once I saw in a film about how they catch monkeys in Africa. The indigenous hunter, if my memory serves me right, puts a piece of salt in a small hole in front of the eyes of the curious monkeys. The hole is just big enough to let the empty paw of monkey through but the monkey cannot pull it out when it is clenched. The curious monkey, of course, sneaks up to the hole immediately when the hunter has cleared off, puts its paw through the hole and grabs the salt. And it is caught immediately. We humans have a good laugh at the monkey and say what a fool it is. All it should do is let the salt go and it would be free. But it does not have the brains to do so. Do we have the brains to do so? Do we have the brains to give up our desires? We do exactly the same thing as the monkey. And in the meantime we go through hell! If an extra-terrestrial creature looked at us, it would be laughing its head off just as we were laughing at the monkey. Or, rather, it would be sad instead. Of course, we need desire as a strategic feeling. The problem is usually that we cannot always tell where the boundary is: when we should not long for something any more, when we should give it up and look for another goal. As a matter of fact, the story is about finding the right proportions. It is natural that the monkey wants the salt but it is not natural that it sacrifices its freedom for a small piece of it. When we long for something, we are not free anymore. We are the captives of our desire. Thoughts that used to flow free all now concentrate on the goal. The world around us disappears just as if we were huddling up in a cell. And our soul has got the blues in the meantime.

Many people have tried to define the notion of 'freedom'. Why would I be the exception? I think you are as free as you want to be, or to the extent that you can get rid of your desires. Since everyone is different, we long for different things or, even if we long for the same thing, the strength of our desires might still be different. Therefore, we can talk about relative freedom and relative captivity. We can use the difference between the strength of the unpleasant feeling of desire to dominate another person. When we are forcefully dominated, we obey to avoid unpleasant feelings. When we are dominated through our desires, we will obey in order to get rid of the unpleasant feeling of desire. When we are forcefully dominated, the dominators, or dictators, must concentrate continuously lest their victim find a loophole and escape the grasp. When we are dominated through our desires, the dominators can sit back comfortably to watch and enjoy our struggle. All they have to pay attention to is never to satisfy our desires. We ourselves will constantly fight for their mercy and do everything so they free us from our tormenting desires. This is the donkey effect. You can drive a donkey in front of your cart with a whip, but it will stop immediately when you stop cracking; or you can also convince it to pull your cart if you sit on the cart and hang a bunch of fresh grass in front of donkey's nose in a way that it can never reach it and then it happily will pull your cart all round the world.

The possibility of dominance is also there in male-female relationships. This possibility is caused by the asymmetric nature of the need-indicating and orienting feeling systems of the male and female participants: i.e. the fact that men are primarily motivated by the lack of sex, while women are more tormented by the feeling of partnerlessness. This circumstance makes it possible that both parties use their high position, or abuse it, should the occasion arise. At the beginning of a relationship, men have more opportunity to influence the activities of women because women have no choice but to go to bed with men if they want to find a partner. There are few men who are willing to invest more energy in a relationship with a woman without sex, even though they are also tormented by the feeling of partnerlessness. If the woman satisfies the sexual desire of the man, she also satisfies his desire related to the indicating feeling of partnerlessness, which is not very difficult to satisfy because it is weaker than hers. So, as a result of the procedure, all the man's desires are satisfied, whereas the woman's desire for a partner is only partly satisfied, so women are still exposed to pressure and dominance. Some men exploit this opportunity as much as they can and after their sexual desires have been satisfied, or if the given woman does not say yes to the game, they immediately look for another "victim".

But life has also given a "weapon" to women which many of them do not hesitate to use. This weapon becomes live after cohabitation has started. Because with cohabitation women are given what they long for the most, their most important desire has been satisfied. The tables are now turned! While the woman satisfies the man's sexual desire, she also satisfies her own sexual desire, which is not difficult to satisfy because it is weaker than his. So all her desires are satisfied, whereas the stronger sexual desire of the man is not necessarily satisfied. So men remain exposed to pressure and dominance. This weapon can be especially effective once the couple is married and the first child is born. The man can choose between meeting the woman's wishes or being left without sex. Naturally, the man can also decide to leave his partner but by that time he is already connected to the woman with many strong ties, which are very difficult to break, or the breaking of which would cause disproportionate damages. The man is tied by the unpleasant orienting feeling of partnerlessness, the love he feels for the woman, the love he feels for his child, the legal ties of marriage, the vow he made to God if he is religious and other matters of conscience as well as financial issues. Of course, the woman may also drive the man to get his sexual desires satisfied by other women, which, of course, will result in the processes described above.

Remember though, that these processes do not necessarily happen! These weapons, just as with real weapons, lay a responsibility on those whose finger is on the trigger. Millions of men and women live a peaceful and balanced life without driving one another into a corner. So if the shoe does not fit, do not wear it. But if you experience any of the phenomena above in your own life, recognise it!

Love

Dear readers, before starting on the discussion of this topic, we must make a detour. The Hungarian language uses a different word for the strategic feeling of love and for the description of male-female relationships. In other languages, for example in English, this difference is not present. In English, you use the word 'love' in both cases. This is an unfortunate situation because it can give rise to misunderstanding. In English, sometimes you can use the expression 'true love' to describe a male-female relationship which helps a little in differentiation but the use of the word 'true' can also give rise to misunderstanding because it immediately makes you think of 'untrue love'. Since I do not feel fit to make decisions and create words for millions of English speakers, I would suggest a compromise. Let us follow the established practice of mathematics and let us denote the love found in male-female relationships with the word 'love$_1$'.

We use the word 'love$_1$' every day, although nobody has ever defined what psychological processes and feelings belong to the symbol of 'love$_1$'. One thing is for sure, however: the strategic feeling of love definitely belongs to the set of feelings denoted by the word 'love$_1$'. Love$_1$ cannot exist without the strategic feeling of love. Most people, without being aware of it, use the word 'love$_1$' to describe a special case of the desire trap, when somebody travels in time to experience the orienting feelings related to the indicating feelings of sex and partnerlessness and thereby generates a strong desire in him- or herself for a given person. Due to its nature, the desire trap is primarily connected to the feeling-based control level. It can connect to this level individually through the orienting feelings of the branches of needs indicated by the indicating feelings of sex and partnerlessness but it can also connect to them collectively. The conditions of the formation of the desire trap are also valid here: a desire trap cannot be formed if we can achieve the object of our desire immediately. So we cannot "love$_1$" somebody who we can get any time. So in order to fall into a desire trap for someone, the given person must be out of reach for us at least until the desire trap is formed.

The desire trap is a psychological process we should beware of because it can cause much suffering. However, it can do good to a male-female relationship. Many young people go to bed with each other the first night – sometimes they may not even wait until the night comes. Of course, they can do that and they have every right to do so. But they must take into consideration that, exactly by doing so, they deprive themselves of an enormous adventure. Because this way, the desire trap cannot form. They will have a sexual experience but it will not even be close to the adventure you can have with someone you are in a mutual desire trap with, i.e. when you are captives of one another. Because a desire trap whips up desires and multiplies the intensity of the orienting feelings experienced during the satisfaction of those desires.

How can you lure somebody into a desire trap? The recipe is simple. Find someone who likes you, tease him, then start backing off, then tease again and back off again. That is, make yourself out of reach, and the rest depends on the "victim". He himself will dig himself into the desire trap. But if you have cooked someone, you must also eat him! Do not cook people you do not want to eat! You must not play with the desire trap. We are responsible for one another. It is irresponsible and wicked to drive others into a desire trap, keep them there and feed them with promises. The person stuck in a desire trap can harm herself and others.

"Does $love_1$ not exist then?" you may rightly ask. I would save this word for the most superior male-female relationship. You often hear people say: "I'm in $love_1$ with someone, but he does not return it." My opinion is that the given person is wriggling in a desire trap but it is completely out of the question that he or she is really in $love_1$. It is impossible to be in $love_1$ alone. It is just as impossible as it impossible to be kissing alone. I use the word '$love_1$' for highest degree physical, mental and spiritual relationship and union of a man and a woman. Since it is a physical, mental and spiritual union, love can eventually culminate in sexual intercourse but I must stress that it is far from being limited to it. During the sexual intercourse, the two bodies unite as if the chests of the man and woman literally melted into one another, the external world disappears, time disappears too and their souls unite: there is no you and me any more, only us as if we had dissolved in, and become united with the universe.

What do you need for $love_1$?
- Take a partner who triggers pleasant sexual orienting feelings in you and in whom you trigger pleasant sexual orienting feelings;
- who triggers pleasant life partnering orienting feelings in you and in whom you trigger the same;
- who has a balanced and healthy mind set;
- who has a lot of love;
- who has a similar personality, IQ and EQ as you;
- who has a similar view of the world (religion, politics etc.) as you.

Add a healthy dose of attention and a pinch of desire trap. Mix them all and leave them to mellow for a while. But be careful! Do not leave them for too long because they can go sour. And if you are lucky and you have fate on your side, you will have something that tastes very nice.

Will everybody find $love_1$? Unfortunately, not. $Love_1$ is a harmony; a beautiful song both partners give their share to. But you cannot give what you do not have. You can only give what you have. If there is meanness, hatred and envy in your soul, that is all you can give. And what will come out of it? Nothing that is good. Everything but $love_1$. If you long for $love_1$, you must first sweep in front of your own door. And if it is fate's will, it may introduce you to someone with whom you can experience the great feeling of true $love_1$.

The child

The complexity and intricacy of the need to reproduce and the male-female relationship are all aimed at making sure that children get born and survive to adulthood. As I have pointed out in the discussion so far, the new-born human baby cannot survive in the world alone when it is born. The help of both parents, but primarily that of the mother, is necessary to keep it alive. What makes parents feed, protect and raise their child? Naturally, you need to look for the answer in the form of a feeling: the strategic feeling system of love is the key. And this is where I would like to emphasise again that this is the feeling of true love and no other feeling of love exists! Since we have discussed the properties of the feeling of love in the chapter about strategic feelings, I suggest that now we should pay attention to the way it is developed in human beings.

Although it is likely that the capability for the feeling of love is there in every new-born baby, we can definitely declare that the immediate environment of the baby has a decisive influence on the further development of this germ of love. So it makes a huge difference what environment a child is raised in. Love, however, is not only important for a child because this is what makes its parents to raise it but also because love plays an important biological role for the baby. Parents experience pleasant orienting feelings of the three variables while carrying out certain series of movements. These movements include, for example, hugging, stroking or kissing the baby. Although it has not been scientifically proven, it is nevertheless very likely that mothers, while experiencing the feeling of love, transfer energy to their children. The larger the surface the body of the parent that is in contact with the body of the child, the more intensive the energy transfer is. This energy transfer is extremely significant in the early development of the child. Children that receive more love, and therefore more energy, will develop more.

While a child is experiencing the love of her parents, a pleasant orienting feeling is generated in her, to which she gets accustomed and will seek and expect to have later on. Apart from learning how to experience the love of others, she also learns how to give love to others and what pleasant orienting feelings are attached to this activity. Yes, you need to learn to love! Just as you need to learn to walk. We are all capable of walking but we need to learn the appropriate order of technological feelings that accompany the movements of our body parts. Tactical and technological feelings also belong to the strategic feeling of love, and these tactical and technological feelings are essential in the implementation of the series of movements and verbal statements that belong to love and that express our love to another person. We need to acquire all of them and we need to be able to differentiate them from other activities. It would not be a good idea to confuse activities related to the strategic feeling of anger with activities related to love.

It is important from the point of view of learning to love that we should learn to feel the pleasant orienting feelings that are generated in us while carrying out activities related to love because these feelings are going to motivate us later on to exercise love. So parents have a crucial role in teaching their children to love. "But why would somebody not teach their children to love?" you may ask. The answer is simple: because not all the parents love their children. If the parents did not learn how to love in their childhood, how could they teach it to their children? The basic principle also applies here: you can only give what you have. So if you do not have love, you cannot give love. Another important reason is that there are "unwanted" children. That is children whose birth was not wanted for some reason. The reasons can be manifold: unwanted pregnancy, the breakdown of the relationship between the parents, career, the disapproval of or contempt for the environment and so on. In these cases, parents perceive their children as obstacles or burdens; their children are only "a pain in the neck" and this will bring about a predictable outcome: a negative one. Would you like your children to become happy? Love them! That is all. The rest is up to good fortune and fate.

Love, however, must not be confused with 'doting love'. 'Doting love' is not love. When I say doting love I mean when parents give everything to their children unconditionally, i.e. when children are showered with everything they can possibly want. This is not love; this is the selfishness of parents. Because, in these cases, parents are not interested at all in the fate of their children, they only want to experience and enjoy the pleasant orienting feelings generated in them in connection with exercising love. So the main goal is to experience the pleasant orienting feelings related to the feeling of love and not the interests of the child: children are only the means to experience these feelings. What is more, the whole thing is represented at the symbol-based control level as if the parents did everything for their children and this has an impact on the satisfaction of the need to meet our own expectations, i.e. the parents are proud of themselves.

The feeling complex of true love serves the interests of the object of the love and not the interests of the person who experiences love or its orienting feelings. So if your children do not learn enough in school, do not buy them presents but punish them instead. And do it because you love them. Because, by forcing them to experience unpleasant feelings through the punishment, you can protect them and prevent them from experiencing the inevitable and much more unpleasant feelings in the future. Although you yourself may experience unpleasant orienting and strategic feelings in the meantime because of the punishment – i.e. it hurts that you have to punish your own children since you love them – you still do it in order to do them good even though that is not what they feel at the time. I think the two main pillars of raising a child are love and strictness.

9.5 The need for a group
(On what basis do we choose friends?
What are the feelings that keep friendships together?)

The indicating feeling of the need for a group is the unpleasant feeling of loneliness. Even if we have everything in life and we lead the life of Riley, if we end up living alone, it is not the real McCoy. It is much easier to face the challenges of life shoulder to shoulder with others. Be it everyday work or especially dangerous situations, it feels good to ask somebody's advice or help, to discuss life or just simply to spend time with somebody. As a matter of fact, humankind owes its achievements partly to this need. This need is the basis of the formation of smaller groups of people, tribes, nations and countries. This need made it possible to organise human knowledge in higher levels and to form developed societies.

Before we start dealing with feelings that keep human groups together, let us have a look at the feelings that appear in the relationship between two people, as the smallest possible group. The feelings that appear at a given moment in two people are defined by what needs those people are trying to satisfy and how each person influences the satisfaction of the needs of the other. That is to say if we meet someone, we immediately assess how the given person can contribute to the satisfaction of our needs. See Figure 28 for the details.

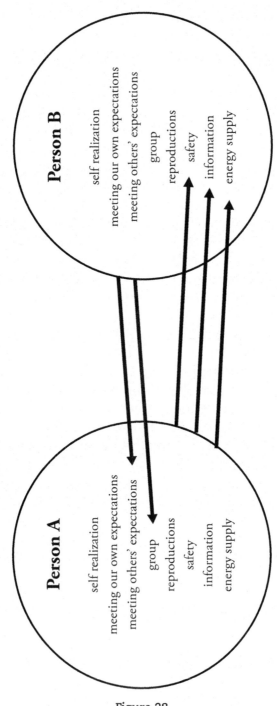

Figure 28

For example, person A can satisfy the needs for energy supply, information and safety of person B, and person B can satisfy the need for a group and the need to meet others' expectations of person A. A given person can have multiple unsatisfied needs at the same time just like the other person with whom she interacts. These needs are ranked within us and we try to involve – or avoid the involvement of, for that matter – the other person in the satisfaction of our needs according to the ranking of our needs and opportunities. During the satisfaction of our needs, we may be forced to stay for shorter or longer periods of time with other people: i.e. to form communities. In this chapter we are going to examine a special version of the situation above, when the partners in the interaction only want to satisfy their need for a group.

The indicating feeling of the need for a group is the feeling of loneliness which, naturally, we try to get rid of. How do we select partners for ourselves? With the help of the orienting feelings, of course. In the selection of partners, just like in the selection of life partners, the data provided by the optical channel are very important. In the initial phase of the selection of partners, the human face is one of the most important criteria on which basis we decide whether we find someone nice or not. Finding somebody nice is nothing other than an orienting feeling. Then come the orienting feelings generated by physique and clothing. Other incoming feeling channels also play an important role in the selection: we tend to avoid people with unpleasant voices or smells. A given face, physique or clothing generates different orienting feelings in different people. Why a given sight generates a given feeling in somebody would be really difficult to say but one thing is certain: the extension of feelings plays an important role in the process.

We have already discussed the extension of feelings but let us now have a closer look at it. If you have ever visited a dentist, you must have experienced a few unpleasant feelings. The source of these unpleasant feelings is mainly the dentist's drill, pliers and hypodermic needle. That is, these are the tools that cause the pain directly and, of course, that nasty dentist. However, the unpleasant feelings in us are not only connected to these objects and to dentists themselves but are also extended to the dentist's chair and white coat, to the whole room and, indeed, to the whole building. Next time we will experience unpleasant feelings when we enter the same building even if we are not visiting the dentist.

The same phenomenon can also be observed in other walks of life. If we experience an intense feeling, that feeling will not only be connected to the phenomenon triggering it in our mind but will also cover the direct vicinity of the phenomenon that triggers it. Although I called this phenomenon the law of the extension of feelings, it is very important to understand that the process of extension actually takes place by connecting these feelings to one another. For example, on our first visit to the dentist, we connected a very unpleasant orienting feeling, and also the need-indicating feeling of fear, to the unpleasant feeling of sound triggered in us by the dentist's drill. It is very important to understand this mechanism because feelings do not just vegetate or linger around in us independently. Neglecting the law of the extension – or connection, if you prefer – of feelings has led science into a misbelief, or a dead-end street, the influence of which is still felt even today.

Now we will take a little detour but what follows is important to understand. We need to go back in time to 1884 in the US where the brothers William and Henry James were living. The James brothers worked out a strange theory which still leaves its mark on the way scientists think and causes a lot of confusion in doing so. I am in a difficult position because, in order to understand the problem, first we need to try and "translate" their assumptions and claims. Why do we need to translate them? Because they use inaccurate terms that may look clear at first but, because of their inaccuracy, they are easy to misinterpret, and they are actually uninterpretable even by a careful reader. If we try to make out what the bottom line of their theory is, they say that our interactions with the environment generate physical changes in our body which are necessary to solve the given situation and feelings are generated in us incidentally, as a result of these physical changes, as a by-product, and they just vegetate in us without any function. What is more, with their misinterpreted experimental results, they also considered this statement grounded. One of their famous experiments was the "grin" or, to put it mildly, the "smile" experiment. This experiment was meant to prove that after certain physical changes in the body – in this case the arrangement of facial muscles in a certain shape, more accurately a shape resembling a smile – the related feeling, in this case cheerfulness, will appear in us. (Although, I would definitely burst out in laughter sooner or later, if someone tried to arrange my face in a smile.) So what they say is that the physical changes in the body are the primary and the feeling of cheerfulness is only generated incidentally, as a by-product of the physical changes.

Scientists were misled when they assessed this experiment because they did not take the law of the extension, or connection, of feelings into consideration. So they did not remember that, just as negative orienting feelings and fear connects to the sound of the dentist's drill, the somatic feelings appearing in our facial muscles when we are smiling or laughing may also connect to the feeling of cheerfulness and vice versa. So the somatic feelings generated in the facial muscles can also draw forth the status-indicating feeling of cheerfulness that was connected to them previously. That is all! There is no magic here and no ludicrously intricate theories. There are other contradictions in the James brothers' theory but it is not the intention of this book to discuss them.

Getting back to the law of extending, or connecting, feelings, we will see that this is a very useful phenomenon which helps us recognise situations that are important to us in time and thus gives us the chance to avoid them if they are unpleasant and to search for them if they are pleasant. Think of somatic markers. So our past experiences play an important role in the creation of orienting feelings, at least at the feeling-based control level. But what is the case at the symbol-based control level? Things happen in different way at the symbol-based control level. Does the phenomenon of the extension of feelings not exist at this level? It certainly does! That is what we call prejudice. Prejudices only exist at the symbol-based control level. Prejudices are just the marker feelings connected to various words at the symbol-based control level. How can feelings connect to symbols? We have already looked at this in previous chapters: on the one hand, they can connect as a consequence of the assessment at the symbol-based control level of events that we ourselves have experienced or, on the other hand, they can connect when we attach feelings to certain symbols on the basis of some-one else's accounts. After attaching a feeling to a symbol or word, if we connect this word to any other symbol, this word will extend the feeling attached to it to the new symbol we connected it with.

Let us take an example. Let us make up a name, for example: Allala. No feeling has been attached to this name in the past because I have just come up with it (although an orienting feeling may appear in you due to the melodic or other properties of the word itself). So theoretically no feelings from the past are attached to this word. Now please concentrate on what you feel when you read this: Allala, Allala is nice, Allala is beautiful, Allala is a murderer. Yes, indeed, different feelings are attached to the word Allala each and every time, that is we extend different feelings to it. The true masters of the language, poets and writers, who can play on our feelings as a virtuoso can play his piano, can do this exactly because they are aware of what feelings are attached to which words. Without the feelings attached to the words, literature would not be worth a button. If a vile magician deleted all the feelings related to the words from the minds of humankind, the literature of the world would become an enormous pile of boring information.

Getting back to our original subject, i.e. the feelings triggered in us by other people, we will see that prejudices play a very important role here. However, based on what we have said above, we must say that the word 'prejudice' is not completely accurate. The word 'postjudice' would be more accurate because these judgements are, in one way or another, based on past experiences. They are either based on our own experiences or on other people's experiences passed on to us in the form of words, or rather of marker feelings connected to words. We often condemn prejudices but they are very important. We owe our mere existence to these prejudices or postjudices. If we have never met a tiger in all our life, it is our prejudices that hold us back from approaching the first tiger we see in the jungle to stroke it. Although those who hold prejudices in contempt might walk there bravely: maybe it won't bite at all.

But we are on a detour again! The judgement we make about a given person from the symbol-based control level is decisively influenced by the marker feelings connected to the symbols or words we use to describe her build, the ethnic features of her face, the colour of her skin, her origin and so on. Another group of prejudices are connected not so much to the physical appearance of the given person, but rather to her education, religious conviction, political views and cultural outlook. This is also simply the extension of feelings. We extend marker feelings used to describe the given religion, political approach or outlook to the given person to whom the given religious, political or general approach can be connected. So if pleasant marker feelings are connected in us to a symbol or word denoting a given religion or political school, we will extend those pleasant marker feelings to the people sharing the given approach. If negative marker feelings are attached to the given word, we extend the negative marker feelings to the people in question.

In the next phase of meeting people, however, as we start getting to know a particular person, the orienting feelings attached to his personal traits will start to dominate more and more and marker feelings will be pushed to the background and will be modified on the quiet, i.e. our prejudices will be transformed. So the openness, kindness, good humour and helpfulness of the given person will become more important than the prejudices activated by his face or other physical features as well as marker feelings. And this is perfectly reasonable because it is personal traits that define what role a given person can play in a community. These traits define if somebody will be the driving force or the detractor of a community, whether he builds or distracts the given community, i.e. if that person can become useful to the community and the members of the community. And the feelings listed above will also define whom we admit to the "group", whom we will form a community with. But what keeps the group together? Naturally, feelings, more precisely: floating orienting feelings.

It is orienting feelings such as belonging, power, complicity, devotion and trust that ensure that groups of people stay together. These are pleasant and very useful orienting feelings that we experience every day. Schoolmates and colleagues can feel them but also people who do dangerous sports like climbing or caving in groups. These are the feelings that forge soldiers together in the battlefield. But there are less noble forms of these feelings, for example those experienced by different gangs, rings of criminals or spontaneously assembled mobs that set cars on fire, break shop windows and participate in riots. Naturally, these deeds can have different motives. I would not like to talk about the deeds driven by the understandable agitation of oppressed people revolting against their hard fate but hooligans and troublemakers who riot just for fun, for kicks and for the hell of it. You must have noticed that people usually do not do these things alone but organised in groups. Why? Because people participating in these actions do not have a motive that would drive them to carry out these actions alone. A revolutionary rebelling against oppression has enough motivation to fight against the oppression alone, if necessary, and they often have the devotion and courage to do so. The mob has neither the motives, nor the devotion, nor the courage for individual action. For a revolutionary, the action is the means to achieve his goals. For the mob, action is the goal itself. Why is it good to go on a rampage in the streets and set cars on fire? Because you can experience pleasant orienting feelings during that sort of "party".

One of the preconditions for the generation of these feelings is danger that is ensured by the presence of the police. Of course, this is not a serious danger, this is just something that can produce adrenaline. If it was a real danger, these people would be the first ones to clear off. But here they have a mutual enemy they can join forces against. I am sure if all these things were legal, nobody would care. If these people were taken to the junkyard and given the task of turning cars over all day, they would get a fright from the job. But in the street, there is a little excitement and not too large a risk. They feel strong, they hold together, they protect each other against the police, they screen each other and they trust each other and they experience pleasant orienting feelings in the meantime that ensure the sense of belonging of the group. They can feel like heroes and that satisfies the need to meet their own expectations. This is a cheap circus where somebody else pays the bill. To stand up alone and defy real danger just feels embarrassing, then they shit bricks and find no fun in the whole thing.

But it is not only mobs but also politicians that use this strategy when they incite conflict and hatred between people on the basis of their nationality, ethnicity or religion. When they need a common enemy, and a minority you can unite against, someone whom you can kick and stamp on without the majority risking anything. And then the majority is excited by the feeling that they belong together, they wink at each other in complicity while their chest is swollen with the feeling of superiority. Does it ring a bell? (Third Reich)

But let us get back to our original topic. A typical feature of feelings keeping groups together is that their intensity increases proportionately with the growth of difficulties. The more difficult or dangerous a given situation is, the stronger these feelings become and the stronger they keep the group of people together. If the danger reduces, the intensity of these feelings reduces also and the group may dissolve. These feelings, however, will never disappear completely. If we get into a difficult situation together with someone, we will treat that person as our comrade and trust him even years after, and our earlier feelings will revive.

So far we have discussed feelings that keep groups of people together. But in order to ensure higher efficiency, it is not enough if groups hold together, they also need to organise in structures. In the formation of structures, the goal is to achieve the most efficient form of organisation. So the group must be led and guided and you must choose the person for the job who is the best for it. The feelings of humility and dominance may play significant roles in the formation of the group structure. These feelings, however, are orienting feelings that are more connected to the need for safety, even though they definitely have an impact on the structure of the community. The feeling of humility can be pleasant but only because a pleasant orienting feeling is attached to any action that reduces danger during the satisfaction of the need for safety. People humiliate themselves if they assess that the other person has an overwhelming supremacy and threatens their safety and they do not see any chance to get out of the way or avoid them. The assessment of the situation may be based on their own experience or on feelings connected to the enemy at the symbol-based control level, i.e. if it seems better to avoid confrontation on the basis of the feelings attached to the attributes they have heard about someone. But fear, that is the indicating feeling of the need for safety, definitely has a role in the formation of humility. No matter if one person has an overwhelming supremacy over the other, if the other person does not feel threatened, the feeling of humility is not formed in her. However, humiliation depends on other factors as well so it is not inevitable, it is just an option.

The structuring of human groups is normally ensured by the scale of feelings ranging between respect and contempt. In their personal development, a value system develops in human beings. This value system is not an absolute one: it changes in cultures, strata of the society, persons and eras. If we think that the person we are examining better suits our value system than we do, we will feel respect for him, if we think he suits it less than we do, we will feel contempt for him. The intensity of these feelings is in direct proportion to the magnitude of the difference.

I was using the expression 'value system'. I think it is clear for everyone. Or is it? A value system is simply a list of the phenomena of the world prioritised according to their values. But what does the word 'value' mean? What is more valuable, iron or gold? "Oh, come on! Not another silly question! How can you ask which is more valuable, iron or gold? Of course, it is gold!" you must be answering now. Are you sure? Let us suppose that a mighty magician conjures all the iron away from the world. What would happen? Life would stop. And what would happen if he conjured all the gold away? It would not cause nearly as much of a problem. (Of course, some ladies would definitely be devastated) What is more valuable and what we pay more for are two different issues. Why do we still pay more for gold than for iron? Because different feelings are attached to gold than to iron. Let us take a scientist, for example, who invents a medicine that could save the life of millions of people. Who cares? It is possible that she can hardly make ends meet from her salary. But if a famous Hollywood actor plays the role of the tough guy of the season in an action movie (with the help of stunts, of course), he immediately earns $20 million and he will be the best-known person on the planet. But is he going to be the most valuable as well?

The value systems of people do not necessarily reflect real values. We should rather be talking about feelings systems than value systems. That is to say items that have the most pleasant feelings attached to them will be at the top of the scale of the feelings system and the ones with the most unpleasant feelings will be at the bottom of it. Whereas on the scale of the value system, items that are the most valuable are at the top and items that are the least valuable are at the bottom.

Once a child was asked what he wanted to become when he grew up. He said he wanted to become a bank robber. It is clear that, due to his impoverished environment and the impact of the media, the feelings related to the bank robber had top priority in his feeling system. It is an exciting job, he can drive a big car, he is a very tough guy, has a lot of money, the girls want him, what else do you need? This is a prestigious job! Why should only children want to be bank robbers? Are you sure that adults never cherish the idea?

A true value system can only be worked out in a strictly speculative and logical way. Or rather, it could be but it cannot. We are humans and, like it or not, feelings are connected to words in us. Naturally, individuals can work out a more or less realistic value system, but it is heavily influenced by the mental capacities of each person, how comprehensive her database-type knowledge is and how much she can make her thinking at the symbol-based control level independent of the feelings attached to the symbols. People having value systems, as opposed to people having feelings systems, are extremely dangerous. They are dangerous because they cannot be fooled. Their value system cannot be reprogrammed at will and dictators, the manipulators of other people, particularly hate it. People with feelings systems are easy to mislead. All you need to do is to replace certain elements of their feelings systems with those that are the most suitable for you. But what can you do with someone who has a value system? Do you replace the elements of reality with nonsense? It does not usually work. Shame on you!

While self-humiliation and subservience can also be found in the animal kingdom because, as I mentioned, this feeling comes from the need for safety, the feelings of respect and contempt are only typical of human beings. The explanation may be that you need thinking at the symbol-based control level in order to have these feelings because they are created by extending positive and negative marker feelings to a given person with the use of words. We could say while self-humiliation is a hardware-type, factory-wired feeling every human being may experience in emergency situations, respect and contempt are software-type feelings and depend on the education of each of us and on the value and feeling system that has been developed in us. A hierarchy is usually formed in groups on the basis of how many positive and negative feelings are attached to the members of the group, i.e. how much the members of the group respect the others or hold them in contempt. Sometimes, however, the hierarchy fails and does not ensure the most efficient operation of the group. This can happen because the members of the group do not develop respect on the basis of the appropriate groups of feelings. For example, in a football team, it is right if the player who plays football the best is on the top of the hierarchy and not the one that can produce the best theories about football. The hierarchy between football coaches, in turn, should not be decided on the basis of who plays football the best but on the basis of who can best train the team.

9.6 The need to meet others' expectations

(Do we need to meet others' expectations? Why does it hurt when we are scolded? What is relative devaluation?)

Before beginning our discussion of the need to meet others' expectations, we need to clarify a few important things. While the needs for energy supply, information and safety, the need to reproduce and the need for a group are hardware-type needs, the need to meet others' expectations, the need to meet our own expectations and the need for self-realisation are software-type needs. We use the term 'hardware-type need' for needs that are genetically encoded in us. That means these needs are present all the time throughout our life and the activation of the previous levels is not a precondition for the existence of any of them. Their continuous and parallel existence is proven by the possibility of the constant appearance of indicating feelings that belong to the bottom and top limit values.

The situation is completely different with software-type needs. The primary precondition of software-type needs is the existence of a language – a programming language, if you like – and, consequently, the existence of the symbol-based control level. That is to say these needs simply cannot come into being without thinking in words or symbols. And software-type needs are not always present in our life, they only get activated under certain conditions. A condition of their activation is that the need directly below the given need must be previously activated. So the need for self-realisation can only be activated if the need to meet our own expectations has been activated previously; and the need to meet our own expectations can only be activated if the need to meet others' expectations has already been activated previously; and the need to meet others' expectations can only be activated if the need for a group has been met, i.e. we are among other people. But, at the same time, if several software-type needs have already been activated, you can observe their parallel presence. So even a person at the level of self-realisation needs the satisfaction of the needs below the need for self-realisation in the hierarchy. Those at the level of self-realisation would also like to meet their own expectations and others' expectations although, in this case, emphases can be radically shifted between the different levels of needs. The last important difference in comparison with hardware-type needs is that in the case of software-type needs, there are no need-indicating feelings. This fact can cause severe problems, especially the lack of the upper limit indicating feeling that would prevent over-charging.

Well, then let us start the discussion of the need to meet others' expectations. We see in personal development that the first years of a child's life are dominated by feelings that only exist at the feeling-based control level. This is perfectly natural because children cannot speak at this early age so they do not have symbols to carry out operations with at the level of symbol-based control. At this early age, children do, or do not do, something to experience pleasant feelings, or avoid unpleasant feelings, at the level of feeling-based control. That is to say children obey their parents to avoid punishment. As a consequence, however, we need to modify, or rather clarify, what we said a few lines before. The need to meet others' expectations is not a fully software-type need. As a matter of fact, it is a borderline case between hardware-type and software-type needs. Meeting others' expectations can be achieved with software-type means, i.e. the use of a language, but also with "traditional", or rougher methods, with hardware-type means, so to speak: with the help of physical pain.

As children grow, they learn more and more symbols or words. These symbols, however, are only "empty" symbols at first: no feelings are attached to them. And an important circumstance is that although this set of symbols is gradually increasing, children still cannot carry out logical operations with them. But as time passes, more and more symbols get recorded in their memory and more and stronger feelings are connected to them, and this process is further helped by the development of their logical operation capacity. The child gives names, i.e. symbols, to the phenomena found in the world and attaches various feelings to them. Specifically, she will attach orienting, strategic, tactical and technological feelings and somatic markers to the phenomena she has experienced herself and she will attach marker feelings to phenomena and notions learnt from others. As she grows older, apart from labelling the phenomena of the world around her or attaching symbols to them, she also recognises her own existence that is separate and autonomous to a certain extent from the rest of the world: her 'Self' image forms. She attaches the symbol 'I' to her own self. But just like the other symbols, the symbol 'I' cannot remain an empty symbol either: she must fill it with feelings. How then does the process of filling the symbol 'I' with feelings take place? Feelings related to each distinct phenomenon of the external world are generated in us when we interact with that phenomenon. If we interact with another person, it is not at all certain that the interaction will generate the same feelings in both of us. During the interaction, the feeling generated in us is generated and recorded in us, whereas the feeling generated in the other person is generated and recorded in that person. The feeling generated in us is connected to the other person, although the feeling was generated in us; the feeling generated in the other person is connected to us, even though it was generated in the other person. The problem with regard to the feelings attached to the symbol 'I' is rooted in the fact that we cannot interact with ourselves. If we come into contact with another person, we will only have feelings in connection with the other person, at least at the feeling-based control level. Or we can ask the other person what feelings we generated in them. The information gained this way, however, is received by our symbol-based control level. So we do not have, and cannot have, any feelings related to our own person at the feeling-based control level.

As for the symbol-based control level, we have many more symbols related to our own personality there. However, we did not create these symbols, other people attached them to us when we were interacting, based on the feelings they felt during our interactions. These words, therefore, symbolise how other people see us. But as we know, feelings are also attached to the symbols associated with the symbol 'I' and these feelings are extended to the symbol 'I'. So if you attach a symbol carrying an unpleasant feeling to the symbol 'I', an unpleasant feeling will be extended to the symbol 'I' and if you attach a symbol carrying a pleasant feeling to the symbol 'I', a pleasant feeling will be extended to it.

In order to be able to understand the following processes, we need to go back a little to strategic feelings and, more precisely, to the feelings of joy and non-physical pain. The function of the strategic feeling of joy is to urge us to accept things, whereas the function of non-physical pain is to urge us to keep things. What do we need to accept or keep? An interaction or a relationship. How do we "know" that we are interacting with a phenomenon? Naturally, we know it from the feelings appearing in our incoming feeling channels and the emerging orienting feelings. We can draw conclusions about the status and the future of the interaction from the intensity and the temporal changes of our feelings, respectively. If the feelings related to a given interaction intensify, we are moving into the interaction, i.e. the interaction is intensifying, whereas if the feelings are weakening, we are moving out of the interaction, i.e. the interaction is weakening, too. If a particular interaction is important for us, the intensification of the interaction is accompanied by the strategic feeling of joy, whereas the weakening of it is accompanied by the feeling of non-physical pain in order to guide our activities in the appropriate direction. The form of the appearance of the feelings of joy and non-physical pain greatly depends on the course of the process. Joy and non-physical pain appear in different forms and with different intensities in the case of unexpected events versus gradually forming events. The more important the interaction is, the more intense the feelings we will experience. The importance of an interaction will be defined by the quality and intensity of the orienting feelings experienced throughout the interaction. The stronger the pleasant orienting feelings we experience during an interaction, the more important a given interaction is and the more we strive to maintain the interaction and the more vehemently we react to changes in the intensity of the feelings accompanying the interaction. For example, we react differently to the death of an unknown person, a close friend or our parents.

Let us now examine the processes taking place at the symbol-based control level. We have found that various feelings are attached to various symbols. Marker feelings, i.e. compressed feelings of general validity attach to notions and certain attributes. Feelings connected to the words 'good' and 'bad' are typical representatives of marker feelings. The marker feelings connected to the words 'good' and 'bad' are universal and convey the orienting feelings connected to the given phenomenon with more or less accuracy during the communication. Although a bad steak generates completely different orienting feelings at the level of feeling-based control than a bad car, an approximately appropriate feeling is still generated with the help of the marker feeling attached to the word 'bad', based on which you can behave appropriately with respect to the steak and the car. So you will not take your steak to the garage and will not to try to roast your car longer. As a matter of fact, all that happens in this case is that the marker feelings connected to the words 'good' and 'bad' are extended to the steak and the car.

If you tell somebody that his car is bad, he can rightfully ask why you are scolding his car. What does scolding mean? Scolding is a verbal action during which we attach a symbol or word carrying a negative marker feeling to the symbol of the given phenomenon at the level of symbol-based control. The negative marker feeling attached to that symbol weakens the positive feelings of the given person towards the given phenomenon and he experiences this weakening of his feelings as the loss of an interaction at the level of feeling-based control and therefore, the strategic feeling of non-physical pain will appear in him. But not only words, movements or facial expressions can have negative marker feelings attached to them but also intonations. A grimace, a raised index finger or a scornful intonation can all carry negative marker feelings. So if you scold or disparage a person, an object, an idea or a phenomenon close to someone's heart, it will trigger non-physical pain in the given person. The stronger her positive feelings towards the given phenomenon are, the more intense the non-physical pain she experiences will be. At the same time, you can scold things that she is indifferent to, or that she finds undesirable, day and night, she will not experience non-physical pain at all.

In human beings, the symbol that is the closest to the feeling-based control level is the symbol of 'I'. This is the symbol the greatest number of pleasant feelings connect us to. That is why if somebody scolds, disparages or hurts us, i.e. extends negative feelings to the symbol of our 'Self', it can really hurt. To ensure better understanding, I borrowed a few figures from my book *Words*. Let us have a look at Figure 29 first. The white patch shown at the feeling-based control level symbolises the positive marker feeling connected to the symbol 'I', whereas the black patch symbolises the negative marker feeling connected to the symbol 'clumsy'.

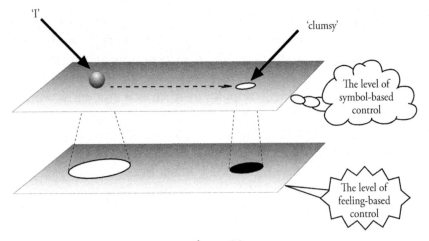

Figure 29

We are okay, thank you very much, until somebody calls us clumsy, i.e. until somebody connects the symbols 'I' and 'clumsy' at the symbol-based control level. Because at the moment this connection takes place, it is not only the symbols that get connected but also the marker feelings attached to the symbols at the feeling-based control level, as you can see in Figure 30.

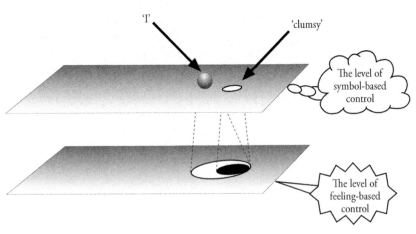

Figure 30

As it is shown in the figure, the black patch simply "swallows up" a fairly large part of the white patch. Translated into the language of feelings, the negative marker feeling attached to the symbol 'clumsy' weakens the positive marker feeling attached to the symbol 'I' and, as a result, the strategic feeling of non-physical pain appears.

The case is much better in Figure 31. The situation is similar to the one in Figure 30, but with the difference that there is a nice white patch at the feeling-based control level under the word 'clever' that symbolises the positive marker feelings attached to this word.

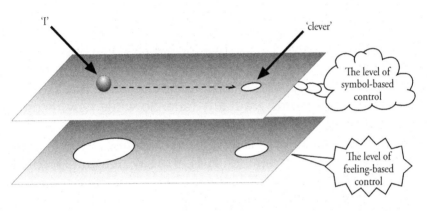

Figure 31

If someone says we are clever, he simply connects our 'I' symbol with the symbol 'clever' at the symbol-based control level and, in doing so, he automatically connects the positive marker feelings attached to these symbols at the feeling-based control level. The positive marker feeling attached to the symbol 'I' will be supplemented, or enlarged, with the positive marker feeling attached to the symbol 'clever' as shown in Figure 32, and this process is accompanied by the strategic feeling of joy.

265

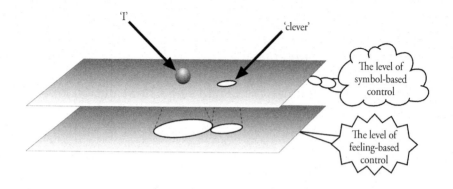

Figure 32

There is, however, a "relative" or indirect way of scolding. In our memory, as we have discussed previously, we record various feelings related to various phenomena. But as time passes, these records gradually fade. So while new records contain strong feelings with almost real-time intensity, older records contain increasingly weaker feelings which might even get completely deleted. That is to say, real-time records always contain stronger feelings than older ones recorded at the same level of intensity. If we attach the same pleasant feeling in real-time mode to phenomenon A as we did previously to phenomenon B, our feeling-based control level will experience it as the weakening of the feeling attached to phenomenon B, which, in turn, it interprets as a sign of us moving out of our existing interaction with phenomenon B. So, if pleasant feelings were connected to phenomenon B previously, a feeling of non-physical pain will be generated which urges us to keep the interaction with phenomenon B. An exception to this rule is the case when you can replace the interaction with phenomenon B with a more pleasant interaction with phenomenon A. In more simple language, if we continuously attach positive feelings to one of two phenomena that belong to the same category, the other one will automatically become relatively devalued. So I suggest that we call the process described above the phenomena of relative devaluation.

At the level of meeting others' expectations, a similar relative devaluation takes place when the environment attaches symbols carrying positive feelings to a third person that are then extended to that third person and therefore our own person will become relatively devalued. And it all happens without hurting us with a single word. Although the result will be much the same as if we ourselves had been scolded. That is why we can experience praises given to others as a scolding for us. So we can experience non-physical pain because our feeling-based control level experiences the relative weakening of the feelings connected to the symbol 'I'.

And now let us get back to childhood. When children start learning words and start attaching feelings to those words, not only will they obey their parents in order to avoid punishment but also to avoid being scolded, i.e. attaching symbols carrying negative marker feelings to their symbol 'I'. When raising our children, we need to pay attention to the intensity of the load of feelings connected to certain symbols. It is no use if you attach the symbol 'bad' to your children's symbol 'I': if the symbol 'bad' is not loaded with feelings, there is no point in extending it to the 'I' symbol of the child. In these cases, the symbol 'bad' is an empty symbol and will not have any impact on the child's behaviour. It is important that the symbols we use carry expressly polarised, clear and strong marker feelings because that is the only way in which they can have an impact on the behaviour of the individual. The use of symbols with vague, indistinct or weak marker feelings will produce a vague, indistinct or weak impact.

Due to the nature of things, you can only scold somebody with words to which negative marker feelings are attached in the given person's mind. No matter if you call a mean scoundrel a mean scoundrel if no negative marker feelings are attached to the expression 'mean scoundrel' in the mind of that mean scoundrel. Since his great-grandfather, grandfather and father were all scoundrels, no negative marker feeling is attached to the word 'scoundrel' for him at all. So your scolding is like water off a duck's back for this kind of a person.

But let us not only focus on the negative side of things because, apart from hurting people, you can also reward people with words. If you attach words carrying positive marker feelings to somebody's 'I' symbol, the strategic feeling of joy will appear in the person you praised. There is a saying: "If nobody praises you, praise yourself". Not a very nice saying, is it? But we play this game every day. It is called boasting. When we boast, we simply associate symbols with positive marker feelings with our 'I' symbol. A good proof of this is the technique of boasting itself. I don't know if you have noticed what silly things people boast about sometimes. For example: "my ancestors were peers", "the son of my neighbour knows a man who has shaken hands with the President" and so on. When somebody says these things, no logical connection can be made with the personal qualities of the given person and these statements. All that happens is the boasting person attaches symbols to his 'I' symbol that have positive marker feelings in his mind and he expects these positive marker feelings to be extended to his 'I' symbol.

We have mentioned relative devaluation but there is also something we can call relative revaluation. Some people belong to the group of "the great champions of truth". I am sure you have met people who keep a saying that they always give their opinion about anything. The interesting thing is that their opinion is always negative and always refers to somebody else. These people are always looking for faults in others. And they find them. And then they rub it in to the given person with no mercy: "You see what a useless person you are! But look at me!" All these people do is they attach words carrying negative marker feelings to the person of their victim and, as a result, the feelings attached to their own 'I' symbol will appear relatively positive to themselves and to their victims alike. So they drag others in the dirt so they can feel a little better. This is much more comfortable than always measuring your strength against your environment. You do not need much brain, talent or effort to do so and if you are clever enough you can even make a virtue of it. These are the champions of truth. Mind you, these people, God knows why, are not so enthusiastic anymore when their "sins" are presented to them with the same sort of "frankness".

Why are we talking about the need to meet others' expectations at all? Because, at a certain point of our personal development, we do not have much choice. As a matter of fact: we can choose among three things:

1) We live alone. But a higher priority need, the need for a group, works against this solution.
2) We live without adapting to others' expectations. But then we must expect continuous conflicts that would lead, at best, to our being stigmatised, which only causes non-physical pain, but, in the worst case, we could even end up in prison or on the scaffold.
3) We live by meeting others' expectations which will call forth others' positive acknowledgement which is pleasant for us.

The need to meet others' expectations, however, has an interesting characteristic. The unpleasant non-physical pain lasts as long as you do not meet the expectations of your community, which is not always that easy. But the pleasant feeling of joy that follows meeting others' expectations disappears quickly. It disappears because it has achieved its goal: an appropriate symbol has been attached to the symbol 'I' and, as it has served its purpose, it naturally vanishes. But this is still nothing! Since it is a pleasant feeling of joy, it is easy to take to this feeling, to get accustomed to it or to become a captive of it. Therefore, we want to experience this feeling more and more often. And if there is ever an opportunity, we expect to be praised, stroked, glorified and celebrated. Those who cannot resist this temptation will become vain. But it is still not the end of the list of bad things. Because according to Weber's law, it is not enough that the nice feeling of joy disappears, but you also need a much stronger stimulus to trigger it again. So if you praise someone and tell her that she is clever, the next time you want to produce a pleasant feeling of joy of a similar intensity, you must tell her that she is a genius, then the wise leader of the people, then the Vicar of Christ on Earth and so on and so forth and there is no stopping for some. Of course this is because, in this case, we do not have a hardware-type need but rather a need generated in the software-type way. While hardware-type needs have two kinds of indicating feelings: one of them is activated when there is a lack of something and the other is activated when there is too much of something, software-type needs do not have the upper or lower limit switches. So you can praise someone to the skies and he will still not come to his senses and will not recognise that you are making a fool of him. At best, he will look puzzled when his followers drive him away and hurl down his statues. Craving for fame is simply the wish that other people acknowledge you and as many people as possible attach as pleasant as possible marker feelings to your 'I' symbol.

And there are the humble ones. Not that humble people do not like it when others attach positive marker feelings to their 'I' symbol but they are more self-critical. That is, the processes taking place at their symbol-based control level more or less have control over how justified the words loaded with positive marker feelings to be attached to their 'I' symbol are. So they do not accept the connection of marker feeling attached to the word 'clever' to their 'I' symbol just because they can scratch their right ear when their left-hand. On the other hand, these people have not got accustomed to the feeling of joy that companies the worship of their 'I' symbol. I do not know if you have noticed that there is not one puffed up fathead among the great thinkers of the world. These people are always deeply humble.

9.7 The need to meet our own expectations

(Why do we need to meet our own expectations? Why does someone sacrifice his own life? What is a guilty conscience?)

During the development of a child, as she starts interacting with the external world, she begins to map the world in her mind. The process of mapping is based on experience, i.e. feelings appearing at the feeling-based control level as a result of interactions with certain phenomena, and logical operations carried out with the symbols related to these feelings at the symbol-based control level. But during the process of mapping, feelings might appear at the feeling-based control level that can significantly influence, and distort, the logical operations taking place at the symbol-based control level. The whole process is a little like when an aesthete is trying to do a jigsaw puzzle. He has the entire picture in front of his mind's eye, he is holding the next piece in his hand, he knows exactly where the given piece fits in the half-made picture but still he finally decides not to put it there because he thinks it would not be aesthetic like that. The problem is that although tastes might be different, there is only one reality.

The mapping of the external world shows other similarities to jigsaw puzzles as well. When we are trying to do a puzzle, we concentrate first on the piece in our hand and try to find out all its characteristics. The process is similar in real life: if we come across a new phenomenon, we thoroughly examine it first. In the second step, we examine the part of the picture we have already completed from the point of view of where the new piece would fit. It is the same in real life: we examine how the new phenomenon can be connected to the image we already have and if we find a connection point, we fit the new piece, or phenomenon, in. Then we pick up the next piece and the whole thing starts again from the top. We do not pay much attention to the pieces already fitted in, except for when we are looking for connection points for the newest piece. And we do not care at all about pieces that are already deeply embedded. We do not re-examine them again and again and we do not contemplate if they are in the right place or not. The situation is exactly the same with the mapping of the world or building our data network. If we have successfully mapped the phenomena of the world and organised them in a consistent system within us, we do not examine the individual elements any more. We do not deal with them after they have been embedded. And the emphasis is on the word embedded. In our everyday life, when we encounter a phenomenon already mapped and embedded in our mind, we act automatically with regard to the given phenomenon. So if we have been eating apple pies regularly for years, we no longer think about whether it is edible or not, we just bolt it down and the thought that the apple pie might not be edible does not even flash through our minds.

It is not only the apple pie we handle this way but anything that has already been embedded in our mind including ethical, religious or political views. If somebody has negative marker feelings in connection with the symbols of 'lying', 'theft' or 'fraud' embedded in her image of the world in her mind, she will not revise these things from day to day, instead, she will automatically evaluate things based on what she has learnt before. So a relatively fixed map of the real world is developed in the individual, a data network based on which she will evaluate the events of the world around her.

But why are we paying so much attention to this image of the world or this reference data network? While at the discussion of the need to meet others' expectations we saw that an external person was judging the actions of the individual and punished or rewarded the individual based on his judgement. However, in the case of meeting our own expectations, the individual judges and punishes or rewards himself. So the role of the external leader, teacher or guide has been made redundant, the individual can already exist in a "self-propelled", autonomous mode adapting to the image of the world, the data network, the coordinate system, the value system or feeling system mapped in his mind. This, however, can only be done if the individual has a stable embedded database in his mind.

But let us not overlook an important fact. This database, created over the years, to describe the world is not uniform. A part of it is developed by us but the rest we receive ready-made from our parents and environment. The ratio of the parts developed by us to that developed by our environment changes from person to person. This ratio greatly depends on the mental capacities, lexical knowledge, feeling system and age of the given person. Those whose databases are primarily programmed by others do not actually meet their own expectations at the level of meeting your own expectations, they meet the requirements preprogrammed in them instead. That is, these people who are apparently meeting their own expectations actually want to meet others' expectations, only they subjectively feel that their preprogrammed value system or feeling system is their own and does not belong to somebody else. The need to meet our own expectations and the need to meet others' expectations, however, work on the basis of totally different mechanisms.

How does the process of self-control operate? Let us take a specific example: murder. There is a definition of the word 'murderer' at the symbol-based control level in the database of an individual that describes with more or less accuracy what deeds are considered murder and who is considered a murderer on the basis of those deeds and negative marker feelings are attached to the word 'murderer' at the feeling-based control level. Let us suppose that somebody else dies during the activity of this individual. The individual analyses the events from her symbol-based control level. With a series of logical operations, she excludes accident and self-defence and classifies the event as a murder. After the classification of the event, this person analyses her own role in the events from the symbol-based control level and, as a result, she draws the conclusion that she is the murderer. At the instant the word 'murderer' appears in the thoughts of the individual, the marker feelings attached to this word activate. As the outcome of her logical operations was that she was the murderer, the marker feelings attached to the word 'murderer' extend to her 'I' symbol. If a negative marker feeling is attached in the individual to the word 'murderer', this marker feeling extends to her 'I' symbol, which significantly weakens the positive feelings attached to her 'I' symbol which triggers the strategic feeling of non-physical pain in her.

The operation of the system rests on two conditions: 1) negative marker feelings must be attached to the word 'murderer' in the coordinate system or feeling system of the given individual and 2) the person must classify the event as a murder and her own person as a murderer. If these two conditions are met, the process that is commonly known as a guilty conscience will start. At the level of meeting others' expectations, the first condition is not met, i.e. no negative marker feelings are attached to the word 'murderer' in the coordinate system of the individual. The negative marker feelings appear in the external judge or guide who, after having assessed the events logically, uses other words for the person committing the murder to which negative marker feelings are already attached in the murderer's mind, for example rascal, vile, brute or scoundrel. Then the person committing the murder will extend the negative marker feelings attached to these words to her 'I' symbol and experience non-physical pain as a result. She experiences non-physical pain but not because she condemns murder as a deed and she has a guilty conscience but because she was offended in her self-esteem.

A person controlled by the need to meet others' expectations can avoid non-physical pain in two ways: either he avoids the person who criticises him or he does not carry out the deed triggering the criticism. The person controlled by the need to meet his own expectations, however, can only avoid self-reproach if he does not carry out the deed that is not in keeping with his feeling system or conscience. So the person in the first case needs continuous control and supervision, whereas the person in the second case does not need any external supervision at all.

The other important difference between deeds based on the two different levels of needs is seen in the duration of the unpleasant non-physical pain after committing the given deed. While the people that act at the level of meeting others' expectations only experience non-physical pain as long as an external person is bombarding them with negative marker feelings connected to their 'I' symbols, the situation is completely different for the people that act at the level of meeting their own expectations. People violating their own value systems can suffer until the end of their lives because of the moral weight of their deed. They will bombard the positive feelings attached to their 'I' symbol with negative marker feelings every time they think of their deed, a murder in our example, and its consequence: that they are murderers. So they will constantly punish themselves. And you cannot run away from yourself, you must live with yourself.

There are three ways to get rid of self-reproach. The first, and probably the easiest, way to do it is to try and reclassify your deed with logical manipulations carried out at the symbol-based control level. In our example, the perpetrator may try to come up with arguments by which she can reclassify the murder as an accident or, if it is completely hopeless, she may try to present the case as self-defence or acting under orders. Totally different marker feelings are attached to the symbols of an 'accident', 'self-defence' or 'acting under orders' which will not bombard the positive feelings attached to her 'I' symbol with negative marker feelings. The second, much more difficult, way is to overwrite your embedded coordinate system or feeling system. In our example you could say things like: "Murder is not such a deadly sin, everybody has to die sooner or later." The third option is if you squeeze the events that have happened out of your feeling-based control level. You can achieve this by preventing them from emerging from your memory. This way, if the events cannot be recalled from memory, they must not have even happened at all. And you cannot classify events that have not happened at the symbol-based control level so no symbols loaded with negative marker feelings can be attached to your 'I' symbol.

The need to meet our own expectations has great significance: our peace of mind often depends on this need. We humans actually exist at our symbol-based control level: this is where we live our life. What science calls consciousness is nothing other than the symbol-based control level. If you ask someone who he actually is, he will not say he is actually two size 10 feet, a torso, a size 16 neck, a head and two hands. In his answer, he will primarily describe his mental properties and he will look at his body as the tenement of clay of his spirit and soul. And he will be convinced that he controls his tenement of clay and not the other way round. Therefore, the symbol 'I' is particularly important at the symbol-based control level.

Let us now turn back the wheel of time and let us examine the famous Japanese pilots of the Second World War, the kamikazes. It is a well-known fact that these pilots took off with the intention of flying into American ships with their aeroplanes and thus sinking them by sacrificing their lives. What could possibly make them do so? Naturally, they had to go through long and complicated psychological processes until they reached that state of mind but it is beyond doubt that the need to meet their own expectations played a paramount role in these psychological processes. The training of these pilots was not only focused on learning how to fly an aeroplane. Their worldview, value and feeling systems were also carefully transformed. Very strong positive marker feelings were attached to the words 'Emperor' and 'homeland' – and to the persons who were protecting the Emperor and the homeland – and very strong negative marker feelings were attached to anything that could threaten the Emperor and the homeland. On the basis of the feeling system created in this way, they had two choices. The first choice was to walk tall into a glorious death, i.e. to be able to attach very positive marker feelings to their 'I' symbols and thus ensure that their life had a "meaning" they could realise through their death. The second choice was to turn tail like a coward, attach very strong negative marker feelings to their 'I' symbols and spend the rest of their life with a guilty conscience in constant self-reproach and damnation. As a matter of fact, these pilots were manipulated by transforming their value and feeling systems.

Although Albert Einstein created his relativity theory to describe physical phenomena, one may observe that the notion of 'relativity' is also valid for the human mind. Although the images of reality objectively exist in human minds, these images are not universally valid but relative. Japanese pilots were acting according their own particular value and feeling systems and American soldiers were also acting according to their own particular value and feeling systems and they could not do anything else. There is one important lesson to draw from the fate of kamikazes. Since the need to meet your own expectations – just like the need to meet others' expectations – is a soft-coded need, it does not have a top limit switch either, i.e. there is no warning feeling that would signal overcharging as in the case of hard-coded needs. Therefore, it may happen that individuals want to meet the expectations of a system of thoughts, a value and feeling system imprinted into their minds by others even to the extent of sacrificing their own lives. This fact underlines the responsibility of those who are in a position to form and shape the value and feeling systems of millions of people. And I primarily mean rulers, politicians and religious leaders.

Fortunately, we do not only meet sad things during the satisfaction of the need to meet our own expectations. This need is one of the driving forces of human development. We owe the birth of a number of scientific, artistic, sporting and other achievements to this need. That is to say if you want to feel good about yourself, and why should you not, you need to attach symbols carrying positive marker feelings to your 'I' symbol. While in the case of the need to meet others' expectations this is done by somebody else, in the case of the satisfaction of meeting your own expectations, you do it for yourself. Naturally, you cannot hang those symbols on yourself just like that, you need to be able to justify with logical operations at the symbol-based control level why you attach a certain symbol, and the related marker feelings, to your 'I' symbol. So no matter if you lie to the world that you have climbed Mont Blanc, this way you can only satisfy the need to meet others' expectations (by a little deceit) but you can never satisfy your need to meet your own expectations because your symbol-based control level will object and will not let you to attach the positive marker feelings connected to climbing Mont Blanc to your 'I' symbol.

And look, in the meantime we have discovered one of the reasons for lying. We often lie to others to satisfy the need of meeting others' expectations and we lie to ourselves to satisfy the need of meeting our own expectations. Lying, however, is just like fake money: apart from not satisfying our needs, it actually triggers the opposite reaction. Instead of growing in others' eyes and in your own eyes, you shrink down to a teeny-weeny size. Liars deceive themselves!

But the need to meet our own expectations can mislead us and can also cause unhappiness. The traps work in a similar way to the case of meeting others' expectations. After achieving the goal we set, we proudly attach the symbol carrying the current positive marker feeling to our 'I' symbol. "Yes! I've climbed Mont Blanc!" and, as the old American Indian would say, "My heart's flying like an eagle!" The prob-

father and father were all scoundrels, no negative marker feeling is attached to the word 'scoundrel' for him at all. So your scolding is like water off a duck's back for this kind of a person.

But let us not only focus on the negative side of things because, apart from hurting people, you can also reward people with words. If you attach words carrying positive marker feelings to somebody's 'I' symbol, the strategic feeling of joy will appear in the person you praised. There is a saying: "If nobody praises you, praise yourself". Not a very nice saying, is it? But we play this game every day. It is called boasting. When we boast, we simply associate symbols with positive marker feelings with our 'I' symbol. A good proof of this is the technique of boasting itself. I don't know if you have noticed what silly things people boast about sometimes. For example: "my ancestors were peers", "the son of my neighbour knows a man who has shaken hands with the President" and so on. When somebody says these things, no logical connection can be made with the personal qualities of the given person and these statements. All that happens is the boasting person attaches symbols to his 'I' symbol that have positive marker feelings in his mind and he expects these positive marker feelings to be extended to his 'I' symbol.

We have mentioned relative devaluation but there is also something we can call relative revaluation. Some people belong to the group of "the great champions of truth". I am sure you have met people who keep a saying that they always give their opinion about anything. The interesting thing is that their opinion is always negative and always refers to somebody else. These people are always looking for faults in others. And they find them. And then they rub it in to the given person with no mercy: "You see what a useless person you are! But look at me!" All these people do is they attach words carrying negative marker feelings to the person of their victim and, as a result, the feelings attached to their own 'I' symbol will appear relatively positive to themselves

At the level of meeting others' expectations, a similar relative devaluation takes place when the environment attaches symbols carrying positive feelings to a third person that are then extended to that third person and therefore our own person will become relatively devalued. And it all happens without hurting us with a single word. Although the result will be much the same as if we ourselves had been scolded. That is why we can experience praises given to others as a scolding for us. So we can experience non-physical pain because our feeling-based control level experiences the relative weakening of the feelings connected to the symbol 'I'.

And now let us get back to childhood. When children start learning words and start attaching feelings to those words, not only will they obey their parents in order to avoid punishment but also to avoid being scolded, i.e. attaching symbols carrying negative marker feelings to their symbol 'I'. When raising our children, we need to pay attention to the intensity of the load of feelings connected to certain symbols. It is no use if you attach the symbol 'bad' to your children's symbol 'I': if the symbol 'bad' is not loaded with feelings, there is no point in extending it to the 'I' symbol of the child. In these cases, the symbol 'bad' is an empty symbol and will not have any impact on the child's behaviour. It is important that the symbols we use carry expressly polarised, clear and strong marker feelings because that is the only way in which they can have an impact on the behaviour of the individual. The use of symbols with vague, indistinct or weak marker feelings will produce a vague, indistinct or weak impact.

Due to the nature of things, you can only scold somebody with words to which negative marker feelings are attached in the given person's mind. No matter if you call a mean scoundrel a mean scoundrel if no negative marker feelings are attached to the expression 'mean scoundrel' in the mind of that mean scoundrel. Since his great-grandfather, grand-

with the negative marker feelings connected to the words at the symbol-based control level. That is, she slates the second lady and marks her down below herself. She belittles her with words carrying negative marker feelings until her feeling-based control level perceives the second lady as someone to whom negative marker feelings belong and therefore the feelings attached to her 'I' symbol will be relatively more positive. Her 'I' symbol will be relatively revalued. The pleasant orienting feeling of the mentally committed verbal aggression can also add to these positive feelings. She wants to hurt the second lady and cause her non-physical pain in order to take revenge for the non-physical pain she suffered because of her. The process of relative devaluation was perfectly automatic and unconscious in the first lady. You can see this phenomenon quite often in your everyday life. One of the most certain signs is that you compare yourself with others and try to find error in others in order to relatively revalue yourself.

It is often said that you should be proud of your achievements. You can do this, of course, because it is not forbidden by law, but you should not. Or, at least, I would not. You should be aware of your achievements. Yes, you should be aware if you are the best but you should not let the feeling of pride take control over you because you will have to pay a serious price! Be modest instead. Those who take to the feeling of pride, sentence themselves to eternal damnation. They will have to be alert all the time in order to maintain the pleasant but rather fragile feeling of pride. The cleverest, the strongest, the coolest or the most beautiful person has to prove day after day that he is the cleverest, the strongest, the coolest or the most beautiful. The pressure to prove is constant because the world is full of phenomena that trigger positive orienting feelings at the feeling-based control level that indirectly hurt the feelings attached to the 'I' symbol at the symbol-based control level. As a matter of fact, the two levels are in a constant fight with one another here. This is a war that cannot be won and only the individual can incur the losses. Moreover, to make the situation even more hopeless, as time goes by, it will be increasingly difficult to prove the impossible. Because you will actually become less and less clever, strong or beautiful as you grow older.

The other big problem is that the pressure to prove often follows completely unsettled, in some cases idiotic or explicitly harmful, value and feeling systems. Sometimes people pursue "values" that are not real values through their entire life. They want to be the first in things that have no value at all or that are simply idiotic. Just think of the great conquerors! In his book *What do you say after you say hello?*, Eric Berne rightly says that in the end the fate of proud people will be that they will eventually be left alone in a hermitage, a prison, a public hospital or in the mortuary and it does not matter anymore whether it was their religion, money, race or sex that made them so proud.

9.8 The need for self-realisation
(What is self-realisation?)

Throughout its history, humankind has created an enormous knowledge base and, although the scientists of the past did everything they could to discover our world as accurately as possible, we must admit that this effort was not always successful and sometimes they were wrong. They were wrong just as many of today's scientists must also be wrong. We can all be wrong because we are humans. And the ones who created moral rules and other systems of thoughts may also have been wrong or, even if they were not wrong, they might not have been able to foresee every possible situation. It is physically impossible to create rules and regulations for each and every moment of everybody's life. Rules and regulations do not fit, and cannot possibly fit, each and every moment of everybody's life: this is impossible. If you have a driving licence and you drive, you must have seen that it is impossible to follow traffic regulations literally. If everybody obeyed traffic regulations literally, traffic would stop. Naturally, this does not mean that you do need to follow traffic regulations generally. Those who are act from the level of meeting others' expectations do not worry about all the various regulations. They do not care about regulations at all. They only meet regulations because others make them do so. Only those people worry about regulations who act from the level of meeting their own expectations. They are the people that bombard their own 'I' symbol with negative marker feelings if they cannot meet the regulations set by the society. But this is sometimes a Mission Impossible. Still, it would be a serious mistake to draw the conclusion from the statements above that there is no need for moral or other rules. We indeed need these rules. Without them, the society simply could not operate. It is only that the rules must be brought closer to real life and you must not program expectations into people's minds when it makes no sense to meet them, is impossible or is explicitly harmful.

During our personal development, first our parents and later our wider environment program us with the feelings we should attach to the different phenomena of the world. As we have discussed already, the world image created this way, gradually, layer by layer, does not always reflect reality since the way individual elements connect to one another is heavily influenced by the feelings attached to these elements (see the example of the aesthete doing a jigsaw puzzle). The divergence between the real world and the distorted image we create of the world creates tensions because we do not react appropriately for the real world but carry out actions controlled by the feelings wrongly attached to the phenomena of the real world in us instead. This situation naturally creates tensions in the individual. The intensity of the tension is in direct proportion to the divergence between the real world and the image of the world developed in us. The more wrongly we perceive the world, the more unpleasant a situation we get into. The agony triggered by our incapability to meet the requirements becomes insufferable after a while. The tension between the natural need of the individual to reproduce and the habits and traditions of society can often trigger this kind of agony. The individual does not want to, and cannot, live in continuous suffering and this is the reason people are forced to move on from the level of meeting their own expectations to the level of self-realisation.

As a matter of fact, we can choose between two options: either we transform the real world or we transform the world that exists in our mind. Since it is impossible to over-write the real world, only one option remains and that is to overwrite the image of the world that exists in our minds. You would be surprised to learn how many people still try to transform the real world in order to meet the requirements of the world programmed into their minds. Some people, for example, try to solve the conflict triggered by the need to re-produce by castrating themselves. This phenomenon clearly demonstrates the fact that their own internal image of the world is the primary governing force for everybody, which is quite understandable.

I personally recommend the second solution for every-body! (Let us not waste time!) But it is really difficult to transform such a massively embedded image of the world anchored by millions of feelings. Sometimes it is impossible for the individual. In order to solve the problem, you need to have certain mental capacities and the imprinted doctrines must not hinder or forbid free thinking and, finally, you need to have the appropriate factual knowledge. One of the ways of overwriting world images is to overwrite them on a logical basis. The individual starts examining the world around her, draws conclusions and, based on these conclusions, lays a mental foundation that she can use as a starting point for building her own coordinate system. Building a new coor-dinate system, however, can only be successful if she tries to clean the building blocks from the feelings attached to them. Then, holding onto her own coordinate system, she tries to reinterpret the world and, if necessary, rewrite the feelings attached to certain phenomena. Naturally, this is no easy task: it is a very contradictory process that lasts for years. It is a difficult delivery. Not only does the given person have to cope with the difficulties of the task itself, but sometimes – due to the disapproval, fault-finding and possible expulsion from her environment – her financial or personal safety may also be threatened. And this is all the consequence of the fact that different feelings are attached to a given phenomenon in the minds of the people in her environment than in the mind of the person creating her own value system.

In fact, self-realisation is nothing else but the liberation of the individual from the meaningless and harmful bonds that limit and restrict her mind. This is the step that makes it possible to interpret the world around us appropriately, to assess our own possibilities and capabilities and to satisfy the first five hard-coded needs and the needs of meeting others' expectations and our own expectations. As a matter of fact, this is an optimum game that is based on the factors listed above. This way the personality of the individual can become accomplished, her goals can align in harmony with realistic achievements and her capabilities, and this way she can get rid of most of the problems that have caused her tension so far. Not primarily because she managed to change but because she managed to understand the world. Although the possibility is open to everyone, it is only the privilege of a few to reach the level of self-realisation. Millions of people fight against starvation and struggle for survival in war-torn areas. Tens of millions of people are illiterate but enormous masses of people live and mental poverty and mental plainness also in welfare societies.

The careful reader must have noticed that from the level of the need for self-realisation we have arrived back at the level of meeting our own expectations from a certain point of view or, more specifically, to an extreme form of it.

In the discussion of the need to meet our own expectations we have mentioned that people whose world image does not primarily come from their own resources but is based on fundamentals given to them by others, when they act at the level of meeting their own expectations, they still actually want to meet others' expectations. When we talk about people at the level of self-realisation, as a matter of fact, we are talking about the other extreme: the person who tries to form his own image of the world instead. Due to the nature of things, developing a complete image of the world is impossible, the mental capacity of a single person is not enough for the task. But you don't really need it. It is enough for an individual to see clearly what he sees. Everybody does not have to become a nuclear physicist, a chemist, a neurobiologist, a psychologist and so on at the same time. You do not need to know everything in the greatest possible detail. A comprehensive but realistic knowledge is enough.

Why do we talk about the need for self-realisation instead of the need to meet our own expectations? As a matter of fact, the human beings at the level of self-realisation do not want to meet their own expectations, they want to meet the expectations of the world. They want to understand the world and they want to become a part of it. Why do we call it the need for self-realisation then and why not the need to meet the world's expectations? Because we need to create and implement our internal world, i.e. ourselves, in a way that fits the world around us and creates a uniform entity with it. And nobody else can do it for us but we ourselves.

10.

THE VALUE

*(What is value? How much is a work of art worth?
Do you know what a "hamster feeling" is?)*

We have already spoken a lot about values, pseudo-values and real values. What should be considered a real value people have been debating for thousands of years. And they have been doing so in such a way that the knowledgebase of the given age and the feelings attached to the words in this knowledgebase have left their mark on their way of thinking. Since the knowledgebase of humankind has been continuously broadening throughout our history and different feelings have been attached to different words in different eras, the definition of value has accordingly been different era by era.

Let us now make an attempt to define the notion of 'value' in such a way as to deprive words of the feelings attached to them. My definition for the word 'value' is as follows: If an existing interaction between a given system and its environment can cease and its cessation negatively influences the operation of the given system or the given system has the chance to start an interaction that positively influences the operation of that system, then we assign the word 'value' to these interactions at the symbol-based control level which is meant to denote an attribute of interactions maintaining or creating that which is practical or advisable from the point of view of the given system.

We can draw important conclusions from this definition. Events simply occur, or do not occur, in the world around us in a way that is independent of human beings and, as a result, the negative or positive influence of those events on a given system is either exerted or not. But human beings are adaptable systems that can avoid situations that are disadvantageous for them and can out seek situations that are advantageous for them. Although there may be objectively advantageous or disadvantageous interactions for a given system, the word 'value' is still a symbol that only exists objectively at the symbol-based control level of human beings. So value, as such, does not exist in the absolute sense. It is not a natural, tangible thing, it only exists in the minds of human beings as a series of feelings of sound or the undefined nervous stimulus state symbolising the word 'value'.

The second important conclusion is that value, as a desirable interaction attribute, is system dependent. That is to say an interaction that brings positive changes for a given system, may bring negative ones for another system. So we cannot talk about absolute values even at the symbol-based control level of human beings. Naturally, systems may overlap. What is of value for one system can also be of value for another one. Although the notion of 'value' can be interpreted equally for interactions that have been lost, that currently exist or that may yet arise, the notion of 'value', due to its definition, mostly plays an important role when we are in the position to lose or obtain things. This is something we can experience ourselves day by day. We are often only able to value what we have when we no longer have it or before we have got it.

It is advisable to mark the conditional sense in the definition. The phrase "the system has the chance" is very important. Interactions that are impracticable for us do not represent something of value for us. However, they may still represent something of value for others. So no matter if there is a beautiful, ripe banana on one of the planets of the next solar system, if we do not have a chance to get it, it will not represent something of value for us, but the small monsters with green legs who live on that planet will love it.

In creating the notion of 'value', we have, like it or not, also created the notions of 'valueless' and 'harmful'. We must interpret the word 'valueless' literally. That means this word refers to an interaction that does not have value so we do not need to strive to get it and we do not need to keep it. It simply makes no difference. We use the word 'harmful', on the other hand, to describe the opposite of the interactions denoted with the word 'valuable', i.e. interactions that we should refrain from because they have a negative influence on a given system.

Having clarified the notion of 'value', it is now time to focus our attention on value systems. Why do we talk about "value systems"? Are values organised into systems? Exactly! Values are organised on the basis of a certain order. In the definition of value, we said a value is an attribute of any interaction that it is practical to keep or to get, and the emphasis is now on the word 'practical'. It means these are the interactions that we set as goals for ourselves. Now, as I explained in Chapter 6 about synchronisation, many subprocesses, or an entire system of subprocesses, may be formed while we are achieving a goal, depending on what obstacles we must face on our way to our much-wanted goal. Each and every new obstacle starts a new subprocess the goal of which is to overcome the given obstacle. So not only do new subprocesses appear, but also new subgoals. Each and every subgoal that belongs to a subprocess creates a new value system, a new value coordinate system, that is typical only of that particular subprocess. This is completely natural because different interactions may serve the purpose of achieving one individual goal. So, if we go back to the example of the discovery of the cure for cancer, the main process runs in a completely different value coordinate system from the process of finding your socks (you bet!). So when a process is running, we use the value coordinate system valid for that process. That is to say the currently valid values are always defined by the goal of the given process.

The main question to decide is whether the goal of the main process has real value or not. As a first step, let us examine what goals people set for themselves. If we examine goal-setting, we will see that people do not just set goals at random, these goals are usually connected to their needs: they serve the satisfaction of them. Accordingly, adapting itself to the division of our goals on the basis of our needs, our value system is also divided by the levels of needs. Every level of need has its own value system and every goal, and subprocess belonging to that goal, at any level also has its own value system. If we are working on the satisfaction of meeting our own expectations, we are using the value system of meeting our own expectations; if we are buying sausages at the butcher's, we are using the value system of the need for energy supply and, more specifically, the value system of buying sausages and not the value system of buying apple pies.

In the formation of a value system we do not only differentiate between valuable interactions on the basis of their outcome but also of their importance. There are more valuable and less valuable interactions. So our value system is not only divided according to the levels of needs and goals but also according to the order of importance. The value system used during the achievement of a goal arising from a certain need also takes into account the order of importance of interactions. How valuable a given interaction is, is defined by the strength of its influence on the given system. So if losing, or getting, an interaction A has a bigger influence on the given system then losing, or getting, an interaction B, we will declare interaction A more valuable than interaction B and, therefore, we will choose interaction A as we prefer more valuable interactions to less valuable ones.

If we examine the levels of needs, we will see that the lower ones can work without the higher ones but the higher ones cannot work without the lower ones. That is to say, failing to satisfy the lower needs can result in the destruction of the entire system, while failing to satisfy the higher ones leaves most of the system operable. Accordingly, the interactions serving the purpose of satisfying fundamental needs are more interesting in general than the ones serving the satisfaction of higher level needs. But this is only true in general. Sometimes we partly and temporarily give up the satisfaction of our primary needs in order to satisfy other needs. For example, we give up satisfaction of our need for energy supply in order to satisfy our need for safety. But in the long run, we cannot go on doing that, we must take risks in order to survive.

Another constraint is that the classification of the values of interactions only works this neatly in the field of the first five hardware-type needs: the needs for energy supply, information, safety, reproduction and group. Animals live only under the control of their hardware-type needs and they can easily decide on the basis of their feelings which food, information, safety situation, partner or group is the most valuable for them. They still live in Paradise. But humans were expelled from Paradise because we ate the fruit of the tree of knowledge, so we are done for (Oh, that nasty snake!). The levels of software-type needs – that is the levels of meeting others' expectations, our own expectations and self-realisation – can create quite a mess because software-type needs, should the occasion arise, can overwrite the satisfaction of hardware-type needs. For example, the most valuable interactions for the individual, as an independent system, are the ones that ensure its own existence, the ones that the individuals must maintain at all costs, because they can only satisfy any other needs, and it only makes sense to do so, if they are still alive. But the satisfaction of the need to meet our own expectations can lead individuals into situations where they sacrifice their lives in order to satisfy the need to meet their own expectations. "How is it possible?" you may ask. This phenomenon is partly caused by the lack of need-indicating feelings, or top and bottom "limit switches", and partly by the contradiction between the operation of the feeling-based and the symbol-based control levels. At the feeling-based control level, the search for valuable interactions is carried out with the help of feelings and, more specifically, of orienting feelings. At this level we make relatively few mistakes. At the symbol-based control level, the search for valuable interactions is carried out by logical operations. For these logical operations, we use symbols to which different feelings are attached just as they are to the symbols we get as the output of these logical operations. So the output has twice the chance to be faulty. We may make a mistake while carrying out the logical operations and we may make another mistake when we attach an inappropriate feeling, or feeling of inappropriate intensity, to a given symbol. If we follow a strictly logical thread, there are four options:

1) Both the feeling-based and the symbol-based control levels select the valuable interaction correctly.
2) Both the feeling-based and the symbol-based control levels select the valuable interaction incorrectly.
3) The feeling-based control level selects the valuable interaction correctly and the symbol-based control level opposes the selection.
4) The symbol-based control level selects the valuable interaction correctly as a result of its logical operations, but the feeling-based control level urges us to act differently.

In the two latter cases, a conflict is generated between the two levels. In these cases, we must make decisions. We must decide whether we should "listen to our heart or listen to our head".

When we were discussing the role of feelings in Chapter

7.4, I already mentioned that these two control levels sometimes make themselves independent and break free from each other. These situations are nothing else but decisions between "heart" and "head". These decisions are often not real decisions. More specifically, the "heart" and the "head" do not decide the problem according to the rules of a "parliamentary democracy" but one of them mounts a coup instead. Frequent examples are the situations when we know we should not do something but we still do it. In these cases, the feeling-based level takes control over, and the symbol-based level just watches things happening helplessly. Then comes the guilty conscience!

But this situation can also take place the other way round. In these cases, it is the symbol-based control level that rules supreme and suppresses the feeling-based control level completely. This is the normal "mode of operation" of human beings. This is what our environment and our society expects from us. That is why we consider someone a thinking human being. (It is a different issue that thinking human beings are also controlled by their feelings because our thoughts are nothing other than chains of series of feelings of sounds, only we might not know about it, that is all.) So the answer to the question of why people sometimes prefer the value system connected to the software-type-need levels over the value system connected to the hardware-type need levels even though the values connected to hardware-type needs are more important than the ones connected to software-type needs is partly that we human beings primarily "live" at the symbol-based control level: our conscious life takes place at this level. We spend most of our time at this level and therefore we prefer using the value system connected to software-type needs which belong to the symbol-based control level.

Another thing that can cause a problem is changing between value systems connected to the different levels of needs. When we are absorbed in a given problem, sometimes it is really difficult to switch value systems. In these cases, our consciousness narrows down and we concentrate on the given task. Let us take the example of the kamikazes again. The pilot squeezes himself into the cockpit, fastens the seat belt, switches the mains on, and the gauges come to life. In the meantime, the technician starts turning the propeller by hand in order to break up the cold oil in the engine. The pilot shouts at the technician to move away from the propeller and starts the ignition. The propeller begins to move slowly and reluctantly. It is rather bouncy first, and the cold engine, among big bangs and flames, gradually revs up. The pilot takes a last deep breath from the air laden with the fragrance of flowers and then closes the cockpit. He accelerates, the plane pulls away and starts their last journey. What thoughts may cross the pilot's mind no one knows. He is bidding farewell to his parents, his love and his life. And he does it all because he feels he must do it. Thousands of people did and do so in human history no matter what race, nation or religion they were or are serving as soldiers. Allah's soldiers, the Crusaders, the American, the Japanese, the German and the Soviet soldiers all did it. Although the soldiers were all fighting for different goals, they were actually driven by the need to meet their own expectations when they sacrificed their lives. When thinking at the level of meeting their own expectations, soldiers only use the value coordinate system typical of this level. The characteristic features of this value coordinate system are symbols such as 'homeland', 'honour', 'manliness', 'resolution', 'toughness', 'persistence' and 'heroism' (although which of them are real values is another question). The opposites of these symbols are 'statelessness', 'dishonour', 'sissyness', 'weakness', 'cowardice', 'desertion' and so on. Naturally all the soldiers would like to have symbols that carry marker feelings that are positive in this coordinate system attached to their 'I' symbols. That is to say, they would like to deserve the symbols 'hero', 'brave', 'tough', 'resolute' and so on. The responsibility of military commanders is to keep soldiers at the level of meeting others' expectations and their own expectations so they measure themselves according to the coordinate system valid at these levels. It would not be appropriate if soldiers started using the coordinate system valid at the level of the need for safety. In that case, everyone would pack up and go home.

I am sure you have noticed in films, and those who have served as soldiers may have experienced it themselves, that sergeants keep howling at and cursing soldiers. They continuously disparage them and compare them to little girls about to receive their first communion. Do you think it is a coincidence? No, it is not. This is how commanders try to keep their troops at the level of meeting others' expectations and their own expectations. They want to ensure that soldiers use the value coordinate systems of these needs and do not even think about other values. Who is the self-respecting young man that would like to resemble a little girl? In order not to have to suffer this humiliation, each soldier tries to behave properly, both in others' eyes and in his own eyes also: to behave like a hero, a tough and brave man. As long as soldiers are using the value system that belongs to the need to meet others' expectations and their own expectations, they are willing to sacrifice their life. That is why it is in the interests of monarchs and societies that soldiers live according to the standards of the value system of these levels of needs, or rather die following them. I know it sounds cynical and I do not want to offend anyone. There are, indeed, just wars and heroes who sacrifice their lives so that others could live in peace. But this fact does not change the working mechanism of things at all. Those who fight just wars, do your tasks whatever your motivation is; and those who fight unjust wars, notice the powers that manipulate you. Hitler's soldiers did not notice that they were being manipulated. They held onto the symbols from the level of meeting others' expectations and their own expectations such as 'commitment', 'perseverance', 'toughness', and 'loyalty' while killing millions of people in the meantime.

The words 'commitment', 'perseverance', 'toughness' and

'loyalty' do not denote values. These are words that exist at the symbol-based control level and to which very strong positive marker feelings are attached. But they only describe the way of implementing an interaction and not the goal of the interaction. That is to say you can do wicked things with perseverance, toughness and loyalty just as much as you can do noble things. The situation is similar to meeting others' expectations and our own expectations. We can meet others' expectations, and our own expectations too, both if we are committing base deeds and if we are doing the noblest things in the world. This is the explanation of the fact that two soldiers fighting on two different sides of the same war can be equally confident that they are doing the noblest thing in the world and are fighting for a true and noble cause. Actually, they cannot do anything else because both of them are using their own value systems or value coordinate systems. And the two value systems can be completely different.

It is very difficult to break out of a value system or to revise a value system. Usually it is in the interests of the given social system that the people living in it do not even think about questioning the validity of the given value system, that they do not even think about the possible existence of other values. That is why they do everything to cement their value system. Propaganda can be sophisticated enough to block or forbid searching for other values by simply declaring it a sin. It is perfectly understandable that less educated, less knowledgeable people with a lack of up-to-date knowledge, data and facts simply cannot examine the value system of a given society from an external and objective aspect. That is why the soldier in the battlefield cannot and does not want to – and is not allowed to either, for that matter – break out of the levels of meeting others' expectations and his own expectations and the related value system.

What is the difference between retreat and flight? During a retreat soldiers are still striving to satisfy the needs of meeting others' expectations and their own expectations under the control of the symbol-based level. In other words, controlled by the symbol-based level, they suppress the value system of the feeling-based control level. They act deliberately, according to a plan. But in a flight, the feeling-based control level takes over, its value system becomes the ruling one and the value system of the symbol-based control level gets suppressed. During flight, the value system of the level of the need for safety comes into force under the exclusive control of the feeling-based level. Soldiers save their lives and flee in terror. The symbol-based control level is only watching "with its arms open" what is happening. And then comes the guilty conscience.

The question arises of which value system is then the real one, the true one that we should follow. Is it the hardware-type value system of the feeling-based control level or the software-type value system of the symbol-based control level? The value system of the feeling-based control level, the hardware-type value system, primarily concentrates on the individual itself as an independent system and refers to each and every inhabitant of the planet Earth: it is identical for everyone. Some of my readers may be puzzled now to see that animals also live by this value system: "To live by the same norms and standards as an animal?! Phew! Terrible." Only one question: Have you ever heard about any animal that sent others from the same species to gas chambers just because the colour of their skin was different, or raked them with a machine gun, or burnt the flesh off their bones with napalm, or blew them into pieces, or dropped an atomic bomb on them? Honestly, I have never heard of any animals like that. These things only exist thanks to the sophisticated, and highly appreciated, thinking of *homo sapiens*. Animals only kill when they are hungry. We, *homo sapiens*, also kill when another *homo sapiens* has a different colour of skin, follows a different religion, likes the views of another party or simply just for fun! Are you still so proud of being a *homo sapiens*? Many of us are *homo sapiens* but not all of us are HUMAN BEINGS.

What decides if somebody is *homo sapiens* or HUMAN BEING? The software-type value systems connected to the software-type needs. That is, the value system connected to the levels of meeting others' expectations, meeting our own expectations and self-realisation. The question arises of whether we need the value system of software-type needs. The answer is a clear yes. What makes a difference, though, is who shapes the software-type value systems and what values they contain. We definitely need the value systems of both the hardware-type values and the software-type values, only humankind should work out a universal value system for HUMAN BEINGS.

As for the value system of hardware-type needs, here we have an easy task. We need to find phenomena with which we can interact and a given interaction which could be beneficial for us. For example, an interaction with a glass of milk and a slice of bread has value because it satisfies our need for energy supply. An interaction with a good book or a good poem has value because it may satisfy our need for information. Visiting an abandoned corner may be of value because it may satisfy our need for safety. An interaction with a member of the opposite sex may have value because it may satisfy our need to reproduce. An interaction with a true friend have value because it may satisfy our need for a group. These examples can be easily interpreted for the hardware-type need levels, but what is the situation with the values of software-type need levels? In the case of the value system of software-type need levels, the most important thing to keep in mind is also the fact that values are only connected to interactions so it only makes sense to talk about them in this connection. If there is no interaction, there is nothing of value. Without realising this fact, humankind has done nothing but merely to copy the processes taking place at the level of feeling-based control level, i.e. depended on their feelings, but made a few mistakes in the meantime.

At the feeling-based control level, the search for values is carried out with the help of orienting feelings. All that happens is a continuous scanning and monitoring of orienting feelings. If we experience a pleasant orienting feeling, we start interacting with the given phenomenon that triggered the orienting feeling in us. And as a result of the interaction, an outcome desirable for us is created. You must understand that this is an automated process: we always follow the most pleasant orienting feeling. Probably, we can best demonstrate this process with the example of animals. When a monkey is eating a banana, it does not have the slightest idea what it is doing or what consequences and effects it might have, it simply enjoys the pleasant orienting feeling triggered in it by the banana.

What happens at the symbol-based control level that makes humans make these mistakes? To understand it, you do not need to do anything but copy the previous paragraph word by word *without thinking* and replace the expression 'orienting feelings' with 'marker feelings':

At the symbol-based control level, the search for values is carried out with the help of marker feelings. All that happens is a continuous scanning and monitoring of marker feelings. If we experience a pleasant marker feeling, we start interacting with the given phenomenon that triggered the marker feeling in us. And as a result of the interaction, an outcome desirable for us is created. You must understand that this is an automated process: we always follow the most pleasant marker feeling.

As for desirable outcomes, they may be desirable but they are not necessarily valuable and they can even be downright harmful because we can sometimes have foolish desires. Remember one of the famous quotes of His Holiness the Dalai Lama that says "Sometimes not getting what you want is a wonderful stroke of luck".

"And what is the case with logical operations?" you may ask. Yes, logical operations play a very important role but, as we saw, the database necessary for logical operations is not objective: its data selection is carried out by various feelings. On the other hand, the implementation of a part of the available logical operations is also heavily restricted by feelings. There are forbidden logical operations which are blocked by various feelings in individuals and, as a result, the individuals will not want or will simply be unable to carry out these operations. Think of somatic markers and marker feelings. Eventually, the selection of values at the symbol-based control level will primarily be defined by feelings, marker feelings attached to various symbols. We find our way on the basis of these feelings, and these feelings decide what we consider to be of value. And this is exactly the problem! Because we are impressionable: we might attach positive marker feelings to words or symbols that actually have nothing to do with real values and valuable interactions. It is important to point out that positive marker feelings may also attach to the word 'value' itself. So if we attach the word 'value' to a given symbol, that will extend its positive marker feelings to that symbol as well.

What, then, are the mistakes we can make in forming our value system at the symbol-based control level? The answer is very simple: we attach inappropriate marker feelings, or marker feelings of inappropriate intensity, to certain symbols or words. Valuable interactions appearing at the feeling-based control level are mapped at the symbol-based control level with multiple distortions. Taking our example of the banana mentioned above:

1. The first mistake is that, if we humans are eating the banana, we attribute the pleasant taste to the banana. So we say the banana tastes good. As a matter of fact, the banana itself does not taste in any way at all. The

feeling of taste is generated in us when we interact with the banana.

2. The second mistake is that we also attribute the pleasant orienting feeling to the banana, although it is also generated in us when we interact with the banana and, moreover, it is not always pleasant: as we saw, the quality of the orienting feeling changes in time, whereas the feeling of taste is relatively constant.

3. The third mistake we make is that we attribute value to the banana instead of the interaction as a result of which we can ensure our energy supply. That is to say the banana is worth nothing if we cannot interact with it, if we cannot eat it. So we do not need to make efforts to own the banana but to interact with it, to eat it, because it is only the interaction that has any value.

The mistakes of interpretation listed above naturally leave their mark on our way of thinking, on the way our symbol-based control level works. The consequence of the mistakes of interpretation, and of the fact that the feeling-based control level selects interactions on the basis of orienting feelings, is that we often attach positive marker feelings and the word 'value' at the symbol-based control level to words such as 'beautiful', 'delicious' or 'pleasant' which symbolise orienting feelings. But the words 'beautiful', 'delicious' and 'pleasant' only symbolise orienting feelings and not the outcome of the interactions. You can live in a terrible marriage with a beautiful woman, a delicious mushroom stew can be toxic and so on.

To complicate matters further, we also tend to attach the symbol 'value' to certain adjectives, for example big, fast, strong, persistent, tough. We attach very strong marker feelings to all these words. But these words definitely have nothing to do with values. We use these words to describe the circumstances of a given interaction but not the effect or the outcome of the interaction. But it is the outcome or the effect of interactions that is the most important. The circumstances only matter insofar as they have an influence on the outcome of the process. That is to say you can do both mean and noble things fast, strongly or toughly. This extent of misinterpretation of the symbol 'value' at the symbol-based control level causes incredible chaos in the value and feeling system of human beings and it is not without consequences.

The first, and probably most serious, consequence is that our actions during the satisfaction of the needs to meet others' expectations and our own expectations are motivated by achieving goals that make it possible that we attach symbols loaded with positive marker feelings to our 'I' symbol or the 'I' symbol of others that actually do not represent any value, for example beauty, wealth, fame, power, strength, fastness, cleverness and so on. These words have nothing to do with values. These words do not symbolise interactions, they simply have positive marker feelings attached to them.

To illustrate what idiotic and foolish ideas the use of a value system shaped by these words can lead to, let us see a specific example. There was a guy in the United States who decided that, whatever it might cost, he would become famous. He realised this goal by setting out on a nice day and killing a lot of people. What happened? This guy attached an enormous amount of positive marker feelings to the word 'famous' in his value system. He did not concentrate on the interaction but on the positive marker feelings attached to the word 'famous' and thus he created a freak value system. He used practically the same scheme as the monkey with the banana. While the monkey was motivated by pleasant orienting feelings, this fool was motivated by positive marker feelings but neither of them had any idea of what they were actually doing and what consequences and impacts would be.

There is no such thing as a valuable person. There are

only people who can create valuable interactions with others (not with everyone!). You may now say: "Oh, come on! What the heck does this guy want with interactions again? Isn't it much simpler to say that someone is a valuable person than that someone is a person who can create valuable interactions?" Yes, that would really simplify the situation but it would not reflect reality. The value is not connected to the person but to the interaction. A given person may have a positive interaction with one person and a negative one with another. For example, a policeman protects respectable citizens but locks up rascals. Both actions are carried out by the same policeman but the two have totally different outcomes and effects. For a respectable citizen, the policeman is a person that provides him with a valuable interaction. For a rascal, the same policeman is a person that provides him with a harmful interaction. To further complicate the situation, interactions, just like rods, have two ends. And the two ends are not necessarily similar. Participating in the very same interaction may have totally different outcomes for different participants. Using the same example, if a policeman gets wounded while protecting a respectable citizen, then this interaction becomes a positive one for the respectable citizen and a negative one for the policeman.

So we must clearly and finally draw the conclusion from the above that only an interaction can represent any value and not a phenomenon. So, for example, no matter if there is a beautiful, wealthy, clever, strong etc. person, if she never has a valuable interaction with anyone, she is like the banana in the other solar system. To be more straightforward, and to use the old interpretation, you can only become a valuable person if you help your fellow human beings. If you do not help people, no matter what adjectives, titles or ranks symbolising "greatness" you are ornamented with, you will still remain a valueless nobody. Moreover, you can even become a sponger and harmful parasite that snatches worldly possessions from others and passively watches others suffer. Not to mention the beasts that wade through other people's blood and misery so they can hang foolish symbols on themselves like 'great conqueror' that give positive marker feelings to them (now I should apologise to beasts for comparing them to this kind of *homo sapiens* because no beast would ever do anything like that).

Another, less serious, consequence is that people start hoarding objects they think represent values. A painting, a work of art or a piece of music has no value whatsoever. The interaction with them does. That is a different kind of animal. But what is a piece of music worth whose score gathers dust locked up in a cabinet hidden from everyone, a piece that musicians cannot play and people cannot listen to? What is the worth of a painting nobody can ever see? And I could go on with my list... Objects do not have value, only interactions with them have. But then why do people collect objects? There are several possible reasons. The first one of them is probably what we call the 'desire for possession'. The name is already completely inaccurate. We humans cannot possess anything in this world apart from maybe our own bodies, but even that is doubtful. I would replace the expression 'desire for possession' with 'desire for disposition'. As a matter of fact, this is a special type of orienting feeling. The person who has the disposition of something experiences a pleasant feeling when she holds it in her hand, or strokes or touches her favourite object; when only she has the disposition of the given object; when she does not have to share it with others; others cannot take it from her. Actually I would call this feeling the "hamster feeling". Hamsters also stuff their face without even be being able to swallow everything. They collect food in their cheek pouches so no one else can have any (I do not know if you have ever seen a hamster but it is completely ridiculous).

These feelings, in reality, have nothing to do with values. A collector, if he does not know about the trick, can experience the "hamster feeling" with a good fake just the same as with the original painting. The value a painting has can also

306

be conveyed by a good reproduction. "Phew!" Shout the connoisseurs. "It is impossible! You cannot replace the original with a fake!" Yes? Then how could people make fakes that cannot be spotted? Although those insisting on originals are right to a certain extent, although they are not right about the artistic value conveyed by the given work of art but about other feelings attached to the original work of art. When we are looking at a 1000-year-old work of art, the feelings that arise in us can be classified into two groups. The first group consists of feelings triggered by the artistic elaboration of the work of art. These are the feelings that can still be generated by a good reproduction. The second group consists of feelings triggered by the history, the past of the given object. These are the feelings that appear when we think about other people that may have used the same object thousands of years before and when we consider that these works of art may have seen, and been part of, the history of humankind.

Another explanation for collecting objects may be the extension of feelings, when we extend the positive marker feeling carried by the word 'value' to a given object. A very good example of this is the life of several famous painters. While these painters were alive, or were destitute rather, no one cared about them. They almost starved to death because nobody bought their pictures. A shorter or longer period after their death, their pictures, that used to be worthless, all of a sudden became incredibly valuable. Just to be sure, they were the same pictures. No one repainted them. There are two possible explanations for this phenomenon. There were only stupid people living in the world when these painters lived but they became enlightened after the painters died and suddenly became experts and thus they could properly recognise the incredible value of the paintings. This solution does not sound very credible, does it? The other solution is that after the death of these painters, the positive marker feelings attached to the word 'value' were extended to their pictures in a well-managed advertising campaign. How do you extend marker feelings? The recipe is very simple: people to whom the public attaches very positive marker feelings, for example art experts (what they might have been before is a secret), the nobility, the wealthy, people in power and so on make very positive statements about the paintings and buy some of them. And immediately those that would like to be considered part of the nobility, wealthy, or powerful, run and flock to buy them. The question may arise: what do these people buy? Do they buy value? Yes, obviously, the visual interaction with the picture has some impact on them that might have a certain value. Only "might", because, as we know, rods have two ends. It doesn't matter what work of art you have, if the person who looks at it cannot appreciate it. But the same interaction could be triggered in them by a good copy. Then what did they buy? FEELINGS! They merely paid a lot of money for feelings. The more expensive something is, the wealthier and the more distinguished the people who can buy it. So if somebody buys very expensive stuff, she extends, and others can also extend, the feelings attached to the very wealthy and very distinguished people to her 'I' symbol. The more expensive the thing is, the fatter the feeling. This makes me think of a joke. Two nouveau riche people meet. "How much did you pay for your new tie?" asks one of them. "$1000 dollars." answers the other one. "Are you insane? You could have bought the same one round the corner for $2000." And this is no joke. Life is full of these cases.

And what is the case with gold, precious stones and jewellery? The situation is the same. These things have no value at all because the interaction you can have with them has no, or minimal, value. An exception is jewellery that is of artistic creation. But only the marker feelings attached to it make a piece of gold expensive. Expensive but not valuable. And the same applies to money. Money has no value at all. But a piece of bread does. If you do not believe it, I suggest that you move to a desert island. Before you start out, you can choose between taking a suitcase of money or a suitcase of food with you.

To be completely accurate, this is not quite true. It would

only be true if only one person lived on the earth. But as we know, there are quite a number of us living on this ball of mud that races through the space. Due to this fact, we need to introduce the notion of 'indirect value'. We can talk about something having an indirect value if we possess, or dispose of, a thing that has no value for us as individuals but is valuable to somebody else. By exchanging the thing that is valueless for us we might obtain something else that has real value for us so the otherwise valueless thing has an indirect value for us. Or, more accurately, it can have an indirect value because in order to realise that value it will need somebody else for whom the thing that is valueless for us has a real or indirect value. Various objects that we do not use can have an indirect value.

By the way, indirect value is the basis of commerce. A shoemaker does not need thousands of shoes of different sizes (shoemakers usually only have two feet). The pair of shoes that he made and uses represents a real value for the shoemaker but the shoes he made for sale only have indirect value for him and real value for the buyers. As we know, at the outset of commerce, barter was in fashion, i.e. people exchanged indirect value for indirect value. But this was rather cumbersome, that is why we had to introduce money. But what is money actually? Does it have value? What kind of value can a piece of paper have? Well, paper has very little real value. You can use it to light a fire in the fireplace on long winter nights or you can use it in the toilet if it is large enough and not too rough. So why does everybody strain every nerve to get those miserable pieces of paper?

As a matter of fact, with the introduction of money, we also introduced imaginary value. Imaginary things, as we know, do not exist in the world around us, they only exist in our minds. Money, however, does not only have an imaginary value, it also has an indirect value. But while other indirect values can represent real values for somebody, like the shoes sold by the shoemaker, money has no real value.

The real value of money is minimal: it is only worth as much as the piece of paper it is printed on. Therefore, money is an imaginary indirect value that does not represent real value for anyone. That is to say it does not have any real value for us as individuals: it only functions as indirect value because somebody else needs it. But money does not represent real value for others either. Other people also consider money as only having indirect value because they trust that others will accept money as having indirect value in exchange for something of real value that they want to get. If we get to a desert island and find a suitcase full of money, we cannot do anything with it: it is worthless for us. In our imaginations, we may have become rich but actually we will starve to death. If the sea washes another shipwrecked person to the shore and we want to pay her with our money, she will laugh at us because money does not represent either real or indirect value for her either, because there is nobody else on the island she can give it to in exchange for something of real value. The suitcase full of money "comes to life" when the rescue boat appears on the horizon. From that moment, the fight for the money begins. Money is an interaction voucher that you can exchange for interactions at certain places. But apart from buying valuable interactions, you can also buy valueless or downright harmful interactions, like the influence of drugs, with this voucher. Do we need money then? Yes. Is it good if you have money? Yes. Only it matters what you spend your money on.

Not only printed money but also electronic money represents imaginary value. Because what real value could a few electrons have? But all securities also have both imaginary and indirect values. So we can draw the conclusion that what people do in banks and stock markets is nothing else but twisting imaginary values. Bankers live in an imaginary world: that is what they build, piece by piece, i.e. they massage the air, the big nothing, and they are worried in the meantime lest the whole balloon burst. Probably you have already found this out but it is still worth pointing out that the situation is the same with gold and diamond as it is with money, with the slight difference that gold and diamond have real values because they can be used in industry, but primarily they have indirect and imaginary values.

And now let us get back to a rather delicate topic: works of art. What value does a work of art have? The value of a work of art is a combination of different values. The proportion of these values changes from work of art to work of art, from era to era and it also depends on the person examining the given work of art. How much real value a given work of art has for a given person is defined by how useful his interaction with that work of art was for him and how much his spirit and soul developed and was polished as a result of the given interaction. Generally, though, we must say that these interactions have relatively little impact on individuals. If it was not so, wonderful creatures on wings would leave the Louvre or the Hermitage after visiting the exhibitions. But this is not the case. The case is that, apart from the feelings discussed at the beginning of this chapter, individual works of art do not have much impact on human beings (although there may be rare and special exceptions). This is proven by the fact that until a given artist is "discovered", nobody gives a damn about him, although the impact of his works of art is the same on people before he is "discovered" as it is after. What actually happens is that disproportionately strong positive marker feelings are attached to the works of art of an already "discovered" artist and, as a result, people start fetishising the given works of art. But only the original ones not the copies. Although a good copy can have the same interaction with its viewer, the other feelings discussed in the previous part are not attached to it.

I have recently been to the Louvre and I was surprised to see that arrows indicate from the entrance where the Mona Lisa of Leonardo da Vinci is and people flock there and crowd in front of the picture trampling on each other's feet as if no other works of art were displayed in that "small" museum.

Such a disproportionate shift of marker feelings results in the incredible growth of the indirect value of works of art, whereas their real value remains relatively low. As a consequence, somebody will have to pay a lot of money for such a work of art if she wants to have it on the wall of her living room, although she will obtain hardly any real value. And if she is not lucky and, as time passes, people attach fewer positive marker feelings, for various reasons, to the given work of art, i.e. the balloon deflates, and the indirect value of the given work of art also decreases, so she will only be able to sell it for less money.

The influence of marker feelings on indirect values is even easier to understand if we have a look at the value of objects used by famous people. The real value of these everyday consumer articles, like a fountain pen, a pair of sunglasses, a hat or guitar, is nothing more than similar objects used by other people. Why do people still pay more money than the real value of these objects when they buy them? If someone buys them for investment, then he pays the extra money for the indirect value of these objects in the hope that he will find a rich fish that will be willing to pay for the feelings attached to these objects. And the "end-user" will pay the extra money for the feelings generated in him and related to the objects. The saddest, or funniest, thing is that you can make real value from the most idiotic things after a bit of transformation. Recently I found the news on the Internet that Hitler's toilet bowl is for sale. Yes, you got it right, my dear reader: this is the exact faience the Führer used to sit on moaning, or sometimes cracking, every day. The object in question, to use an appropriate phrase, is not worth a shit. Its real value is minimal: due to its dated and worn condition, it is worth less than brand-new similar items. But if an idiot has the idea of offering, say, $1 million for this object because some of his ancestors were affectionately attached to the rear end of the Führer, he will immediately create indirect value. And so the object representing practically zero value so far will gain indirect value for its current owner in a split second. For the $1 million imaginary indirect value given to him in exchange for the indirect value created this way, the owner could instead buy something of real value, for example, something delicious to eat. This is a little grotesque (and disgusting), isn't it?

I must mention one other important value: collective value. Although collective values have some real value for individual members of the community, this value is relatively low. But it still has value for each and every member of the community. Therefore, the community decides to protect this value in their mutual interest. Things of collective value might be works of art, historic buildings, a beautiful environmentally protected area, a species of plants or animals on the verge of extinction and so on and so forth. In these cases, the "little strokes fell a great tree" principle applies.

Well, at the end of this chapter we can draw the following conclusions:

1. Value is a rather complex relative notion that changes according to person, situation and era. There is no such thing as absolute value.
2. The value system of our age is heavily deformed by marker feelings. Sometimes so much so that we cannot talk about value systems any more, only about feeling systems.

This deformed feeling system leaves its mark on our world, our goals and our entire way of existence condemning us to misshapen, grotesque, and indeed sometimes terrible, lives and deaths.

11.

THE WAY
TO HAPPINESS

I could have also given the title ornithology to this chapter because we are going to deal with a very special bird in this one. The distinctive feature of this bird is its blue feathers. We are trying to find the blue bird of happiness. I cannot promise you we will find the nest of this precious bird, but we will be able to locate the places where this bird definitely does not nest. This makes me think of a joke: once a very old man was asked what the secret of a long life was. "The secret of a long life, my son" answered the old man "is that you do not stop breathing." So what is the secret of happiness? To experience the fewest possible bad feelings and the greatest possible number of pleasant feelings. This is absolutely true but, let's face it, the answer to this question is a little more complicated than that. The "game" that is about navigating among good and bad feelings, and whose stake is our life itself, can be traced back to two main motives or drives.

- The first main motive, or drive, is the necessity of satisfying our needs. In this case, the main driving force is provided by our unpleasant need-indicating feelings: this is what we are trying to avoid. These are need-driven processes. As I explained in the beginning of the book, not only need-indicating feelings participate in these processes but also orienting, strategic, tactical and technological feelings. These processes are the fully controlled processes mentioned in Chapter 6.

- The second main motive is the accumulation of reserves. Prehistoric humans had to pay attention to the accumulation of reserves all the time because they never knew when they would be able to satisfy their needs next. Nature could have arranged it so that if a need was satisfied, i.e. the need-indicating feelings of the bottom limit were not present any longer, it would simply "switch off" the related orienting feelings, thus preventing further need satisfaction processes, and would only "switch them back on" if a bottom limit-indicating feeling appeared again. In other words, we would only have felt that an apple pie was delicious, if we had been hungry. But Nature did not do so. Our orienting feelings are also "switched on" when our needs are satisfied. So an apple pie is also delicious when we are not hungry. As a consequence, we may also start satisfying a need when our bottom limit-indicating feelings are not activated, i.e. our needs are met. But since we "further satisfy", or overcharge, an already satisfied need, what we do is simply accumulate reserves (until the orienting feelings turn to neutral or negative or until the top limit indicating feelings start to appear). The bottom limit indicating feelings are missing from the processes ensuring the accumulation of reserves but the orienting, strategic, tactical and technological feelings are present just the same. These are partly controlled processes as explained in Chapter 6. The main driving force of these processes is experiencing pleasant feelings.

The processes mentioned above have actually been discussed in detail in the previous chapters of the book. We only needed to introduce this classification in order to examine things from the perspective of the blue bird: from the point of view of what practical difficulties await us in life and how we can avoid them; and what chances poor and rich people have in their search for happiness or, in other words, in order to try to cash in on the knowledge we have acquired so far.

11.1 The need-based control
(Is potato better than caviar?)

The main driving forces of the need-based control are unpleasant indicating feelings coming from unsatisfied needs and, in the case of software-type needs, the feeling of non-physical pain. As a consequence, until we satisfy our needs, our physical and non-physical status indicating feelings cannot be anywhere near the ideal values so we have, at best, the chance for a roast chicken but not the blue bird of happiness. Naturally, we may experience pleasant orienting feelings or the feeling of joy when we have unsatisfied needs but the experienced reader does not confuse them with the status indicating feeling of happiness.

The need for energy supply

In connection with the satisfaction of needs, certain important questions inevitably arise. We consider a need satisfied when we do not experience the unpleasant indicating feeling any more or, in the case of software-type needs, we do not feel non-physical pain. But does it matter what we use to satisfy a need? Is it all the same whether we satisfy the need for energy supply with potato and water or caviar and champagne? "Another silly question!" you think now, while you are walking to the kitchen to get box of caviar and some chilled champagne out of the fridge. But if we disregard the biologically different nutritional values of potato and caviar – one of them is rich in starch, whereas the other one is rich in protein – we should say both of them are suitable to satisfy the need for energy supply, i.e. we can use both foods to put an end to our feeling of hunger. "Okay, okay, but their taste is completely different!" you shout now. Yes, potato and caviar taste different, but who cares? We are not interested in tastes: they are what they are. We are interested in orienting feelings because that is what we enjoy! So it is possible that in one moment we like the orienting feelings triggered by the caviar, whereas in the next moment we like the orienting feelings triggered by potato. And what is the most important thing, as we have discussed in the beginning of the book, is that both orienting feelings will disappear just the same. What is more, they may even be transformed into unpleasant orienting feelings! To put it more simply, we will get bored with, or find too cloying, both kinds of food, if we eat too much of them. A simple hunter living in Siberia or Alaska will always eat what he has a fancy for in the given moment: either jacket potato with butter and some onions (I personally like this very much) or salmon caviar with a tablespoon (this is not bad either). He will always eat whatever triggers the most pleasant orienting feeling in him in the given moment. We, who live in wealthy societies, behave differently. We do not only care about the orienting feelings triggered by a given food; our choice is also influenced by the marker feelings appearing at our symbol-based control level in connection with the potato and the caviar. That is to say, it is not only the feelings appearing at the feeling-based control level that are connected to the symbol of the caviar, but also marker feelings carried by other words at the level of the symbol-based control are extended to this symbol and, therefore to the caviar itself. To put it more simply and clearly, we are programmed to think that caviar is better than potato, although this statement makes no sense at all.

But actually, the situation is even more complicated! Would you think that potato and caviar have anything to do with the needs to meet others' expectations and our own expectations? Yes, they do! Because potato and caviar not only carry the marker feelings related to the given food but the marker feelings connected to the people who primarily eat the given food are also extended to potato and caviar. I will explain this statement a little to make it easier to understand. In the olden days, the transport of caviar was rather cumbersome and costly because it needed constant cooling. Consequently, only the well-to-do could afford to eat caviar. Potato, however, was available for everyone: the food that everyone could grow and everyone could eat. These facts became common knowledge and now everyone knows that caviar is the food of the rich, whereas the potato is the food of the poor. In some people the positive marker feelings that they connected to the ruling classes were extended to the caviar. That is to say, if someone eats caviar then the marker feelings she finds positive, and that were extended from the ruling classes to the caviar, will also be extended to her. To put it more simply, those who eat caviar may feel like the nobility. But this is not only true for caviar. Some people also like to play sports played primarily by the classes considered the elite of the society such as golf, tennis, horse riding, polo or hunting. You may think there is nothing objectionable in liking these sports. That is right. If someone really likes and enjoys these sports, then why not? But interestingly, these people do not like boxing, wrestling, shotputting or hammer throwing and not even chess (you need to do some thinking there also). And we could go on with many other things: people choose cars, clothes and entertainment they think is typical of people belonging to the ruling or elite class.

This phenomenon is present in childhood as well. If a child puts an army hat on his head, he becomes a soldier and if he puts on a pilot hat, he immediately becomes a pilot. Partly this phenomenon is the explanation of the fact that children imitate adults: they can share the feelings experienced by adults. When children play with dolls or small cars, they do not primarily exercise their symbol-based control level with the implementation of complicated logical operations but try to experience the feelings they will have to experience in real life instead. They try to extend to themselves, and learn, feelings you can experience in real life.

321

They model real life and prepare for it. And that is absolutely right like that.

Getting back to the caviar, if someone eats caviar, she may think that the people around her attach the positive marker feelings connected to the caviar in her mind to her. So the person is trying to boast and increase the positive marker feelings attached to her person in others' minds: she tries to appear something more or to meet others' expectations better. Because those who eat caviar are noble, while those who eat potatoes are bust. Naturally, we can replace the word 'caviar' with the name of any other phenomenon you think positive marker feelings are attached to.

The same applies to the need for meeting our own expectations, only in that case, these people do not play for the people around them but fool themselves. They fool themselves because they do not concentrate on real values, only manipulate their own feelings. And people often do so without being conscious of it. So they do it because it feels pleasant when positive marker feelings are attached to your 'I' symbol. Of course, they always come up with some explanation of why they ape others. You often hear them saying that they simply have high standards. In doing so, they only attach another marker feeling to their 'I' symbol that they think positive.

If we get back to our need for energy supply and concentrate on the feeling-based control level, we can sum up the things we have said so far by pointing out that above a certain level of prosperity, there is not much difference between the feelings experienced by a poor and a wealthy person. So if someone has achieved a level of not starving any longer and eating a relatively varied diet, then he can satisfy his needs for energy supply just as well as a much wealthier person. The difference between the two of them is only expressed in the fact that the wealthy person can choose from many more flavours than the poorer one. In more simple language, the rich person can choose from more types of foods but the orienting feelings triggered by these foods will disappear just the same as the orienting feelings his less well-to-do counterpart can experience. So there is no difference in the pleasantness or intensity of their orienting feelings. Pleasantness will always be defined by the current physical and psychological state of the given person tasting the particular food, whereas the intensity of the feeling will be defined by the maximum law. Remember the experiment with table sugar in the beginning of the book. So we can state clearly that the satisfaction of the need for energy supply does not play a great role on the way to happiness above a certain level of financial prosperity. That is to say, less well-to-do and incredibly rich people have roughly similar chances for happiness in terms of the satisfaction of their need for energy supply.

The need for information

As for the need for information, the situation is completely different here than in the case of energy supply. While in the case of the need for energy supply it is the bottom limit-indicating feeling, i.e. the feeling of hunger, that causes the most problems to humankind, in the case of the need for information, the culprit is the top limit-indicating feeling.

In terms of access to information, today's world is fully open: information can flow freely and is accessible to everyone. Exceptions to this rule are certain nondemocratic states and the state, military and business secrets of countries. This means that, after reaching a certain standard of living, everybody can gain access to the information they are interested in with more or less effort. In the discussion of the need for information we said that only interactions that appear in some form or another at the symbol-based control level can be considered information. In reality, however, we are involved in many interactions that do not appear, or only partly, at the symbol-based control level. Since we are practically swimming in an ocean of interactions, it is not difficult to get rid of the unpleasant bottom limit-indicating feelings related to the need for interactions – what we call, for the sake of simplicity, the need for information. As a matter of fact, this bottom limit-indicating feeling appears very rarely, mostly in extreme conditions. This bottom limit-indicating feeling must not be confused with boredom.

On the other hand, the top limit-indicating feeling appears much more often in today's flood of information and when it appears, we can hardly wait to be left alone a little and to have the chance to retreat into seclusion. But this sometimes seems a luxury in modern societies. Bosses at workplaces are not happy to see their subordinates throw in the towel because they cannot cope with the flood of information that covers everything. And in these cases, we suffer. To make the situation even worse, it is not only the top limit-indicating feeling of the need for information that torments us, but the non-physical pain related to the need to meet our own expectations may also start working because we cannot do our jobs. And the non-physical pain related to the need to meet others' expectations can also start working when we cannot meet our boss' expectations and she, explicitly or implicitly, tells us so. And the indicating feeling of the need for safety, fear, also starts working because you may lose your job and your livelihood as a result. What kind of blue bird can we talk about in these circumstances? Today's modern wealthy societies suffer much more from the superabundance of information than from the lack of it. Who suffer more from the flood of information, poor or well-to-do people, is difficult to tell. Probably it is the very poor and the very rich that are less influenced by the dumping of information. This dumping does not reach the very poor and the very rich can afford to have others solve their problems.

The need for safety

The next need to talk about is the need for safety. Tens of millions of people living in misery experience the feeling of physical pain day by day. But no matter if the indicating feeling of physical pain warns them that their life is under threat, they cannot afford the luxury of avoiding this feeling. Everyone knows the other indicating feeling of the need for safety: fear. Fear is a bottom limit-indicating feeling. The related top limit-indicating feeling is a less conspicuous one. Conventional wisdom in Hungary has come up with a very good proverb for this kind of feeling: dogs get rabies when they have it too good. It means that after you have resolved a dangerous situation, life becomes as boring after a while as still water. You need a little excitement. A burst of adrenaline. I suppose you have already found out which is the limit-indicating feeling that causes the most trouble to humankind. I read somewhere that more people have died since the end of the Second World War in local wars then in the Second World War itself. But you do not even need to fight wars in order to be afraid because death is waiting for each and every one of us at the end of our journey. But even before we get to the end of our journey, we need to face the pressing feeling of fear countless times. The indicating feeling of fear always appears when there is a chance that our fate will take a turn for the worse. Because that is exactly the function of fear: to keep us away from these situations. Naturally, the symbol-based control level tries to modify our fear. Sometimes it can reduce fear but sometimes, on the contrary, it thrusts us into the deep pit of fear.

There are four ways to avoid fear. The first, and the most simple one is to avoid dangerous situations. The second one is to get used to dangerous situations, i.e. to train our feeling-based control level to gradually lower the threshold level of our fear based on the experience that dangerous situations can be escaped. The third way is to try and present the situation with logical tricks at the symbol-based control level in such a way that our fear reduces. There are several "tricks" like this, for example playing the situation down, i.e. describing the situation with words other feelings are attached to; or deliberately not thinking the situation over, as we often say: "I do not even want to think about it!" The fourth way is to openly face danger. In this case we are completely aware how dangerous a situation is. We are afraid, we are trembling inside but we "steel our heart". We take up the challenge. And we often do it to preserve our human dignity. That is to say the need to meet our own expectations is activated. We do not want to live on or die like a lamb taken to the slaughterhouse. We step into the arena or on to the scaffold walking tall. Not everyone can do that although this is the only way out when there is no other way out. The difference between a foolish and a brave person is that the fool does not understand the situation or, even if he understands it, he takes risks in order to satisfy his needs to meet others' expectations and his own expectations. Brave people do not rush headlong into disaster. They do not need to satisfy the need to meet others' expectations and their own expectations this way. If they still get into dangerous situations, they have the strength of mind to analyse the situation in detail and, although they are afraid because it is natural, they take up fight.

You can also get rid of fear with a simple technological "trick". The indicating feeling of fear is only present as long as its function to keep us away from danger can get across. But once it can no longer serve its function, it disappears and other feelings take its place. So if you launch an attack, it is already the feelings of anger and hatred that control you and not fear.

From the point of view of happiness, it is clear that we cannot talk about happiness as long as we have fear in our life. From the point of view of poor and rich people, I must point out that prosperity above a certain level can reduce the chance of getting into situations where you need to fear to a certain extent. Naturally, unfortunate accidents may happen to anyone regardless of their financial situation and standing. But well-to-do people do not need to worry so much about starvation, losing their shelter or illnesses. They may still get ill, but they have access to a much higher level of medical care; in the case of wars they can escape more easily (and if they die, they get buried in much more beautiful coffins ☺). But excessive wealth can also make you a target. Blackmailers, kidnappers, robbers, murderers, assassins, parasites and bloodsuckers start to appear. On the other hand, it is difficult for a poor person to imagine when the top limit-indicating feeling of the need for safety of reach people, i.e. the feeling of being worn out or bitterness appears. In this case, however strange it may sound, wealthy people have no chance for happiness at all. So they take some risk under well controlled circumstances: they travel around the globe with a well-equipped luxury yacht, a hot air balloon or an aeroplane and so on. This, naturally, helps the need for meeting others' expectations and their own expectations as well. They swell with pride (although there would be a good few million applicants that would also do these "heroic deeds", if someone else paid the bill).

The need to reproduce

The indicating feelings of the need to reproduce can also be very unpleasant. The need for sexual intercourse is relatively easy to satisfy one way or another. But the indicating feeling of partnerlessness embitters the lives of millions of people. Finding a sex partner is much easier than finding a partner to share the holidays and workdays, and sometimes the misery, of your life with. Our feeling-based control can very quickly select a partner who is suitable for generation. The orienting feelings triggered by the body shape and the face of a candidate can inflame desire in seconds, that is we can decide in a few seconds if we would like to have sexual relations with the given person or not. As a matter of fact, if both parties are mutually suitable for one another, the intercourse could take place, the offspring could be born and we could live our everyday lives. But, although a little slower, the symbol-based control level also starts working. And we start pondering and collecting arguments for and against the given person. And at this level, a number of other things also appear that do not have much to do with the need to reproduce.

If we take a look at partner selection from the point of view of poor and rich people, we must look for the difference at the symbol-based control level. While the feeling-based control level only sees a man or a woman that is or is not attractive for us, the symbol-based control level mixes things up big time. The moment words emerge in your mind, the feelings related to these words also appear. No matter if you think logically, the output of your logical train of thought is always a word to which, naturally, feelings and marker feelings are attached. And these feelings do their job: they control us. If we spot a pair of identical twins and we have no other information about the two people yet, they will generate roughly the same feelings in us: we only see the man or the woman in them. The moment we learn that one of them is rich and the other one is poor, the symbol-based control level starts working and carries out logical operations. The results of these logical operations will naturally be different for the two people, and different feelings will also be attached to the words symbolising these results.

In today's modern societies, many pleasant feelings are attached to the word 'rich' and many unpleasant, or at least neutral, feelings are attached to the word 'poor'. Accordingly, if we attach the word rich to a person, the marker feelings attached to the word 'rich' will be extended to this person. The situation is similar with the word 'poor' the only difference being that negative or neutral feelings will be extended to the person here. "You see" you may say now "how good it is to be rich because rich people are selected sooner as partners since many more positive feelings are attached to them." This is true. But! There is this little but here. You must have noticed that problems usually start with the word 'but'.

This case is no exception. The problem with marker feelings is that they are too general and do not reflect the traits of a certain person. Marker feelings are compressed packages of general feelings related to the symbol-based control level that do not always have anything to do with the feelings you can feel through direct experience at the feeling-based control level. As a matter of fact, their disadvantage is exactly the same as their advantage. When we talk, we use these compressed feeling packages to mark various phenomena and sometimes we use them to fill the space that is a result of the feeling-based control level not having a chance to generate feelings about the given phenomenon. So, due to their compression, marker feelings are rather inaccurate essences of feelings that can be modified by feelings appearing later at the feeling-based control level. We can gain marker feelings in split seconds, whereas it takes time – and above all, situation – for the generation of feelings at the feeling-based control level. So if we want to know how somebody behaves when we need his help or when he is irritated, we must wait until such a situation occurs. And sometimes it can take years. The problem with marker feelings, or prejudices, is that they make the task of the feeling-based control level – embedding later real feelings into the data network – more difficult in cases where the feelings generated at the feeling-based control level are inconsistent with the marker feeling. So a positive marker feeling will hinder the appearance of negative feelings emerging at the feeling-based control level in connection with the same person at the symbol-based control level and, thus, in the data network. But the fact that a negative feeling emerging at the feeling-based control level cannot appear at the symbol-based control level does not mean that the problem related to the negative feeling does not exist in reality. Indeed, the problem can be very real. Only we cannot express it in words because the feelings already existing in our data network do not make it possible. So we only feel that we feel terrible, that something is not right but what it is, we cannot tell. To put it more simply: it is difficult to get rid of prejudices. The stronger and the more numerous our prejudices are, the more difficult a task we have.

If somebody chooses a poor person as a partner, she obviously does so because she has collected pleasant orienting feelings in her feeling-based control level and not because she has pleasant prejudices about poverty. If someone chooses a rich person as a partner, there is a much higher chance that his choice has been influenced by the marker feelings attached to the word 'richness' at his symbol-based control level and not by the feelings emerging at his feeling-based control level that would assess the real personality of his partner much more accurately. In everyday language: those who chose poor partners probably assessed the personality of their partners more accurately and, therefore, can expect a longer relationship than those who chose a rich partner and may have listened to their prejudices and assessed their partner inaccurately in doing so.

Let us now take our potato and caviar simile again. As we saw, you can satisfy your need, i.e. put an end to your hunger, perfectly with both potato and caviar. You can also do the same with a good stew made of a healthy portion of death caps. Mushroom stew would also put an end to your feeling of hunger, i.e. it would satisfy your need (once and for all). Although both potato and caviar can really satisfy your need, due to their chemical composition, they still have a different effect on your organism. The situation is similar with the indicating feelings of the need to reproduce. We can calm the indicating feelings of the lack of sex and partnerlessness with anybody but the outcome makes a difference. Just think of the mushroom stew. So although you may terminate the unpleasant indicating feeling of a given need, you may cause damage to yourself at another level. And we often do something very similar in the case of relationships. Driven by the unpleasant indicating feelings of the need to reproduce, attracted by pleasant orienting feelings triggered by a potential partner and controlled only by the feeling-based control level, we often consent to relationships that are very much like a poisonous mushroom stew (and their effect is also similar).

In the earlier discussion of the need to reproduce, I mentioned that a good relationship can bring happiness and heaven, but sometimes also hell, to you. What do heaven and hell have to do with these issues? The explanation is that a good relationship can satisfy all our needs and it's packed with the most pleasant feelings, whereas a bad relationship can attack all our need levels and it's packed with the most unpleasant feelings. The more of our needs it can satisfy and the higher number of pleasant orienting feelings it produces, the better and more valuable a relationship is. Relationships that only satisfy the need to reproduce are still useful because, at least, they satisfy one need and they are still way better than the ones that block, or downright compromise, the satisfaction of our other needs.

How is it possible to compromise the satisfaction of a need? For example, if you are reprimanded in front of others and if it is always pointed out how stupid, dumb and completely incapable you are. But it will also do if all your money is spent, you are elbowed out of your own flat and, on top of that, even the Mafia is set on to you (isn't it nice?). So you can calm the unpleasant indicating feelings related to your need to reproduce with many people but it makes a difference what the side-effects are.

In the case of the need for energy supply, it is clear for everyone that you do not eat poisonous mushrooms even if you are starving or you do not drink salty seawater even if you die of thirst. But at the same time we are ready to start a relationship which you can already tell at the outset will not work, it will be harmful and it will be detrimental to your spirit and soul. And there are no miracles. Poisonous mushrooms will remain poisonous and seawater will remain salty.

But apart from "poisonous" people, you may also encounter "poisonous" situations. A typical example is the eternal triangle. For an eternal triangle, you need three people (surprise, surprise): two of them in a seasoned relationship (which is tied up by strong financial, career related and child related bonds and in which at least one of the parties, but sometimes both of them, feels bad) and a third person who is suffering from, and is driven by, the unpleasant indicating feelings of the need to reproduce. The third person – we will now evaluate the situation from his or her point of view – has two options: he or she either moves on, driven by unpleasant need-indicating feelings, on the path fate has laid out or tries to get rid of these unpleasant need-indicating feelings with one member of the couple. If the third person decides to move on tormented by the unpleasant indicating feelings of unsatisfied needs, she or he will either find a partner for life or not if luck does not help. But if this third person tries to satisfy his or her needs with one member of the couple, he or she inevitably walks into the trap of salty seawater and suffering is guaranteed.

Since the couple is tied together with strong bonds, a happy ending is out of question. So the third person who, when she or he walked alone, only suffered from the indicating feelings triggered by an unsatisfied need is now also suffering from desire. And as if that was not enough, sometimes a guilty conscience may be added topped up with some anger, despair and fear. Instead of improving, the position of the third person has become much worse not to mention the other two people who are not in an enviable situation either. Why is it a seawater trap? Because if we are thirsty and drink salty water driven by a need-indicating feeling without controlling ourselves, instead of quenching our thirst, we will become even thirstier. And the case is the same here: the members of the eternal triangle are in a worse position than at the outset. On one side of the scale there are the short hours that are sometimes spent in a pleasant way, and that serve as bait, and on the other side of the scale there are the days, weeks or sometimes years spent in misery. Hours versus years. It is up to you. Make your choice! We could replace the pleasant hours with a piece of salt. If the monkey lets the salt go, it is immediately free, and at worst, it loses the salt. But if it does not let the salt go, it does not get the salt and will also become a captive (in its captivity, it will only get crumbs). The pleasant hours only relieve you from the unpleasant need-indicating feeling of sexuality for a shorter or longer period but they do not relieve you from the other indicating feeling of the need to reproduce: the need-indicating feeling of partnerlessness.

The situation is uncannily similar to a desire trap. Only while you are experiencing a situation in your imagination in a desire trap, you can taste the long-craved goal in an eternal triangle but you still cannot satisfy your need, at least not your need for a partner for life, just the same. So the carrot is held out for you in both cases but you cannot eat it in either one of them. And this leads to the intensification of your desire which, in turn leads to suffering. The parties have three options in these situations. Either they continue drinking salty water and will definitely continue suffering; or the third person moves on, thirsty and a little battered, and will either find a partner for life or not; or the partners own up to the situation and to one another and, making mutual sacrifices, they start a new life together.

As a matter of fact, there are two things you must be very careful with in the selection of your partner. One of them is not to be driven by marker feelings, or prejudices, in your selection; the second one is that you should make sure that your partner-to-be not only satisfies your need to reproduce but also supports the satisfaction of as many of your other needs as possible or, if not supporting it, at least she or he should not block or compromise it.
The need for a group

The indicating feeling of the need for a group is loneliness. The top limit-indicating feeling of the need for a group does not yet have a well-known name, probably the expression 'disgust towards crowds' describes this feeling the best. The situation is similar for the indicating feelings of the need for a group as it was for the indicating feelings of the needs discussed previously. Unless you live on a desert island, it is relatively not that difficult to belong to a group so it is not that difficult to get rid of the unpleasant indicating feeling. The problems come from the side-effects. It makes a difference whether you belong to the honourable group of regulars in the local hideaway (pub for those who didn't get it) or to the group of the members of the Academy. Although both venerable groups can definitely satisfy the need for a group of certain people. Perhaps the topics of discussion are slightly different in these two groups. While in one of them you can discuss the topical issues of space research, genetic surgery and laser physics, in the other one you can join seminars on pimping, mugging or receiving stolen goods (this last one often takes place in pubs).

People usually choose company for themselves that will promote the satisfaction of as many of their needs as possible. In one of the groups above, they are after the royalty paid for their publications, while in the other they might be after their share from the shifting of a recently stolen gold watch. In one of them, you will be acknowledged for a scientific discovery, in the other, for giving a good slap in the face to another guy. Anyway, these things serve your need to meet others' expectations. Ironically, the people in question subjectively will feel pleasant feelings of the same intensity when they hear the words of acknowledgement after the scientific discovery and after the slap in the face. The only difference is that these pleasant feelings are attached to different deeds, and different words denoting certain deeds, in the coordinate system of the scientist and the tramp. In other words, they have different feeling and value systems. The tramp does not try to make it into the Academy and the scientist does not try to become the hero of the pub. They do not do so on the one hand because they have different feeling and value systems and, on the other hand, because they would definitely fail in an unknown territory, i.e. their needs to meet others' expectations and their own expectations would be hurt. People choose their company on the basis of their feeling and value systems, taking into consideration how the participation in a given group may contribute to the satisfaction of their needs other than the need for a group.

If we disregard artificial organisations such as school, workplace or military service, where people are held together by external forces, we can differentiate between two different types of organising into groups. The first group includes group formation initiated by the feeling-based control level. A typical example is package holidays where complete strangers meet for the first time in their life and know nothing about one another. The group of tourists, that is actually a bunch of independent persons at the beginning of the trip, starts to organise into real subgroups as time passes. Primarily feelings emerging at the feeling-based control level, i.e. likes and dislikes towards other group members, contribute to the formation of these subgroups. The second group includes group formation initiated by the symbol-based control level. The second group has three subtypes:

1) A person joins a group because symbols that represent positive marker feelings for him are attached to the group. A typical example is joining political parties. In these cases, the relations of the members of the groups towards one another are of secondary importance. The main cohesion of the group is provided by the feelings attached to the idea of the party, i.e. a symbol. In these cases, even people who otherwise would not like one another can organise into one group. You can observe the phenomenon of the extension of feelings in these cases too. That is to say we extend the marker feeling

that belongs to the primary symbol to other human beings, sometimes even to those we would normally dislike.

2) In this case, a person joins a group because she would like the marker feelings connected to the groups to be extended to her. A typical case is if someone wants to join a group that she rates as prestigious. She tries to satisfy her need to meet others' expectations and her own expectations this way. Typical examples of this case are elegant clubs or the societies of famous or rich people.

3) While conscious decisions, i.e. decisions based on logical operations, did not play a role in the two previous cases, they are conclusive here. In this case, as a result of series of logical operations, an individual draws the conclusion that it is beneficial and practical for him to belong to a given group. This is the "It is good if I frequent the club of successful business people because I may pick up some information." type of thinking.

Naturally these formations of groups do not exist in their "pure" forms. In real life, we encounter different mixtures of them. It is important to point out that, after the formation of a group, regardless of the type of the group, orienting feelings that ensure group cohesion like solidarity, complicity, power, devotion or trust start to appear.

Looking at the issue from the point of view of poor and rich people, poor people are more likely to find true friends, i.e. people will seek their company because they like them. Rich or famous people are surrounded by greater numbers of people, but the number of their real friends is only revealed if they become poor. Rich and famous people are surrounded by those who would like marker feelings attached to the persons of the rich people to be extended to them. Rich and famous people live in symbiosis with this kind of company. The entourage, the so-called friends, are there to prove the greatness of the rich and the famous, at least that is what they want to make them believe, so they help the rich and famous to satisfy their needs to meet others' expectations and their own expectations. In return the rich and famous extend the marker feelings attach to their persons that they consider positive to their entourage. So the entourage, or the court, can also say "you see, I am the friend of a rich and famous person" thereby extending the marker feelings attached to the rich and famous to their own person and thus, they can satisfy their need to meet others' expectations and their own expectations. Naturally there are also "friends" around the rich and famous who are consciously looking for morsels dropping from the table for them.

The need to meet others' expectations

We have reached the first software-type need. As we discussed earlier, there are no unpleasant indicating feelings in the case of software-type needs. So the question arises of what feelings motivate and drive us at the level of software-type needs. In the discussion of the need to meet others' expectations we have seen that at this level, we primarily strive to avoid letting others attach negative marker feelings to our 'I' symbol that would destroy the positive feelings attached to it and our feeling-based control would therefore release trigger the strategic feeling of non-physical pain. In more simple terms, we are trying to avoid being reprimanded, to avoid verbal aggression, in order not to have to experience non-physical pain. Naturally, the opposite is also true: we like it when words carrying positive feelings are attached to our 'I' symbol. We like to be praised. And, indeed, we are willing to do a lot to get others' acknowledgement.

Let us suppose that, meeting the expectations of the people around us perfectly, we can avoid being reprimanded. Is everything going to be all right then? Will we feel at home? If we lived in an isolated community in a remote village in the mountains, we would have some chance but not in today's modern society. You can only avoid suffering, and maintain your peace of mind for shorter or longer periods, with huge effort. What is the reason? The phenomenon of relative devaluation. TV channels, radio stations, the printed press and the Internet are full of news praising others. All we see around us is how sensational, incredible, awesome, gigantic and world shaking Joe This or Jane That is. And naturally, we are given the reasons, too. They are great because one of them managed to scratch his right ear with his left foot and the other one was able to spit into a bowl of soup from a distance of 10 metres with her eyes closed. This is something, indeed! If you have this occasionally, no problem. But this is what you see from dawn to dusk, dusk to dawn every day from month to month for years. And you see: it has its result. We have formed a degenerate, idiotic value and feeling system. Good job! There are those doctors who save millions of lives every day with persistent and tiring work. But what use are they? How many of them could scratch their right ear with their left foot? Who are they? Nobodies! Do you have money? Then you are somebody. You do not have money? Then you are nobody. If somebody thinks that he is bigger, greater or more valuable than others, just because he has more money than others, then there is a big problem. If somebody thinks that she is greater than Buddha or Jesus just because she has a luxury car, a luxury yacht or a private jet, she should urgently visit a mental specialist. Maybe it is not too late. But whose fault is it? Ours. Because we ourselves educate ourselves into being idiots. Of course, in exchange for a little money. What do you think, we are not idiots to do it for free!

I know, I got carried away. But the degenerate value and feeling system of our world imposes incredible amounts of suffering on us human beings. Billions of people are presented as nobodies even though nobody reprimands or disparages them. This is exactly the phenomenon of relative devaluation. What can people do to protect themselves from relative devaluation? Some try to find a flaw in the glorified stars and put them down, i.e. attach symbols to the

'I' symbols of the stars that extend negative feelings and marker feelings to them and try to mark themselves up, i.e. attach words to their own 'I' symbols to which positive feelings and marker feelings are attached. This solution does not require too much effort from the individual. The second solution is to carry out deeds and achieve great successes to which the public reacts positively and decorates you with positive symbols which, naturally, do not always have to do with real values. This solution already requires a lot of effort but can also create real values. The third solution is when you try to form a value and feeling system that is close to reality and try to cut free from the lunatic asylum around you. The fourth solution is to retreat into seclusion. The fifth one is to become neurotic. You must have met wretched people who were telling the night a few home truths in a loud voice alone in the dark and deserted streets. Those are the ones that have already lost the battle and believed they are nobodies. Nobody will heal their souls because who would deal with a nobody? Nobody.

Most people choose their own method of marking themselves up. And they do it merely for self-protection. But what else can a person of average skills do? The world around us is full of single people. If you talk to them about why they cannot find partners, the answer very often is that they won't deal with just "anybody". If somebody else is just "anybody", or nobody in other words, it means that they are somebody. If somebody has become "somebody" it means precisely that he has already attached symbols to his 'I' symbol that carry positive marker feelings for him. He has puffed himself up and now he will only deal with a person who has at least the same level of quality marker feelings attached to her 'I' symbol. But where are human beings here? Who cares about real human values? And these people will be left on the shelf either because no candidate ornamented with the necessary amount of marker feelings turns up or because these marker feelings burst out when they live together and the given person appears in reality without all the ornaments. And all this happens because society forces us to become "somebody" in order to avoid the phenomenon of relative devaluation and to protect our 'I' symbols. It is the phenomenon of relative devaluation that renders the need to meet others' expectations a need. The feeling of non-physical pain related to the need to meet others' expectations regenerates just like hunger and thirst. We need to fight for our balance of mind every single day. You can find the phenomenon of relative devaluation everywhere in the history of humankind but it is today's modern societies that have pushed it to the extreme.

Looking at this issue from the point of view of the rich and the poor, the situation is even more disheartening. Fooling people and forcing a wrong value and feeling system on them cripples the way of thinking of both poor and rich people. However, while poor people do not have any, or have much less, chance to decorate themselves with beads and pseudo-values, well-to-do people can really cover themselves with symbols to which positive marker feelings are attached in the degenerated value system of society but which actually have no value at all. A consequence of this fact is that the position of poor people further deteriorates due to relative devaluation. So poor people feel even more miserable and struggle even more to protect their own 'I' symbols from relative devaluation. But do not believe that rich people are so much better off! Since the knickknacks they have hung on themselves are not real values, they lose their glitter quite soon. Luxury cars, yachts, private jets and palaces wear out and run down. "And what then?" you may ask. You are right: rich people just buy new ones if they can. But for them also, the main problem is relative devaluation. Because there is always someone richer than the rich and richer than the richer. Or, if there are not yet, there will be. So rich people are also driven into a meaningless, idiotic competition nobody can win the same as poor people, only at a higher, and much more expensive, level. And then comes the good old Weber's law. The higher you are and the more expensive your toy is, the more expensive it is to buy another toy that will trigger the same effect. And this one will also lose its glitter soon.

Continuing our investigation of the problem from the point of view of the rich and the poor, we need to examine the role of acknowledgements and praise. Yes, it feels nice when symbols carrying positive feelings are attached to our 'I' symbol. But due to the nature of things, these symbols are often attached to rich people without any grounds. And this phenomenon has another consequence. For example, in historical reviews, you will have a rather distorted picture of monarchs or historic persons. Posterity often does not have the slightest idea what a person living in the past actually did and what sort of a person she actually was because inflated marker feelings cover everything. The feelings carried by the symbols attached to poor people are more realistic and better reflect the actual traits of the given person. But sometimes these can also be glass beads. It is easier to decorate a soldier disabled in a war with an order or medal and say he is a hero than to take care of him and his future. The medal and the word 'hero' do not cost a thing.

The need to meet our own expectations

As we know, we do not find unpleasant indicating feelings in the case of this need either. The need to meet others' expectations is about protecting ourselves from the non-physical pain that originates from others attaching symbols to us that carry negative marker feelings and these feelings being extended to us and from the relative devaluation. The need to meet our own expectations, on the other hand, is about avoiding attaching similar words or symbols to our own 'I' symbols ourselves, and about avoiding our own relative devaluation. And at the same time, we do everything we can to be able to attach words carrying positive feelings to our own person. Why do we strive to attach words carrying positive marker feelings to our own 'I' symbol? There are two main reasons for this. On the one hand, it feels good and, on the other hand, we try to avoid-relative devaluation. Relative devaluation has two main aspects. One of them, an image that we must preserve, is for the external world; the other, another image that we must take care of perhaps even more, is for ourselves: this is our own image of ourselves. Relative devaluation not only destroys the image for the external world but also our image for ourselves. So this is a war on two fronts, where we need to stand our own ground on both fronts. What weapons do we have? The same ones we mentioned in the discussion of the level of meeting others' expectations. This war has to be fought every day because the need to meet our own expectations regenerates in just the same way as the need to meet others' expectations. The main player here is also relative devaluation.

With certain people, you can clearly observe that they are still only fighting this war only on one front. The second front has not yet been formed. These are the people whose level of meeting their own expectations has not yet been activated or, more accurately, whose emphasis is still on meeting others' expectations. These are the people who drive terribly expensive cars but live in hovels. The ones that buy the most expensive clothes but starve in the meantime. They are the ones who play to the audience and fight this war often beyond their power. And they can never win this war because they had already lost it when they started it.

And there are some other people who are already fighting this war only on one front. They are the ones who do not care about public opinion at all. Those who live, and can afford to live, by their own internal value system. I say they can afford to do so because this is a luxury to a certain extent. Only people that have the wealth to be able to live independently of the external world or beggars that have nothing to lose apart from their peace of mind can afford to live by their own value systems. Everybody else is under threat: the threat of expulsion from the community, impoverishment, prison or execution.

Examined from the point of view of richness and poverty, the need to meet our own expectations is very similar to the need to meet others' expectations. The only difference is that in the case of the need to meet others' expectations, the ornaments are hung on the outside of the building, whereas in the case of meeting our own expectations, they are hung on the inside.

Although I have focused on extremes in the discussion of both the need to meet others' expectations and the need to meet our own expectations, let us not forget about healthy minded people who, withdrawn from the limelight, simply do their task and create real and true values. They are the few who have been able to develop a healthy value system and resist the influence of the external world.

The need for self-realisation

The need for self-realisation is nothing else but the need to put things in order, the need to live in harmony: in harmony with ourselves, with the world around us, with the uniform world we are also part of. Why is the need for self-realisation a need? Because we are forced by the unpleasant need-indicating feelings of different hardware-type needs and the non-physical pain of the attacks against our 'I' symbols originating from unsatisfied software-type needs to fit into the existing world in harmony and thus free ourselves from suffering and misery.

At this level, wealth and money no longer play a direct role. At this level, what matters is brains, mental capacities and wisdom: how you can create harmony in your mind and, sometimes, in other's minds. Money and wealth only have secondary or background roles. It is obvious that those who have wealthier family backgrounds could have better education. But better education is worth nothing if you are lazy, careless, half-hearted or malevolent. Willpower, superior mental qualities, perseverance, a fighting spirit and motivation can sweep the disadvantages of an inferior education away.

A good financial background can also be advantageous in the sense that the individual simply has more time to deal with higher level needs and does not have to work to make ends meet every day. Above a certain level of wealth, however, it is clearly mental capacities that will decide. And I do not only mean the capacity to carry out logical operations but also the discipline and concentration of mind and the love that lives in our heart. I put love in the last place although probably this is the most important thing. There is no peace of mind without love. People living in animosity, envy and hatred do not have a chance for the peace of mind and for self-realisation. Buddha smiles at everybody with love. Jesus also preaches love and this is no coincidence. Without love, no one can find peace of mind!

11.2 The control ensuring the accumulation of reserves
(Can the idle also be happy?)

The main drivers of the control ensuring the accumulation of reserves are pleasant feelings. In these cases, the unpleasant orienting feelings related to hardware-type needs and the feelings of non-physical pain related to already activated software-type needs are not present so the goal of our activities is just to experience a pleasant feeling which then has indirect consequences in the form of the accumulation of reserves. A typical example is the case of the apple pie. We do not usually eat apple pies because we are hungry but because we want to immerse ourselves in the positive orienting feelings triggered by the dessert. We will have to face the consequences, too, because our TV-watching muscle will develop and we will grow a nice little pot-belly or middle-aged spread around our trunk, i.e. we accumulate reserves.

Naturally, not only can we accumulate reserves at the level of the need for energy supply but also at all other levels. A bit of extra sex can never do any harm: at worst, the family will grow a little; or if we can squeeze out one or two extra words of acknowledgement from somebody, our confidence can develop and so on. Practically all kinds of pleasant feelings can come into consideration: orienting feelings, strategic, tactical, technological, status-indicating and déjà vu feelings. Since the main drivers of the control ensuring the accumulation of reserves are pleasant feelings, it will not hurt if we get acquainted with a few common properties of pleasant feelings. A common property of pleasant feelings is that they disappear relatively quickly. Perhaps some of the orienting feelings related to the need to reproduce that are responsible for ensuring that the parents stay together for a longer period are exceptions to this rule.

A contradiction follows from the fact that pleasant feelings disappear quickly. Since, as we know, feelings, and among them pleasant feelings, have functions, then once they have completed their functions, they disappear because there is no need for them any longer. But since the main goal of the control ensuring the accumulation of reserves is to experience pleasant feelings, it could easily happen that we would like to relive a given feeling that has already gone. The more times, however, we try to experience a given pleasant feeling, the less we succeed. Or at least within a certain timeframe. It is only natural because the given feeling has served its function and there is no need for it any more. So the more we want to reach our goal, the further away we get from it. Weber's law only adds to this problem. The stronger a given stimulus, the higher the amount of increase necessary to trigger a noticeable increase in the feeling. From your own flat you must move at least to a castle in order to experience the same pleasant feelings you experienced when you moved from a rented flat to your own place.

Another problem may be caused by the fact that feelings have functions. Since these functions play important controlling roles in our life, they do not simply "hang in the air", they are closely connected to our physical body instead. We cannot play with feelings at will and go unpunished. Experiencing a given feeling can have a severe impact on our health. A typical example of these feelings are pleasant orienting feelings related to the need for energy supply. You cannot experience these feelings for years unpunished. If you do not make sure that you burn the excess amount of energy, you will definitely gain weight.

The next, and sometimes really serious, problem is the tormenting strategic feeling of desire. You can rarely experience pleasant feelings the minute you think of them. Satisfaction, if it happens at all, is usually preceded by a shorter or longer wait. As we discussed in the previous chapter, we usually spend much more time waiting, with the accompanying feelings of desire and craving, than we do experiencing the pleasant feeling that was the subject of our desire. This, as we know, we can sometimes enjoy only for a few seconds. The situation may deteriorate further with the appearance of a desire trap.

I suggest that we play with some more philosophical strings now. Let us read a few lines from the *Tao Te Ching*, a book written around the fourth century BC by the Chinese philosopher Lao Tzu, here in the translation of Robert G. Henricks.

"When everyone in the world knows the beautiful as beautiful,
ugliness comes into being;
When everyone knows the good, then the not good comes to be.
The mutual production of being and nonbeing,
The mutual completion of difficult and easy,"

As a matter of fact, our effort to experience pleasant feelings automatically results in an effort to avoid unpleasant feelings. But we are pretty "well equipped" with unpleasant feelings also. Probably nobody would mind if they had to make do with a smaller set of them. Unfortunately, pleasant feelings are dwarfed against the vast sea of unpleasant feelings. And this is due to the fact that only a negligible part of the world around us supports our existence. Just think of the ratio of edible to non-edible materials.

Although we have discussed a number of unpleasant feeling groups in this book, we have left out an important unpleasant feeling. Perhaps the best way to illustrate this feeling is to ask you to imagine that you want to search the nest of the blue bird of happiness in such a way that you remain seated in the meantime, doing nothing at all, only vegetating. Just running on idle. Will you succeed? Not very likely. The search for happiness does not tolerate laziness, sluggishness or inactivity. You may now think that this is some kind of poetic simile. No, it is not. Not at all. This is the strictest reality. There is a very concrete and unpleasant feeling which does not let you sit around kicking your heels. And this feeling is nothing else but boredom.

What causes boredom? The idling speed of the symbol-based control level: the complete absence of carrying out logical operations. But carrying out logical operations is no simple thing. First of all, you need a database to operate on. You need to enter data into your mind: you need to acquire lexical knowledge. And this is not a nice process at all. Then we need to learn how to carry out logical operations with the data we have acquired. But you must not think it can be done without any effort. No way. Thinking, and systematic and purposeful thinking in particular, requires serious effort. And that is why, let's face it, sometimes we don't feel like it at all. What do we do if we are not feeling like it? We switch into idle speed. Yes, but then comes the feeling of boredom. Therefore, in these cases we usually look for an activity that does not require a lot of effort from the symbol-based control level. These activities include watching television, travelling, walking and so on. In these cases, we only use our incoming feeling channels passively. The data inflow is not processed in a way that would force the symbol-based control level to work. Only a few odd thoughts flash up here and there. This is nothing else but latent boredom. Naturally, the top limit-indicating feelings of the need for information, indifference and tiredness can also appear in these cases. The problem with this kind of killing time is that it might work sometimes as relaxation but, in the long run, it leads to the degradation of our mental capacities. Because events primarily take place in these cases at the feeling-based control level and not at the symbol-based control level. In other words, we use only one half of our capacities and the half we do not use is precisely the one that lifted the *homo sapiens* out of the animal kingdom.

But there is another side to this coin. What I mean is you can also go to the other extreme. Due to the nature of things, this phenomenon is not that common. In these cases, the person in question cuts himself off from the world and lives confined in his own mental world. All he does is lay the emphasis on the symbol-based control level. Typical examples of this might be great scientists. They close the door of their office or laboratory on themselves and they do not have the slightest idea what is taking place in the world around them. This is also an extreme. Although the feeling-based control level still shows some activity in these cases, the emphasis is, beyond doubt, on the symbol-based control level. And since we were talking about extremes, we could probably draw the lesson saying that if we want to live a full life we should refrain from either extreme. And here I mean we should live in a way that we load both our control levels equally. In other words, we should set goals for ourselves that exercise both of our control levels.

And talking about setting goals, we have arrived at a very important issue. Let us call this state the state of 'relative happiness'. You can achieve relative happiness if you isolate yourself from the world to a certain extent. But don't do it! You should not think about retiring into a convent or retreating into the seclusion of a cave of a recluse in the mountains. The most pleasant form of relative happiness that is known to everyone is love$_1$. When you are in love$_1$, the world disappears for you. You do not care at all what happens around you. Your house, or even the whole world, could fall apart, you still would not care. You only think about your partner and enjoy each and every moment of the time you spend together. And if you are not with him or her, you keep thinking about when you will next meet and what you will do together. For people in love$_1$, the external world becomes a secondary factor, or a downright disturbance to be got rid of (that is why people usually look for a nice love nest ☺).

A more placid version of relative happiness that activates less stormy feelings, and therefore is less effective, is a hobby. Those who live for their hobbies also isolate themselves from the vexed daily routine of the world to a certain extent and try to create an island of their own peace of mind. And, joking aside, the scientist locking herself up in her laboratory, and even the convent and the life of a recluse, are examples, although extreme, of this same method. I still do not recommend the convent or the cave to you (these are usually wet and cold places and there are no girls there).

What is common in people in love$_1$, people doing their hobbies, scientists in their laboratories, nuns in the convent and recluses in caves? They all concentrate on one thing and only one thing. They only see one goal. But choosing one goal clearly means that they isolate themselves to a certain extent from the rest of the world. What makes a difference is which part, and how large a part of the world they isolate themselves from. Although people in love$_1$ do not care much about the events taking place around them, they would still like to discover all the pleasant things in the world together. The recluse is exactly the other extreme. Although she is also led by one goal, she has already broken off from the world around her physically and, squatting in her cave, she deprives herself completely of any joy (as for myself, I would definitely choose love$_1$ instead of looking at the wet wall of a cave).

There is a fairly efficient, and more pleasant, way to relative happiness which is nothing but a properly chosen goal to live for. Only, as we saw in the previous examples, it matters very much what goal we choose. "How shall we choose a goal to live for?" the question arises. With a good choice we can achieve several results in one go. First, we can satisfy some of our needs. Second, we can get rid of the unpleasant feeling of boredom. Third, our life, instead of idling around from one place to another, becomes a purposeful and organised flow: we will not feel we are only going with the tide and others, or simple chance, direct our fate. And fourth, we get rid of the tormenting feeling of desire.

And here we are again with the issue of desire. There is no problem with the feeling of desire itself: this is a necessary and very useful feeling. The problem lies in the structure of today's modern society one of the key elements of which is institutionalised desire-raising. Our entire society is based on raising desires in everyone and convincing them to spend their money. That is why we have commercials. The great majority of people, however, have much less money than would be necessary to satisfy all the desires raised in them. Therefore, the life of these people is spent in continuous craving and suffering.

If the process of desire has already started, the operations carried out at the symbol-based control level cannot stop it but, by focusing our attention on these logical operations, we can radically reduce the intensity with which we experience the feeling of desire. These logical operations might be aimed at the way to obtain the object of your desire or at completely unrelated things. If the feeling of desire has not yet been formed, you still have a chance to prevent the generation of certain types of desires and save yourself from suffering. This is where the possibility of achieving relative happiness comes into the picture. During the process of achieving relative happiness, the properties of the interaction of strategic and technological feelings play into your hands. The bottom line of the method is that you set a goal the struggle for achieving which you enjoy. Good examples are various hobbies. For example, a model aeroplane does not necessarily have to be completed. Much more important than the fact of completion are the pleasant hours you spend building it. A person who considers his hobby his job is really lucky but even luckier is the one who considers her hobby her goal to live for.

What can we achieve with this approach? The trick is to manage to choose your goal properly. If you can start a main process with the help of it, all of your other processes become sub-processes. And that means the feeling of desire does not appear any longer at the level of the sub-processes as sub-processes are controlled by the technological feelings of tension and slackness instead. The shiny and glamorous objects of the world around us do not raise desires in us and, as a consequence, we do not suffer from our desires any longer and we can experience pleasant feelings during the main process. This trick, however, definitely does not work with the indicating feelings of needs. Needs require their satisfaction. Just as their name suggests, they need to be satisfied. No matter, for example, if you set some sublime goal for yourself, the indicating feelings related to the need to reproduce will drive you to satisfy your need. In these cases, you still cannot escape desires.

Theoretically, your goal to live for can be anything, but since you have a choice, it makes sense to gravitate towards goals that help, rather than block, your personal development. We saw in individual development that people always set their goals so they can preserve their needs corresponding to the levels of needs they have already achieved and can move on in the direction of satisfying the needs appearing in the next level. This process usually takes place moving gradually from one level of need to the other. We are best off if we can find a long-term goal to live for that serves for our entire life and, overarching through levels of needs, can contribute to the satisfaction of higher and higher levels. This way, we can create a pulling force which, apart from saving us from the suffering caused by desire, can also help us through unsatisfied levels of needs.

The difficulty of choosing the right goal for life lies in the fact that individuals have to choose a goal, or goal for life, related to a higher level of need when they are living at a lower level of need and the level of need related to the goal has not yet been activated. The feeling of love can play a giant role in bridging this paradox. Those who have more love in their heart solve this problem more easily. For them, it is natural to help others. They enjoy helping others and therefore, although their level of meeting their own expectations or self-realisation has not yet been activated, they will choose a proper goal for life for themselves sooner and more easily. And their inactive levels of needs will activate faster and the active ones will be satisfied sooner because they can rely on the love and support of the people around them.

I would like to call your attention once more to the necessity to choose a goal you honestly want to achieve from the bottom of your heart: one where the efforts to achieve it will fill you with joy. Do not choose a goal if it will require a struggle which you cannot enjoy. The struggle for your goal for life cannot be mere suffering and teeth grinding. This is what they usually mean when they say: on a journey, the important thing is not to arrive at the next station as quickly as possible but to enjoy the journey itself.

We may ask the question whether we will not be robbed of the pleasant things of life if we concentrate on only one thing. No. If somebody wants to buy the car of his dreams, first he will dream about it a lot, which equals desire which equals suffering, then he will collect the money for it, buy it, and is happy with it. Then the pleasant orienting feelings disappear. A person driven by her goal for life does not dream about a car. For her, a car is a tool that can help her achieve her goal or complete her mission. For her, buying a car is a problem to be solved: something to get over as quickly as possible. She walks into the shop and sees the same car the previous guy bought. She also likes it. Why wouldn't she? If she has enough money, she buys it and is happy with it and gets bored with it just the same. If she does not have enough money, she buys a cheaper car and her world does not collapse at all. She is spared desire. Who is better off then?

A simple potter does not have to think about the problems of cancer research if he hates microbiology and the mere thought of it makes his skin crawl. It is enough if he sets a goal to make pots people like. It is also a good goal if he wants to create the great work of his life but then what will he do when he has succeeded? Setting lower level goals can also help to get rid of desires but if we do not choose a goal carefully enough, it can also be harmful for both the individual and his environment. If, for example, somebody sets the goal for life to become a millionaire, then this is going to be the main process of her life. It will motivate every one of her deeds and it will become the most important thing for her. Everything else will only be obstacles and sub-processes that are only there to complete as soon as possible due to the pressure of tension, i.e. impatience. You must get rid of the problems as soon as possible. But problems can also be people who you must ride roughshod over, who you must trample upon in order to achieve the "great" goal. Achieving lower level goals can sometimes make it harder, or even impossible, to satisfy higher level needs. You are best off if you choose a goal for life based on real values. And real values only come from useful interactions. Do you want to create valuable interactions? Do you want your life to become meaningful? Help others! You do not need to save the world, just do what you can do.

Through our life, we seek to experience as many pleasant feelings as possible and as few unpleasant feelings as possible. So we might consider the ratio of pleasant to unpleasant feelings as an indicator of the quality of our life. But it does not work like that. At least not for humans. In the case of animals that, as we know, live at the level of the first five needs, this statement may be true. But the software-type need levels can radically reshape the picture again in the case of human beings. Feelings generated at the levels of meeting others' expectations and our own expectations and self-realisation can overwrite feelings appearing at lower levels. We are ready to put up with a lot of unpleasant feelings at the hardware-type need levels in order to experience a nice feeling at the software-type need levels. And sometimes pleasant feelings experienced at those hardware-type need levels are worth nothing when we are experiencing unpleasant feelings at the software-type need levels. It makes no difference if we live in a golden castle where we can carouse and have everything that is good on earth, if our software-type need levels are not satisfied: if we are not respected: if we are not satisfied with ourselves and do not find our place in the world, splendour is worth nothing.

Many think if they win a lot of money, they will become happy. A huge folly! You cannot buy others' appreciation with money, only seemingly at best. You cannot satisfy your need to meet your own expectations with money, especially if you have not worked for it. All you can do is ornament yourself with beads and pseudo-values. And do not even mention self-realisation. You cannot buy peace of mind for money. Money can make your life easier and more pleasant but sometimes even the exact opposite may happen. Money is a useful thing. Do not flee from it but do not expect to be able to buy happiness just because you have money, or a lot of money, either. There is a very wise Chinese doctrine that describes money appropriately:

"You can buy a house, but not a home...
You can buy a bed, but not sleep...
You can buy a clock, but not time...
You can buy a book, but not knowledge...
You can buy a position, but not respect...
You can buy a doctor, but not good health...
You can buy blood, but not life...
You can buy sex, but not love..."

Everybody has to fight for their peace of mind. No one else can give you peace of mind but you. This is exactly like asking somebody to drink a pint of beer for you because you are thirsty or to climb Mount Everest for you. They can do both but it will be not you whose thirst is quenched, or who is closer to the stars.

Getting back to pleasant or unpleasant feelings, my readers may rightly expect that we should try and draw conclusions from what we have discussed above. I would say that, in our life, we should really strive to experience as few bad feelings as possible and as many pleasant feelings as possible but if something forces us to choose between feelings to be experienced at the hardware-type and software-type levels, I suggest that we should give preference to software-type needs but only as long as it does not threaten our existence. "Why should it not threaten our existence?" you may ask. So we have a chance to restart if we messed something up. Because the satisfaction of software-type needs, as their name appropriately shows, is highly dependent on the software itself. If foolish or idiotic software, or a value and feeling system in other words, was programmed into our mind, or taught to us, then we might realise, boiling in a cauldron in the other world, that we have been taken for a ride and we have sacrificed our only life on the altar of some bullshit (it would be really hard to get back to life from that place). So the advice above can only work with a value and feeling system based on real values.

11.3 A summary of system optimisation
(What are we talking about then?)

After having examined need-based control and the control ensuring the accumulation of reserves, let us try to summarise the bottom line and distil the lessons. But before starting that, let us turn again to the wisdom of Lao Tzu who, in the English words of Robert G. Henricks, speaks as follows:

> "By not elevating the worthy, you bring it about that people will not compete.
> By not valuing goods that are hard to obtain, you bring it about that people will not act like thieves.
> By not displaying the desirable you bring it about that people will not be confused.
> Therefore, in the government of the Sage:
> He empties their minds,
> And fills their bellies.
> Weakens their ambition,
> And strengthens their bones.
> He constantly causes the people to be without knowledge and without desires."

When you read these lines, you cannot help thinking that people had very similar problems two and a half thousand years ago, although the situation was not as bad as it is today. You also need to see that some of the roots of the problems had already been identified back then. But can we add anything to these wise words?

- First, you must understand that the individual can only be happy if all of her hardware-type needs and her activated software-type needs are satisfied and therefore, she is now free from the main drive of need-

356

based control, the unpleasant top and bottom limit-indicating feelings and the feeling of non-physical pain in the case of software-type needs.

- The satisfaction of a given need is always carried out according to a subjective value system and not an objective value system. This fact is hugely significant. This is the fact that ensures that everyone has a chance for happiness: with a person on a low income living in a modest village in the mountains and a rich person living in Beverly Hills; people who are living today and people who lived thousands of years before. Because, when satisfying a need, we must concentrate on the output of the interactions and not on the marker feelings or orienting feelings that will disappear sooner or later anyway. So jacket potatoes can satisfy our need for energy supply just the same as caviar. The girl next door can satisfy our need to reproduce just the same as Miss World. It feels just as good for the potter in the corner shop when his work is praised as it did for Albert Einstein and both of them are filled with the same good feelings after successfully completing the job. You may be wondering now how you can possibly compare a pot with the theory of relativity. You cannot. And you do not need to, either. What I am talking about is the subjective feelings experienced by the two people and not absolute values. And this is exactly what is so great about the whole thing.

- Beware of desires and the desire trap! We already know that, during the satisfaction of our needs, the search for values is carried out with the help of orienting feelings (in the case of the hardware-type needs). We always select the interaction that triggers the most pleasant orienting feeling. And that is all right. Problems, and suffering, start when we have chosen the interaction triggering the most pleasant orienting feeling but, for some reason, we cannot implement the interaction.

This is when the agonies begin and the strategic feeling of desire appears and starts tormenting our soul. I will try to explain this phenomenon a little more.

In a small village tucked up in the mountains, people lived in happiness. They had plenty of food: fresh milk, lovely cheese, sausages, ham and so on. They never starved and they always ate what they had a fancy for or what they found the most delicious in the given moment (from the assortment of food available, they always ate what triggered the most pleasant orienting feeling in them). One day, a wanderer arrived in the village from faraway lands. The wanderer produced a small jar from his bag with caviar in it. Everybody tasted caviar in the village. Some liked it, some did not. Those who did not like it remained happy, those who liked it became unhappy. They became unhappy because they only had enough caviar to taste it but they could not appease their hunger with it. Desire started to torment their souls. So they upped and set out into the unknown. So that they would not get hungry on their way, they took a bit of smoked ham richly seasoned with forest herbs with them. They walked and walked until they arrived in a small fishing village where they found caviar on the market beyond their imagining. They quickly bought some and started gobbling up the long-craved delicacy. At first, it was really delicious. But after a while it did not taste that good any longer and then finally they could not even look at it. Nevertheless, they thought they would take some with them back to their mountain village so others could also have it. To make sure that there was enough room in their bag, they gave their smoked ham with the forest herbs to the people in the fishing village. The people of the fishing village tasted the ham. Some of them liked it, some of them did not. Those who did not like it remained happy, those who liked it became unhappy...

It becomes clear from this fable that both the people in the mountain village and the people in the fishing village could satisfy their needs because they were not hungry, and it was desire that embittered their life. And this is very often the source of unhappiness so typical of our time. We always desire something. And if not, the abundance of commercials makes sure that we start craving for something still. "You don't have the newest large screen TV set with surround sound? Or a mobile phone with GPS? A car with a hydrogen engine? Without them you have no chance for happiness!" (I wish I knew how people managed to become happy in the old days). Do you, my dear reader, have a gumytoddle? If you are now asking what a gumytoddle is, unfortunately I do not know. I cannot possibly know either because it does not exist yet but I know for sure that without it, we will have no chance whatsoever for happiness. And they will invent numerous things in the future without which you simply cannot live so you should not even dream about happiness! This is bullshit, isn't it? It is indeed!

With commercials, we raise desires, and therefore unhappiness, in people to make a little money in order to buy things to calm our own desires and the unhappiness raised in us by others. Isn't it great? This is a process that fuels itself and, in the meantime, we are surprised that we are more and more unhappy. Why? Because the period of desire is always longer than the fadeout time of the joy and the pleasant orienting feelings. We long for a supercar for years, we toil away for it and, after we have bought it, we feel joy for three days and we get completely used to it in a week. Years versus days! So very often the culprit, the thing that causes most of the torment of our soul, is an unsatisfied desire and not an unsatisfied need. And, unfortunately, this is going to last for a long time. Because it is coded into the system. Which system? The system of our CONSUMER society. I believe the name consumer society is misleading. Although, for the untrained eye, consumption may appear to be the main driving force of the system, as a matter of fact, the need for consumption alone would not generate this messy, perplexing and fierce competition. No way. A much more appropriate name would be SELLER society. In the seller society, the members of the society are under permanent pressure to sell. They are forced to continuously sell either their workforce or their brain power or their bodies or an object or a service. The moment they stop, even for a split second, they are done. They die of hunger. That is why they introduced the notion of 'planned obsolescence'. There is a gentlemen's agreement between manufacturers to maximise the lifespan of various products. Lest something becomes too good! Do you think I am joking? I am not! If you feel like it, check the story of the "Light Bulb Conspiracy" which is about companies reducing the lifespan of lightbulbs on purpose so that they do not last so long and they can sell more of them. If we lived in a true consumer society, a lightbulb would work for ever: you would never have to replace it. But we are living in a seller society so we must replace lightbulbs quite often. That is why there is the permanent, ongoing, premeditated and well-organised war to raise desires on a constant loop: the flood of commercials. From dawn to dusk and from dusk to dawn they are trying to raise desires in us so that they can sell. To put it more accurately: they are trying to make us unhappy on purpose. And they do not just try, they also succeed! They constantly regenerate unhappiness. They must make others unhappy so they do not die of hunger or they simply become richer and have larger castles where they can live unhappy lives until they die. Because they are just as unhappy as those whom they make unhappy. The seller society carries unhappiness encoded in its system! Eternal unhappiness is guaranteed until we change it. So, good job! Keep it up! The biggest basic mistake we can make is to desire happiness. This is nonsense itself. The presence of desire precludes all kinds of happiness.

- Naturally, it is not only the strategic feeling of desire you need to beware of but all the other unpleasant strategic feelings, like disgust and non-physical pain.
- During the satisfaction of a given need you must be careful not to damage the other need levels. A frequent

example is that in order to satisfy their need to meet others' expectations and their own expectations, some people give up the satisfaction of their need to reproduce or only satisfy it partially. But this can also happen the other way round: a bad love₁ relationship can prevent the satisfaction of the need to meet our own expectations.

- The most problematic need levels of modern societies are the levels of the need to meet others' expectations and our own expectations: these levels cause the most problems. Value systems can be very downmarket and often harmful or they can simply contradict real life. Value systems should reflect true values and should be close to reality. Disregarding reality will have a price to be paid.

- Money and wealth only have a direct impact on the first three hardware-type need levels. That is to say, you can only influence the satisfaction of your need for energy supply, information and safety directly with money. At the other levels, money and wealth can only exert their influence through the symbol-based control of humans and more in a negative than a positive direction. In the case of the need to reproduce, the need for a group, and the need to meet others' expectations and our own expectations, money and wealth only make our situation harder and more complicated because they take attention away from real values. At the level of self-realisation, money only provides opportunity or aid but actually it is not at all important in terms of the satisfaction of this need.

- The phenomenon of relative devaluation embitters people's lives at the level of meeting others' expectations and meeting your own expectations. It destroys your image in others' eyes and in your own eyes, too. It forces you to attach symbols that are positive for others and for you to your 'I' symbol or to downgrade others. This is one of the canker sores of our modern age. How can we protect ourselves from relative devaluation? With one exception, the strategies to do so do not concentrate on solving the problem but on avoiding it, playing it down or sweeping it under the carpet. The only strategy that works in the proper direction involves the formation of an appropriate value and feeling system. But this is only a halfway solution. The real solution lies in the optimisation of a properly formed value system, the feelings attached to its symbols and their intensity. In more simple terms: the goal is to form an appropriate value system and minimise the feeling of pride.

As for appropriate value systems, it is obvious that we must concentrate on the value systems of meeting others' expectations and our own expectations in the fight against relative devaluation or, in other words, we must concentrate on interactions that are useful for us at these need levels but, at the same time, do not hinder or harm the satisfaction of needs at other need levels. Minimising pride is a rather hard nut to crack. We can differentiate between two groups of people in this respect. The first group includes children whose pride has not yet been formed: who have not yet attached other symbols they find pleasant to their 'I' symbols. The second group includes adults whose 'I' symbol is packed with symbols loaded with marker feelings they find positive and other feelings. Logically, the goal in the first group is to prevent the formation of pride and in the second group to deconstruct pride. You may now rightly ask why it is not enough to form an appropriate value system and why you also need to minimise pride. If you only form an appropriate value system – which is, of course, inevitable – and still attach symbols that carry marker feelings and feelings you find positive to your 'I' symbol, you are still vulnerable, i.e. relative devaluation will still torment your soul. No matter if, according to an appropriate value system, you become a person that forms many valuable interactions, if you meet another person who forms an even higher number of valuable interactions, the mechanism of relative devaluation will start to work. The only way to avoid it is to seek to attach as few feelings that you find positive to your person, and to the person of other people, as possible. So if you try to attach as few symbols carrying feelings and marker feelings you find positive to your 'I' symbol and you do the same with the 'I' symbols of others, there is nothing to weaken or attack and there is nothing to weaken and attack with. So if someone is truly beautiful, clever, strong and so on and, although aware of these properties, does not attach strong positive marker feelings to the symbols of 'beauty', 'cleverness' and 'strength', she will not suffer if she meets someone else who is more beautiful, cleverer or stronger than her.

Naturally, you already know that beauty, cleverness and strength are not real values but even if you replace these words with the expression 'valuable interaction', you must still not attach too positive marker feelings to it. Naturally, you cannot – and you must not, for that matter – completely get rid of marker feelings and it is also inevitable that you attach feelings to your 'I' symbol and to the 'I' symbol of others. As a consequence, you will not be able to completely get rid of relative devaluation either. But it would not be good anyway since relative devaluation is the driving force of competitiveness. All you must pay attention to is to keep it within healthy limits. In more simple terms: You should not wallow in the feeling of pride from dawn to dusk.

In the case of adults, the way of logical thinking described above can reduce or deconstruct the exaggerated power of positive marker feelings attached to certain symbols. In the case of children, the situation is different. When you raise children, it makes sense to avoid the formation of pride to start with. For example, it is not advisable to tell children that they are beautiful but that you like them instead; not that they are clever but that they think in a very clever way;

not that they are strong but that they fight strongly. What is the difference? It is enormous. If you tell somebody that he is beautiful, you do nothing but attach a symbol carrying a pleasant marker feeling to his 'I' symbol, so you did what you should not have done: strengthened his pride. If you say you like him, you are talking about the effect your inter-action triggered on your side and this does not strengthen his pride. You focus on the interaction. Not to mention the precision of your communication. If you say somebody is beautiful you make a general statement: you declare that somebody is beautiful in the absolute sense, i.e. beautiful for everyone, which is most probably not true. If you say you like him, you are closer to reality. And, naturally, it does not hurt either if you explain the real "value" of beauty, clever-ness or strength: that these things are not real values, only opportunities at best.

What you must take into consideration in the fight against relative devaluation is the law of handicap. We do not start off in life with equal chances. A child born to a poor African family on the verge of starvation has different opportunities than a child born to a well-to-do American family. Accordingly, it would be unjust to measure the ca-reer and the achievements of the two children on the same scale. If you want to live a valuable life, you need to seek to have as many valuable interactions with your fellow human beings and your environment as possible. And the emphasis is on the word possible. You only need to, and should, seek to do things that are possible for you. No one expects, and no one should expect, that you do things you do not have the possibility for. A doctor working in an ultramodern hospital has different possibilities from a tribal medicine man. They should both do what is possible and if, one day, they must give account for their lives to themselves or to their God, they can say with a clear conscience that they did every-thing they could do.

- You should seek to experience as many of the feelings mentioned in the chapter about the control ensuring the accumulation of reserves as possible but try to do it in such a way that you do not become the captive of a feeling and you do not risk the health of your physical body with the consequences (do not threaten your need for safety).

- Beware of feeling traps! It makes no difference if you satisfy all your needs and you are living in clover, if restlessness torments you, if desire, fear, pain, anger or tension is preying on your mind.

- Keep clear of boredom.

- Keep clear of passivity and the laziness that results in passivity.

- Although not everybody gets bored when they are passive, it is difficult to avoid relative devaluation and mental decline when you are passive and it is impossible to satisfy your need to meet your own expectations and of self-realisation on the basis of real values.

- It is not absolutely necessary but it may be useful to set a goal for life for yourself. This method is interesting because, as we saw, it is nothing but a strategy of positive isolation.

- Do not even think that you can become happy alone, without your fellow human beings.

- Try to direct your feelings consciously. In order to be able to do so, you need to learn how to pay attention to your feelings and how to analyse and influence them. Do not forget that you can, within certain limits, decide for yourself what position you take on the scale of the status-indicating feelings ranging between cheerfulness and sadness. Pull yourself out of sadness and work your way up to cheerfulness. Enjoying the position of cheerfulness, the grim events of the world can affect our consciousness less: they almost rebound from us. At such times we are creative and we find solutions for the tasks facing us more easily. Do not forget that, unfortunately, the opposite of this is also true. If you are sad, you will not notice the cheerful things of life, your creativity will disappear and you will be helplessly tossed about by the storms of life.

- It will not do any harm if you prepare for the final settlement of accounts, either. Think sometimes about when you will have to give an account of what you have done in your life on your deathbed to yourself and to your God. Remember the words of Nikolai Alexeyevich Ostrovsky: "Man's dearest possession is life. It is given to him but once, and he must live it so as to feel no torturing regrets for wasted years, never know the burning shame of a mean and petty past."

That is it. You can draw the conclusion from the summary above that you must harmonise quite a number of factors, and quite a number of conditions must be met so you can experience the feeling of happiness. And it is enough if only one factor changes and happiness is gone. Happiness is a rather changeable and unstable state. Although, if you keep the factors above in mind, and you seek happiness consciously, happiness may also be found without purposeful activity. The easiest way to do so is to find a noble goal for life and then you may be able to be happy for a short period of time.

12.

ON RELIGION

(Why do religious people pray?)

You may ask why I need to write about religion in this book. The reason is simply that religion can generate very strong feelings in human beings and you may now have a chance to get acquainted with a new approach to it. I would like to clarify at the beginning that I am not a religious historian or a religious philosopher. Therefore, anything I write below is based solely on my personal experience.

If you have a look at the history of humankind, you need to notice the indisputable fact that various religions have always played a very important role in it. Historical religions have accompanied the entire development of humankind. And not only did they accompany this development but they also contributed to it in a very positive way. Some of my readers must have their doubts with regard to this statement and must be thinking about all the religious wars, the Inquisition and the missionary work. Yes, many unworthy deeds have been carried out in the name of religion but I would not blame religions for these deeds but the religious leaders of the given age who misinterpreted the holy scripts.

I suppose you expect me to explain the grounds of my statement, and you do so rightly. I suppose we use the holy scripts as our starting point. If we have a careful look at them, we will find that these books contain requirements and instructions that cover the first six need levels of human beings, namely the levels of the needs for energy supply, information, safety, reproduction, group and meeting others' expectations. Those who have never held such scripts in their hands should know that these books address each and every need level in very great detail. Who can eat and drink what, when and how? Who can use which resources of information? Who can apply what safety measures in order to protect their religion, home and loved ones as well as themselves? Who can have sexual relationships with whom, and under what circumstances? Who can have a social or friendly relationship with whom, under what circumstances? Who are the ones that can be accepted in the community and who are the ones that should be expelled from it? And finally, what you must do to meet your God's expectations and the expectations of your God's representatives on earth. These detailed guidelines put an end to chaos, rendered things in order and gave a unified system to societies. I do not think you could have organised and formed societies in the olden days this effectively by any other means. And order and organisation gave the chance for humankind to develop. This is what I see as the great achievement of historical religions.

But now I would like to play on darker strings. As we saw, the role of historical religions is undeniably positive but in our age, you very often come cross new religious schools, closed religious communities and sects. Some of them work for their followers without anything objectionable in their operation. But I am not going to deal with those now. I would like to direct your attention primarily to those religious communities that do not serve the development of the spirit but rather the destruction and hamstringing of it. In the media, you regularly see news about closed religious communities carrying out unprecedentedly evil deeds, such as the gas attack against the Tokyo Metro, or force their members to commit mass suicide. How can someone get to such a level? Why can't people escape from the captivity of sects, and why don't they at least let others help them? Although I do not promise I can give answers to all of these questions, we will most probably get closer to the truth.

For my non-religious readers, I must make a short detour. Some of you may rightly be asking questions about the practice of religion. For example, why do you need to pray? Why do the followers of all religions pray? Why is there no religion where people do not pray? Naturally, there are many types of answers to these questions. However, I suggest that we try to find an answer that reflects the spirit of this book. To the question of why people pray, I would answer they do it because of feelings. Mechanically murmuring prayers is not praying. What makes a prayer a prayer is a very special feeling: the feeling of meditation. When saying their prayers, believers get into a very pleasant, soothing and open meditative state of mind which they would like to relive again and again. After a true prayer, believers leave their temple calmed down and purified in spirits, no matter which religion or denomination they belong to. The internal design of temples, religious music and prayers all help us to reach this meditative state of mind. It is partly the pleasant feeling of meditation, related to the prayer, that helps religious people to keep their balance of mind.

Getting back to religious regulations connected to different need levels, we must see that while non-believers only follow a simple "traditional" system of needs, religious people live within stricter limits, by a system of needs that contains additional conditions. Additions – which are actually restrictions – are primarily to be found at the levels of the need for safety and meeting others' expectations. While no next world exists for non-believers, religious people believe in the next world. Non-believers, if they do something good, will be thanked or, at best, will be given some reward for it. Religious people believe that they will go to heaven for their good deeds where a happy existence until the end of times awaits them. While non-believers have to give an account for the sins they have committed in this world only, religious people believe that they will be called to account in the next world too for the sins they have committed in this one. The utmost punishment for non-believers for their sins is death, whereas religious people believe they will have to burn in the fires of hell for ever.

If the things I described so far were not frightening enough for a sinner's soul, some religions also add that it is not only sinners that have to suffer for their sins but their direct relatives will also be given to the fires of hell. You must admit that, for religious people, the level of the need for safety provides much less room for manoeuvre: they need to pay attention to many more things and they need to follow much stricter regulations. They may have far greater rewards and far greater punishments or threats. The level of meeting others' expectations also sets much stricter conditions for believers than for non-believers. At the level of meeting others' expectations, non-believers only have to adjust to the people around them. When the people around them do not see or do not know what they are doing, they can do whatever they want. These limits are much stricter for religious people. Primarily, they have to meet God's expectations, then their priests' expectations and then the expectations of the people around them. While non-believers can relax at the level of meeting others' expectations if the people around them do not see what they are doing, religious people will have to meet their God's expectations because God sees everything. But this is still not the end of the restrictions because religious people also have to avoid sinful thoughts as God also sees thoughts. For religious people, it is much more difficult to satisfy the needs related to their modified need levels than it is for non-believers to satisfy their needs related to their "traditional" need levels. Some non-historical religious communities make the mistake of using too strict rules and creating rules in the name of God that God would never create.

The question arises of why it is not easy to break away from a sect like this. As a matter of fact, there are several versions of explanations that can work one by one or together. In the first version the potential member of the sect becomes familiar with the teachings of the sect of his own free will, without any external pressure. On one side of the scale, there is the fearful, unpredictable, perplexing and messy world where the existence of the individual ends in certain death; on the other side of the scale, there is a comforting, quiet, safe and organised world from which, at the end of your life, you can go to heaven. A world where you do not need to bid a final farewell to your beloved ones because you can meet again in heaven. If you keep all the regulations of the sect, this is a relatively comfortable world. There are no doubts, everything is clear and easy to understand. You do not need to think: if something is not clear enough, you do not need to do anything else, just consult the related teachings of the sect. This is a calm and balanced world, to start with, that connects to calmness and that is further strengthened by the calmness of prayer. If someone was raised in a way that the data network formed in her mind provided an interface where the teachings of the sect can connect, i.e. no feelings that would categorically reject the sect's teaching are connected to the notions already embedded in her data network, the sect's teachings can incorporate themselves into her data network. But the sect's teachings are already connected to very strong feelings that will no longer allow that data loaded with feelings opposing the sect's teachings connect to the newly formed interface. Each and every bit of data the feelings related to which are not compatible with the sect's teachings will rebound from the data network. From this moment on, only data the related feelings of which are compatible with the sect's teachings can be incorporated into the database. The feelings connected to the newly formed interface are so strong that they block every logical train of thought at the symbol-based control level and if somebody else is trying to influence a member of a sect with logical arguments, he will definitely fail. People in psychological crises are particularly responsive to these kinds of teachings. If somebody does not find his place in the world, if he is disappointed or suffering from non-physical pain, if he has lost a close relative or if he is afraid of death, the teachings of sects can serve almost as a lifeline for him: he can find peace of mind more easily because there is something he can hold onto.

The reasons listed above may be sufficient in themselves to make someone a sect member but if a given person does not feel inclined or there is a smaller resistance in her data network against the teachings of the given sect, she can still be "converted" or convinced and so she identifies with the sect's teachings gradually. In the process of "converting" somebody, the level of meeting others' expectations gets activated in the person being "converted". In these cases, the person acts under external pressure. But do not think of the "hot iron"-type methods of the Middle Ages, rather parental instruction, spousal pressure or the expectations of the community. People under external pressure have two options. On the one hand, they can contravene the commands of their leader and face the disapproval of the community, punishment, the promise of eternal suffering in hell and, in some cases, also the promise of the eternal suffering of their close relatives in hell or, on the other hand, they can obey the commands of their leader and have the approval of the community, rewards, the reassuring and soothing "lifeline" worldview, the pleasant feeling of meditation and the promise of heaven in the next world. The life of the future sect member is made even more difficult by the fact that the logical operations necessary for decision-making, i.e. free thinking, are blocked because even looking at the pros and cons is considered a sinful thought that can send you to hell, together with your loved ones. And who would risk that? If it was only you yourself alone, you might run the risk but who would risk his loved ones? The two hands are diametrically opposed to one another. On the one hand, there are pleasant and soothing feelings, on the other, there are fearful feelings that generate a guilty conscience.

In the next stage, after the sect's teachings are incorporated in your worldview, the need to meet your own expectations gets activated. The member of the sect will already be obeying the leader's commands so that he does not hurt his own 'I' and will be busy working on meeting the regulations of the sect as best he can so he can attach even more pleasant feelings to his 'I' symbol. Naturally, he enjoys the benefits of the "lifeline" worldview and he may also form a feeling of superiority thinking that he is the clever one who is enlightened, whereas the others are idiots and will go to hell where they belong. Although the indicating feeling of the need for safety, fear, already plays a secondary role, all the sinful thoughts are blocked just the same. In connection with the need for safety, pleasant orienting feelings related to humility can also appear.

This is now a relatively clear situation for an outsider but do not forget that sect members cannot see the situation from outside. Only one reality exists for them: subjective reality. And their subjective reality is completely different from the one of outsiders. Moreover, that subjective reality was formed in such a way as to protect itself from external interventions. A very well-designed, internalised self-defence system protects the subjective reality of sect members, and the task of this self-defence system is exactly to ensure that sect members cannot break away and cannot re-form their subjective world, and that people from outside also cannot "tamper with" the system. If someone wants to give external help to sect members by informing them about their situation, she will come up against several obstacles. First of all, the mere mentioning of any subject that is against the sect's teaching will trigger unpleasant feelings in sect members because it would destroy their data network and worldview. Second, sect members may also experience non-physical pain because things they find important are being abused. Third, these are sinful thoughts to start with which, in themselves and together with their consequences, threaten the safety of sect members. Fourth, discussions like that can directly or indirectly attack the 'I' image of sect members. And we could go on and on. Logical arguments are also completely in vain because sect members simply delete them and do not let them incorporate themselves into their data network because feelings they find unpleasant are attached to the outcome of these logical arguments. Based on this, we can draw the conclusion that sects close their members almost hermetically into a very tight, self-defensive system of thoughts which – if infected with harmful ideas for some reason – can become very dangerous.

Although historical religions are also closed systems of thoughts, they are still not as closed as sects and they serve human beings. Exactly because of their closed nature, historical religions can partly protect the people of our age from the intellectual mess we are living in. I would compare religions to small coves protected from the ocean by huge rocks that keep the raging waves away. In these places, sailors can sail up and down in safety. At the same time, these protected coves have their own disadvantage, and it is exactly the same as their advantage. Rocks not only keep away the waves of the ocean, they also keep adventurous sailors back from sailing to open waters. There are questions of life and science the answers to which cannot be found within the boundaries of religions. Nothing proves it better than the fact that religious leaders have to revise and reinterpret the doctrines of their holy scripts from time to time to reflect the current situation.

13.

POLITICS

(Are you sure we are not ripped off?)

The answer is the same here as it was in the case of religions. I am giving a full chapter to politics in this book because politics can trigger quite violent feelings in human beings. Politics is nothing but an activity aimed at influencing people. People live in societies so it is clear that their activities must be coordinated in some way and to some extent. This coordination is partly done by statutory regulations, morals and religions. Politics is responsible for coordinating some of the remaining territories.

People can be coordinated, or in other words controlled, in various ways. In some societies, it is one person that defines the direction of the activities of the society, in other societies a larger or smaller number of people participate in decision-making. But simply making decisions is not enough, decisions must also be implemented. The more members of a society support a given decision, the easier it is to implement it. You can get the support of people in two ways. One of them is to convince people on a logical basis. The problem with this is that you can only convince those on a logical basis who are capable of carrying out certain logical operations. That is, they have the appropriate knowledge and they are educated enough to carry out the logical operations typical of the given fields. More specifically, they have sufficient knowledge and comprehensive, up-to-date information about economics, foreign affairs and military affairs and they are professionals so they know what logical operations to carry out with certain data.

From the point of view of the ruling class, the advantage of professionals is exactly the same as their disadvantage. Good professionals usually know what is good and what is bad. If the ruling class would like to guide society in a direction professionals find advantageous, professionals are useful for the ruling class and for the society. If the ruling class wants to guide the society in a direction professionals consider disadvantageous for that society, and the ruling class insists on the move even though professionals have warned them, those same professionals can easily become a pain in the neck for the ruling class, one that they will want to get rid of. As a consequence, sense is not always useful for ruling classes and decision-makers. Sometimes it becomes a pain in the neck. Another problem with this method of getting people's support is that only a very thin layer of a society has the necessary knowledge and capacities for it and the rest of the society is impossible to convince on the basis of logical arguments.

The other method of getting support is to manipulate people with the help of feelings. The people in control of the process seek to attach pleasant feelings in people's minds to the symbol (it can be an object, a person, an idea, a deed or anything) that is advantageous to them and to attach unpleasant feelings in people's minds to the symbols that are disadvantageous to them. The stronger and more intense the feelings you can attach to a certain symbol, the stronger the effect you can achieve. This method utilises the fact that human thinking is gradual, so to speak. I mean if people think about, and deal with, the given topic at all. They rarely make it to the second grade, or the next level. And this is simply because they forget about a word. The word – and also the shortest sentence of the world – that made it possible for us became human beings. This word, or sentence, is as follows: Why? If we ask this simple question of ourselves, it is no longer that easy to manipulate us through our feelings. Let us not forget Lao Tzu's words: "When everyone in the world knows the beautiful as beautiful, ugliness comes into being;" Strong feelings can polarise the society. Together with the very good come both the very bad and animosity. Systems formed this way are usually self-reinforcing and high inertia systems. We find it difficult to attach unpleasant feelings to symbols pleasant feelings are already attached to in our minds; and the opposite is also true. Consequently, we have a tendency to neglect information containing feelings that are opposing the feeling systems we have formed. What we should keep in mind in connection with the entire process is that not only the value judgement of others, but also our own value judgement can be manipulated. Never take it for granted that you are right. Always think about why another person represents another point of view and think about the possibility that your opponent may be right. Another important thing is that, in order to achieve its goals as easily as possible, politics seeks to form a polarised worldview. Politics usually thinks in dichotomies like good-bad or black-white but there are millions of shades between the two extremes. Let us discover these millions of shades.

Now I am asking you to think about the biggest enemy of your country: the power, the organisation or the country that is the biggest threat at the moment. And now try to put yourself in the place of an average mortal citizen of that country. What can she think? WHY does she think what she thinks? What has her life been like so far? How did she get where she is now? How could they stuff her head with what nonsense? Or is it really nonsense what she was influenced with? Is it possible that the leaders of your (our) country are at fault? Always be alert! Do not accept feelings conveyed to you without checking them, even if they look straightforward. In fact, that is when you should be the most doubtful.

Because it is the leaders' task to be straightforward, clear and easy to believe in order to create unity instead of doubts. The question is what sort of unity do they create. Will we end up unified for 'good' or 'bad'? And is 'good' really good and 'bad' really bad, and for *whom?*

It is important to know that usually it is not everyday people who deal the cards matters. It is not everyday people who try to influence others' opinion. Everyday people are the ones who usually follow the piper. They are the ones that will have to lie in the bed those in power have made. Everyday people are usually just extras, props or dead bodies in the battlefield: they are only the means with which the plotters of the play reach their goals. But it is them the whole play should be about. Do not become extras! And do not become paid extras, in particular! There would be no problem with politics if leaders kept the interest of the entire society in their minds. But, as the proverb goes: charity begins at home, and, as we all know, politicians are very charitable people. But leaders can also be manipulated. Maybe not manipulated by a specific person but by a historical age. They cannot cut themselves off from the feelings they experience during their lives, from the things that they learn from their parents, teachers, friends and the people around them. The most important thing that everyone must understand is that leading people is not about glory but about the biggest possible responsibility of all.

14.

ON THE ARTS

(Plastic feelings?)

Artists are simply the magicians of feelings. They sacrifice their whole life to present us with feelings. Works of art are nothing other than hibernated packages of feelings that wait for somebody to restore them to life. Often entire chapters in various studies are sacrificed to discuss what works of art are trying to say. But works of art are not primarily about words but about feelings. Treatises on economics, history or science have messages to say but have no messages to feel. But when you discuss a work of art, the most important thing to talk about is the experiencing of what feelings it is meant to serve. Of course, this is rather inadequate also because every person will feel something different in connection with a certain work of art.

Artistic forms all use different means and, therefore, each one of them can restore different feelings to life. However, based on their common properties, we can classify the feelings triggered by works of art into two groups. The first group includes feelings triggered in us by the choice of subject or the plot of a work of art. The second group includes feelings triggered in us by the form of the work of art. Feelings triggered by the choice of subject and the plot are more the essences of feelings to be experienced in real life, whereas feelings triggered by the form of works of art are more the various types of orienting and déjà vu feelings. In connection with the choice of subject and plot, we can experience the full spectrum of feelings we may encounter in real life: orienting, strategic, tactical, technological and status-indicating feelings. Artists can sometimes conjure us into situations that – sometimes unfortunately, sometimes fortunately – are not given in every people's life, and sometimes just show us a mirror. This way, they make it possible – if only for a short period of time – to be part of the fate of other people, to stand in other people's shoes and learn from their mistakes and successes. As for the orienting and déjà vu feelings, they can give us many pleasant hours.

I was talking about artists. But just like any other job, art has its own dross. They are the profiteers of feelings. They mass-produce flimsy, plastic goods. "Roll up, roll up! One for the price of two! Roll up, roll up!" They sell themselves for money, they prostitute themselves. In our time, the pinnacle of this mentality is to be observed in filmmaking (I did not use the phrase 'film art' on purpose). Although there are art films, but not too many of them and they do not reach big audiences. On the other hand, they have succeeded in re-educating the audience in such a way that there is less and less demand for this type of film. But, at the same time, there is a growing demand for the "up and at 'em!" type of film. But it is not only "artists" who are responsible for these "beautiful" achievements but also the general lunacy of modern-day societies. Do not forget: If you take the courage to create something, you take on responsibility as well. Responsibility, because you start teaching and educating and therefore you become responsible for other people's fate.

AFTERWORD

Dear reader,

First of all, I would like to thank you for the honour of your attention. I really hope that there was something in my humble thoughts that grabbed your attention and that something will prove to be useful in your, or in our, life. Although many things were left out from this book, I still know that I have started off in the right direction and that what I have written down might open a new perspective in human thinking. The further development, and introduction into the primary school curricula, of sensology, or the science of feelings, is of the utmost importance for the development of humankind. I hope we will have the opportunity to continue on this road for the benefit of us all.

Quotes: **Eric Berne,** *What do you say after you say hello?*
Lau Tzu, *Tao Te Ching,* translated by Robert G Henricks

The Author

How would I live my life, if I could start it again? I do not think I would change many things. I was born in August in the year 1955 of our Lord. We lived on the outskirts of the forest, right above the paper mill, you know, in Szilvás-völgy. Where is Szilvás-völgy? In Miskolc, Hungary, a little back from Lillafüred, towards the city. It felt good to be a child there. We used to go rambling in the forest or pilfering the orchards on the other side making the farmers grumpy. Then the school started and we had a young and very pretty teacher and, as a matter of fact, I owe it to her that I took to physics and maths. Later on, I went to a secondary school which specialised in maths and physics and then to university. With my degree in electrical and mechanical engineering in my pocket, I set out into LIFE. I thought I understood everything. As time passed, I came to realise I did not. Do you know how much that pisses off an engineer? Engineers hate confusion. Their soul is happy if everything is in its place and if they have answers for their whys. As time went by, I got one slap in the face after the other from life. "It cannot go on like that any longer!" I thought. So I sat down and started thinking. This book is the result.

CPSIA information can be obtained
at www.ICGtesting.com
Printed in the USA
LVOW13s2101020317
525958LV00015B/492/P